DATE DUE

NO 2 9 99			

DEMCO 38-296

The
Japanese
City

THE JAPANESE CITY

日本の都市

P.P. KARAN AND
KRISTIN STAPLETON

EDITORS

THE UNIVERSITY PRESS
OF KENTUCKY

Publication of this volume was made possible in part by a grant
from the National Endowment for the Humanities.

Copyright © 1997 by The University Press of Kentucky

Scholarly publisher for the Commonwealth,
serving Bellarmine College, Berea College, Centre
College of Kentucky, Eastern Kentucky University,
The Filson Club Historical Society, Georgetown College,
Kentucky Historical Society, Kentucky State University,
Morehead State University, Murray State University,
Northern Kentucky University, Transylvania University,
University of Kentucky, University of Louisville,
and Western Kentucky University.

Editorial and Sales Offices: The University Press of Kentucky
663 South Limestone Street, Lexington, Kentucky 40508-4008

02 01 00 99 98   5 4 3 2 1

Library of Congress Cataloging-in-Publication Data

The Japanese city / [edited by] P.P. Karan and Kristin Stapleton
        p.   cm.
    Includes bibliographical references and index.
    ISBN 0-8131-2035-7 (cloth : alk. paper)
    1. Cities and towns—Japan.   2. Land use, Urban—Japan.
  3. City planning—Japan.   4. Urban ecology—Japan.   I. Karan,
  Pradyumna P. (Pradyumna Prasad)   II. Stapleton, Kristin Eileen.
  HT147.J3J39   1998
  307.76'0952—dc21   97-27312

This book is printed on acid-free recycled paper
meeting the requirements of the American National Standard
for Permanence in Paper for Printed Library Materials.

 ✪

Manufactured in the United States of America

Contents

Figures, Tables, and Photographs

Figures

Tables

Photographs

Preface

This book brings together a series of contributions that examine the Japanese city from the perspectives of a number of disciplines—geography, sociology, political science, urban planning and law, and literature. A central theme of the book is to consider the city in Japan from a range of disciplinary perspectives and situations in order to understand the process and characteristics shaping the modern Japanese city. Areas of particular concern include the urban landscapes, changing landmarks, quality of life in the suburbs, spatial mixing of social classes in the city, land-use planning and control, environmental pollution in urban areas, urban restructuring in a depressed mining and industrial city, and the images of the city in Japanese literature. The chapters in this book frequently make comparisons between the Japanese city and the American city, to highlight our understanding of the urban dynamics in Japan.

We acknowledge the support of Richard Edwards, Dean of the College of Arts and Sciences at the University of Kentucky. Grants to the Japan Studies Committee from the College of Arts and Sciences, the Graduate School, and the Vice Chancellor for Research and Graduate Studies, made it possible to sponsor two conferences on the Japanese City at which the papers included in this book were presented. For information, ideas and advice, we are indebted to our colleagues in the Japan Studies Committee: Gregory A. Waller (English), Larry L. Burmeister (sociology), and Douglas Slaymaker (Japanese language and literature); and our friends and colleagues in Japan—in particular Einoo Shingo (University of Tokyo), Shigeru Iijima (Professor Emeritus,Tokyo Institute of Technology, Tokyo), Yuji Yamamoto (Osaka International University), Sugiura Kazuko (Fukui University), Hiroshi Ishii (Institute for the Study of Languages and Cultures of Asia and Africa, Tokyo), Kyoko Inoue (Institute for Developing Economies, Tokyo), Toshiaki Ohji (Kyoto University), and Biren K. Jha (Barrister-at-Law, Tokyo). Christopher Jasparro and Jon Taylor, doctoral candidates in geography at the University of Kentucky, provided research assistance.

We also owe a debt of gratitude to our contributors, who graciously granted us the patience and forebearing we needed to bring this undertaking to fruition, and we are thankful to all conference participants for enthusiastic discussions on the Japanese city. Brian Mayfield prepared the maps. For assistance with illustrations we are indebted to Gyula Pauer, Director of the Geographic and Cartographic Information Laboratory at the University of Kentucky.

1 Introduction

P. P. KARAN

Despite the size of Japan's economy and the long history of urban life in that society, very little has been published recently in English (or, one might add, in the other European languages) on the Japanese city. With the notable exception of books by Jinnai (1995), Shapira, Masser, and Edgington (1994), Cybriwsky (1991), Fujita and Hill (1993), Bestor (1989), and Eyre (1982), most of the publications date back to the 1960s and 1970s. *The Japanese City* provides nine well-documented essays by social scientists on various dimensions of the urban scene in Japan. It does not claim to fill the great gap in Japanese urban-studies literature but makes a contribution toward the understanding of the Japanese cities from the vantage point of several disciplines.

This volume provides interdisciplinary views of the urban experience in Japan. The contributors to this book have written for the intelligent layman, avoiding the quagmire of definitions and frames of reference in which social scientists sometimes bog down. It contains contributions on the Japanese city by four geographers (Karan, Mather, Cybriwsky, and Okamoto), three sociologists (Hall, Fujita, and Kidder), an urban planner and lawyer (Callies), a political scientist (Gilman), and a scholar of Japanese literature (Burton). Together, these contributions provide a unique view of the social and cultural landscapes of the city, the impact of environmental pollution, urban planning and restructuring, and efforts to revitalize the local economy. In each contribution, the authors provide comparisons with American cities so that the reader can appreciate the nature, characteristics, problems, and images of Japanese cities.

These papers were presented at the Japan City Conference, which was hosted by the University of Kentucky's Japan Studies Committee in April 1995. The paper by Burton was presented at the second Japanese City Revisited conference, also organized by the University of Kentucky's Japan Studies Committee, in March 1996. Both conferences were organized to examine the Japanese city from several disciplinary perspectives. Thus, there are papers on urban landscapes, landmarks and cultural symbols, suburbs, social classes, environmental pollution, land use and planning, urban restructuring, and images of the city in literature. The authors represent a diverse group of disciplines. Behind these choices lay the pluralist assumption that a multidisciplinary approach brings forth fresh insights to our understanding of the Japanese city. Thus, this volume breaks out of the intellectual mold that analyzes the city from the perspective of a single discipline. With few exceptions, the multidisciplinary study of Japan's urban areas is just now beginning.

Each paper has been revised and rewritten for this book. At the 1995 conference papers were also presented by two historians—Mary Elizabeth Berry of the University of California at Berkeley ("Images of Kyoto in Diaries, Paintings, Maps and Guide Books") and Henry D. Smith of Columbia University ("Great Urban Earthquakes in Modern Japanese History: Edo 1855, Tokyo 1923, Kobe 1995"); a Japanese geographer—Toshiaki Ohji of Kyoto University ("Urban Morphology of Japanese Cities: An Historical Analysis"); and an architect—Botond Bognar of the University of Illinois ("Architecture of the Japanese City"). These presentations were not made available in essay form for inclusion in this volume.

THE CITY IN JAPAN

A general discussion of city in Japan by Karan (chap. 2) provides a framework for the individual essays in this volume. Karan discusses the development of the Japanese city from the Nara period (eighth century), geographic layout of early cities, and the influence of the Chinese model. He also describes the changing forms of Japanese cities over time, from the formation of Japan's first capital cities—Nara and Kyoto—to the development of cities built for political and military purposes, as trading centers, post or stage towns, ports, and religious towns, are described. Then, the discussion turns to emergence of the modern city and the development of the Japanese megalopolis. Chapter 2 traces the dynamics of economic change in cities and towns of the megalopolis. Finally, Karan notes the role of telecommunications, which provides a new "glue" integrating megalopolis cities into the wider global "networked economy" of information, service, high-tech industries, and capital flows.

URBAN LANDSCAPES, LANDMARKS, AND SUBURBS

The next three chapters are the contributions of geographers, who examine the urban landscape of the Japanese city (Mather), Tokyo's changing landmarks and cultural symbols (Cybriwsky), and the structural transformation of Tokyo and the quality of life in Japan's metropolitan suburbs (Okamoto).

Mather points out that the landscape of the Japanese cities frequently provides intensive spatial experience within relatively small confines. While Japanese cities and American cities contain basically the same sort of functional areas, their arrangements are quite different. American cities do not mix business, commercial, government, and industrial land uses with housing, and in the United States different kinds of housing are kept distinct. In Japanese cities, by comparison, different types of land uses are mixed, with a relatively small amount of space given over to specialized uses. To be sure, there is in any Japanese city of moderate size a downtown business area, a civic center of sorts, and perhaps a bar and cabaret district, but the salient characteristics of the urban landscape are its diversity, intensity of use, and interdigitated character. A street whose principal identity during the evening is that of bar and cabaret district becomes, during the day, a street of houses with children playing outside. Grocery stores and stationery shops appear from between the thriving entertainment houses. In the afternoon, many of the erstwhile bars become coffee shops where teenagers hang out and listen to recorded music. During the hot summer evenings, it is not uncommon to see neighbors—older people, students, young folks, and merchants—carry chairs out onto the narrow streets where they discuss events of the day and other common interests.

In Japanese cities, there are no sidewalks. Cars and people pass up and down the narrow streets. Goods and services frequently spill over from the shops onto the street. In some neighborhood centers, an arcade is created by spanning the roofs of buildings on either side of the street with a skylighted roof, thereby accentuating the sense of containment, intensity of action, and identity of place. Because stores and shops are serviced from the same street, sometimes motor traffic causes an inordinate congestion.

One is always made aware that the Japanese city is a place for all kinds of people and activities, and multiple use of spaces and objects is the rule. Utility poles, for example, supply electricity and telephone service to both businesses and houses. They also provide anchorage for all manner of business signs, traffic and fire-fighting directions, posters, and street lights and occasionally provide support for clothes-drying racks put there by a household member a few inches away. Exclusive use is not characteristic of the crowded urban landscape of Japanese cities, and the multiple use of objects and spaces, as Mather points out, is at once a means of intensifying activity and the result of it. The study of the intensification of use of space in Japanese cities may provide clues that will better allow countries such as the United States to anticipate future urban space use possibilities as available land inexorably diminishes (Mather, Karan, and Iijima, 1998).

Cybriwsky discusses the ways in which contemporary architects are changing the face of Tokyo's landmarks in ways that shock some and delight others. The twin towers of Tokyo's new metropolitan government offices in Shinjuku (designed by the world-famous architect Tange Kenzo), the Tokyo Metropolitan Art Space, the Tokyo Budokan Complex for Martial Arts, and the spacecraftlike shape of the Tokyo Metropolitan Gymnasium exemplify a wave of new construction that swept Tokyo in the late 1980s and early 1990s. Ambitious plans abound for the redevelopment of the waterfront and the bay. In the fast-growing commercial center of Ikebukuro, the 60-storied Sunshine City complex was completed in 1980.

Many of the Tokyo's landmark buildings were designed by Tange Kenzo (1913-), who prepared the Tokyo Plan of 1960. Tange gave Tokyo boldly shaped landmark buildings and urban complexes that show that functionalism need not demand a rigidly geometric style and that buildings can blend modern expression with traditional Japanese esthetics. In addition to the massive new Tokyo government offices, which were completed in 1991, examples of Tange's extremely dramatic urban landmarks include the Yoyogi National Stadium, designed for the Tokyo Olympic Games (1964) and the Hanae Mori Building (1978). While Kyoto embodies the spirit of old Japan, Tokyo's new landmarks resonate with the dynamics of modern life. Tokyo's urban landmarks give one a feeling for the future, but the past is the adhesive that holds the city together as it enters the twenty-first century. The city unfolds as a series of densely built districts, each centered around a subway or train station. Tokyo's political, economic, and cultural history can be traced in these districts. Despite modern landmarks, many districts with winding back streets lined with neat, tiny houses and stores retain a flavor of their original character.

Okamoto's paper deals with the suburbanization of Tokyo and the daily life of its suburban residents. Beyond the densely inhabited commercial and residential core of the Tokyo metropolitan area, comprising the 23 wards of the city located within a radius of about 10 miles from the center, are the suburbs, which stretch into the western two-thirds of Tokyo Prefecture as well as into the surrounding Saitama, Chiba, and Kanagawa Prefectures, covering a distance of 40 to 50 miles from the city center. Okamoto describes the quality of life in Kawagoe, a commuter suburb of Tokyo about 20 miles to the northwest, located in central Saitama Prefecture. Most of Tokyo's suburbs are an outgrowth of farm villages, market centers, or post towns. With a population of 304,854 in 1990, Kawagoe developed as a castle town on the diluvial terrace of the Ara River. The city still has traditional warehouse-style merchant houses, built of wattle and daub (*dozozukuri*). When the Pacific War ended five decades ago, most of Tokyo's suburbs were small agricultural and commercial settlements of 20,000 to 30,000 residents. Since then, many towns like Kawagoe have grown into cities of 200,000 to 300,000. Politically, the suburbs form autonomous administrative entities or municipalities, but their residents are economically dependent on the larger central city of Tokyo, where they commute to work. The population densities of these suburban cities are lower than those of the central city but higher than those of the rural villages of the countryside beyond the suburbs. Middle-class, white-collar workers—*sarariimen* (salaried men)—in the tertiary sector and their families, as well as blue-collar workers employed in the production lines of corporations and their families, form the dominant social groups in the suburban cities such as Kawagoe. They are the product of economic and social changes that have taken place in Japan during the post–World War II era. With about a third or more of Japan's population living in suburban cities, these settlements have assumed considerable demographic importance. An understanding of the quality of life in suburban cities provides an essential insight on Japanese urban areas. Most works written in English have focused on the larger cities of Japan and urbanization. Studies of suburban cities are still relatively rare; Okamoto's essay on the quality of life in Kawagoe enhances our understanding of Japan's growing suburbs.

In the Tokyo metropolitan region, commuting is mainly by trains, and development is clustered near the railroad stations. The transportation system helps push development in high-density centers. In the New York City area, by contrast, some railroad stations, as in Princeton, are surrounded by parking lots, not buildings, and highways in the outlying areas are better developed, resulting in development far from the center. The restoration of central cities in the New York area may be a way to slow suburban and rural sprawl, but Tokyo has its own version of sprawl, with the commuting area spread over a wide region. Many people endure commuting up to two hours each way on trains that are so overcrowded that commuters must be pushed into the cars by conductors. There have been some attempts to create urban cores outside of central Tokyo. In the 1980s, the national government created Tsukuba, a research and science city about 45 miles from Tokyo. The latest and most audacious proposal is to move the capital out of Tokyo. While removing government offices from the city center would help relieve overcrowding, the driving force behind this proposal is not so much urban planning as the desire to decentralize power by separating Japan's political capital from its business capital. Building a new capital would also stimulate Japan's weak economy.

SOCIAL CLASSES IN THE CITY

Fujita and Hill discuss the spatial mixing of social classes in the Japanese city from the perspective of urban sociology. Within the Japanese city, the houses of the poor and the rich, the mechanic, the clerk, and the mayor are essentially the same. They each share the same dimensions, proportions, materials, and plan matrices. They are products of the same system, and they show it. Fujita and Hill point out that class-organized place stratification is practically nonexistent in Japan's second-largest city, Osaka. Despite an acute awareness of status, class consciousness is relatively weak. Horizontal social affiliations based on occupation or class lines appear here and there, but the great majority of people share what they believe to be middle-class incomes, ambitions, attitudes, and lifestyles. Fujita and Hill provide interesting comparisons between the political and social ecology of Japanese and American cities as they explore reasons why class segregation is so much lower in Japan than in the United States.

SOCIAL AND PSYCHOLOGICAL EFFECTS OF ENVIRONMENTAL POLLUTION

Kidder points out the sociological and psychological effects of environmental pollution caused by urban-industrial development. He describes the experiences of air-pollution victims in Amagasaki, a city in southeastern Hyogo prefecture, situated on Osaka Bay. Amagasaki has been an important port since the Heian period (794-1185). A castle town during the Edo period (1600-1868), in modern times its proximity to Osaka made Amagasaki a major industrial center. Steel, electrical goods, and chemicals are the principal industries. In the period of rapid growth following World War II, environmental pollution accompanied industrialization, and the area became one of the most polluted regions in Japan. At first there was widespread ignorance on the part of the public and apathy on the part of the government, which was loath to permit anything that might interfere with the rapid economic growth of the postwar period. By the late 1960s, however, the degradation of the environment had deeply struck the national consciousness, and a series of environmental protection measures were taken (Barrett and Therivel, 1991). In major lawsuits regarding pollution-related diseases, the right of the victims to compensation was established. The lawsuits clarified the responsibility of the companies to ensure that their activities were nonpolluting and to prevent pollution from actually taking place. Kidder notes that in Amagasaki air-pollution victims view litigation as a means of exerting moral and political pressure on government and industry leaders.

He argues that, contrary to sociological theory, which suggests that catastrophies such as environmental degradation sap the cohesion of communities, the victims' movement in Amagasaki has created stronger communal feelings among people who had previously had little to do with their neighbors.

Japan's adoption of the polluter-pays principle in the 1970s, in which polluting enterprises had to accept financial responsibility for damages they inflicted on the community, gives priority to health protection and then addresses the conservation of nature. The enforcement of the antipollution policies takes place at the local prefectural or municipal level, which designates and classifies pollution or environmental protection zones. Tolerable limits remains high for many substances, and, when environmental goals conflict with "stable" growth, the latter prevails.

URBAN LAND USE AND CONTROL AND CHALLENGES FACING CITY PLANNING AND GROWTH

Callies's study of urban land use and control in the Japanese city points out the new challenges facing city planning and urban growth management in Japan. His essay uses the examples of Hiroshima, Osaka, and Kyoto to explain the problems of urban planning in Japan. A city planning law to facilitate the sound and orderly development of cities was enacted in 1968. It replaced the old urban planning law of 1919. There are seven main provisons in the 1968 legislation. First, city planning is defined as planning related to land use, maintenance of city facilities, and urban development projects to facilitate the stable and orderly growth of cities. Second, the law applies only to city planning areas designated by prefectural governors. Third, the law divides urban areas into urbanization promotion areas and urbanization control areas to promote planned growth. Fourth, in order to undertake development activity, it is necessary to receive development approval from the prefectural governor in advance. Fifth, city planning includes city structures such as streets, railways, parks, and plazas as well as urban-development projects such as land-regulation projects or residential-development projects. Sixth, the decision-making authority for city planning is delegated to the city, town, and village mayors, the prefecture governors, and the minister of construction. Finally, the law establishes an approval system for city planning projects. The City Planning Act of 1968 was amended in 1980 to introduce selective district planning on a detailed block-by-block basis.

In addition to the impact of the city planning law, the revision of the Building Standard Law (1950) in 1963 changed the face of big Japanese cities. Until that time, buildings in urban areas were limited to a height of 34 meters, but the progress in construction technology had made it possible to build extremely earthquake-resistant high-rise buildings, which eliminated the need for height restrictions. The first skyscraper of the new era was erected in 1968: the Kasumigaseki Building, a 36-storied structure in downtown Tokyo. That same year, the Urban Policy Council of the ruling Liberal Democratic Party (LDP) produced a Guideline for Urban Policy that emphasized the principle of keeping housing in proximity to working places in urban areas and encouraged the redevelopment of urban areas with the erection of high-rise buildings. Until that time, there had been no attempt to impose order on redevelopment, and, as a result, buildings were laid out in a chaotic jumble. The Council, therefore, advocated the creation of city Master Plans, redevelopment in units of a certain size, with redevelopment areas containing high-rise housing, other necessary amenities such as clinics and restaurants, adequate roadways, open space, sunlight, and efficient urban facilities such as common tunnels for utility lines.

It was from these proposals that the Urban Redevelopment Law was drafted, in 1969, paving the way for integrated redevelopment of both the buildings and infrastructures of designated areas. The Urban Redevelopment Law of 1980 obligated the governments of Tokyo and other major cities to draft "Urban Redevelopment Master Plans." Although it is not legally binding, a master plan functions as the guideline for urban redevelopment. Tokyo's master plan, finalized in 1986, aims to deal with the problems, including long-distance commutes and traffic congestion, brought on by a highly centralized urban structure in which businesses and services are densely concentrated. This is to be done by converting to a multicenter city, and creating an environment that is resistant to disaster while being filled with energy and vitality. Methods to achieve this include incentives and land-use regulations to promote redevelopment that will lead to the creation of subcenters, a better balance between residential and business areas, the erection of fireproof buildings, the formation of safe, "disaster-resistant urban areas" surrounded by firebreaks,and the creation of environments that enjoy economic vitality.

The "Comprehensive Economic Measures" approved in 1983 to relieve economic friction with the United States by promoting domestic demand, viewed urban redevelopment as a powerful tool for encouraging private-sector activities. By relaxing floor-area-ratio restrictions and promoting high-rise construction, the government used urban redevelopment as a tool to expand domestic demand. The redevelopment of public employees housing projects was also encouraged so that the government land would be used more effectively. In 1986 work began on two projects—Redevelopment of the Tokyo Waterfront and Redevelopment of the Tokyo Station Area—that had been suggested by the LDP Policy Research Council as vehicles for introducing private-sector capital to public-sector projects. Urban redevelopment programs became a major part of national economic policy in Japan during the 1980s.

Advances in internationalization of Japanese corporations and expansion of Tokyo as a global economic center in the middle of the 1980s caused central management functions to concentrate more in Tokyo. Central functions on a national level have traditionally been overconcentrated in Tokyo, while Tokyo has also recently assumed a more important role on a global level. As a result, the development of cities and urban regions tends to be more uneven in Japan. In Tokyo, with the demand for office space far exceeding supply, land prices skyrocketed. A further result of the surge in business office demand was that redevelopment projects tended to be office buildings rather than urban living spaces, which were often dropped entirely. This in turn triggered a reduction in Tokyo's resident population. When the bubble burst in 1991, however, economic recession began to have a detrimental impact on Tokyo's development. In 1997 the Tokyo metropolitan government scaled back the Tokyo Bay Development project after finding it impossible to meet the costs of the original plan.

Urban redevelopments, which are adopted as a means of making space for both global functions and increasing domestic demands, have changed urban land-use patterns within Tokyo on a large scale. While this spatial restructuring has made urban space an enormous resource for capital accumulation, it has changed the class formation of residents and has provoked conflicts about the future image of each neighborhood among residents in many areas.

In addition, an increase of foreign laborers during the 1980s has added a new factor to the social structure of Tokyo and other large cities.

Callies concludes that Japanese urban land-use planning is top-down and is based largely on economic considerations, but recent changes appear to reflect an increasing concern for the protection of both the natural and built environment. In Hiroshima, Osaka, and Kyoto, the prefectural governors, in consultation with the national government, have designated lands into (*a*) urban promotion areas, where development is encouraged, and (*b*) urban control areas, where development is restricted. Plans are designed to guide the orderly development of these areas, but exceptions are frequently allowed. Although Japan's city planning is modeled after America's urban planning, the planning process in Japan has not been able to control and coordinate the outward sprawl on the urban fringe, because of the segmentation of land ownership with small farmers and property developers, tax laws, subsidies, rising land prices, and a vibrant capitalist market economy with powerful political and financial interests (Harada, 1996). However, the result of this planning failure is not as serious in the Japanese city as it is in the American cities (with low-density strip development on the edge), because of the intense interdigitated urban landscapes of Japan (discussed by Mather in chap. 2) with their mixture of agricultural, industrial, service, and residential uses that characterize Japan's cities.

IMPACT OF GLOBAL RESTRUCTURING AND REDEVELOPMENT EFFORTS

Gilman discusses the impact of global economic restructuring and the resulting decline of the Japanese coal-mining and industrial town of Omuta in Kyushu and the loss of jobs in Flint, Michigan, resulting from the demand for smaller, fuel-efficient imported cars following the oil crisis of 1973. The Japanese residents of Omuta, like their American counterparts in Flint, made efforts to revitalize the local economy. Gilman points out that redevelopment efforts in both Omuta and Flint failed because of a lack of innovation in the revitalization process.

Omuta City, in the southern Fukuoka Prefecture, is located on the Ariake Sea. The city developed rapidly after the Mitsui Company took over the government-run Miike Coal Mines in 1889. Coal was discovered in the area in the late fifteenth-century. In 1873 the mines were taken over by the Meiji government. From 1876, Mitsui Bussan, the trading arm of the Mitsui business group, was the sole exporter of Miike coal, and in 1888 the government sold the mines to Mitsui. The Mitsui Mining Co., Ltd, established in 1892, formed the basis of the Mitsui combine's wealth. On the basis of the local coal resources, the chemical, metal, and machinery industries flourished in Omuta. Since the 1960s there has been a general decline in coal consumption.

At the same time, Miike mines were the scene of several large-scale labor strikes, which culminated in the strike of 1960. It was Japan's most protracted labor dispute, lasting for 282 days. In the spring of 1959, Mitsui had called for the "voluntary" retirement of 6,000 miners, in line with its policy of rationalization in the face of competition from cheap imported oil. The union rejected this proposal, and several intermittent strikes took place. In December 1959 the company issued a list of workers it wished to dismiss, which included many of the union activists. In January 1960 management declared a lockout. Responding to the perceived threat to employment security, the union called for a full strike. Some 4,000 miners formed a new union, with company assistance, and returned to work, but picket lines were set up, and a pitched battle ensued. The strike was settled in November 1960. Mitsui agreed to train miners for new jobs provided by the company and the government. Although the coal mine and other Mitsui-affiliated enterprises are still in operation, Omuta became an economically depressed area.

Gilman's essay describes and interprets the process and characteristics of Omuta's economic restructuring. He compares that with a similar attempt to revitalize the economy of Flint, Michigan, and demonstrates the difficulty of revitalizing and building a new economic and technological base in a traditional industrial city in both Japan and in the United States.

IMAGE OF THE CITY IN LITERATURE

Burton describes the late-Meiji-era image of Tokyo as depicted in Natsume Soseki's novel *Sanshirô,* which was published in 1908 and translated into English in 1977. Literary creations by writers in the form of novels, short stories, poems, plays, diaries, memoirs, and essays are rich resources within which are treasured, extremely valuable, and unique sources of information regarding perceptions, views, values, and attitudes associated with landscape and place. Literary creations form a rich source of information about a place, stored by sensitive and imaginative writers. Expressions of a writer's emotions and sentiments about space as revealed in a literary creation offer a bond between the landscape and literature. In Burton's essay, the view of Tokyo during the last decade of the nineteenth century and early years of the twentieth century is described, on the basis of the work of Soseki.

Born in Tokyo in 1867, Soseki scrutinized Japan's rapidly modernizing society during the Meiji era and the contradictions of life in a backward country during modern times. He ranks as a major figure in modern Japanese literature. Soseki's early education included intensive studies of classical Chinese. By the time he entered the English Department of Tokyo University, he had already decided to become a scholar of English literature. He began to compose haiku. Soseki went to England as a government student in 1900. On returning to Japan in 1903, he joined Tokyo University and lectured on literary theory and criticism. In 1907 he joined the newspaper *Asahi Shimbun*. During the time he worked at the newspaper, he wrote one novel each year. Soseki's work reflects an understanding of the changing times during the Meiji period. He died in 1916, but his works provide an elegant insight into the modern city and portrays human relationships during a period of rapid change and modernization. In *Sanshirô*, Soseki criticizes the developing modernization of Japan through the portrayal of various types of youths. It depicts the shifting psychological state of the main character, Sanshiro, and his relationships with intellectuals of different ages in Tokyo. A recent study of Tokyo's residential structure by a geographer using historical data offers many similarities to accounts of the city by Soseki (Ueno, 1985).

REFERENCES

Barret, Brendan F. D., and Riki Therivel. 1991. *Environmental Policy and Impact Assessment in Japan*. London and New York: Routledge.

Bestor, Theodore. 1989. *Neighborhood Tokyo*. Stanford: Stanford University Press.

Cybriwsky, Roman. 1991. *Tokyo: The Changing Profile of an Urban Giant*. Boston: G. K. Hall.

Eyre, J. Douglas. 1982. *Nagoya: the Changing Geography of a Japanese Regional Metropolis*. Chapel Hill, N.C.: Department of Geography, University of North Carolina.

Fujita, Kuniko, and Richard Child Hill, eds. 1993. *Japanese Cities in the World Economy*. Philadelphia: Temple University Press.

Harada, Sumitaka. 1996. Urban Land Law in Japan. *Social Science Japan* 6:30-31.

Jinnai, Hidenobu. 1995. *Tokyo: A Spatial Anthropology*. Translated by Kimiko Nishimura. Berkeley: University of California Press.

Mather, Cotton, P. P. Karan, and Shigeru Iijima. *Japanese Landscapes: Where Land and Culture Merge*. Mesilla, N. M. and Baltimore, Md.: The Geographical Society and John Hopkins University Press.

Shapira, Philip, Ian Masser, and David Edgington. 1994. *Planning for Cities and Regions in Japan*. Liverpool: Liverpool University Press.

Ueno, Ken'ichi. 1985. "The Residential Structure of Tokyo in the 1910s (the Taisho era)." *Geographical Review of Japan* 58:24-48.

2   The City in Japan

P. P. KARAN

Cities, in their infinite variety, express the complexity and intensity of the human experience. Nowhere do we find the history, economy, and cultural heritage of a nation more vividly enacted than in its urban areas. Cities are also the fundamental prerequisite of civilization. The histories of ancient Greece and Renaissance Europe bear this out, for it was urban dwellers and urban lifestyles that supported the flourishing arts and letters of these cultures. Cities are not just agglomerations of people, they are the providers of services and functions that are necessary for civilization to thrive. In Japan, cities have grown over several centuries in different geographic regions and economic settings and, therefore, reflect diverse characteristics. Specific features of site and topography modify the form of the city. However, despite intra and inter-regional variations, recurrent national patterns of urbanization are, in their particular characteristics, a reflection of the social values and economic life of the country (Scholler, 1984). During the last 25 years, as a result of increasing trend toward globalization of the world economy and the important role Japan plays in it, contemporary large Japanese cities and urban areas have emerged as places where the many separate and superimposed social, technological, institutional, and economic networks that link them coalesce, cross, and intersect with wider interconnected groups of global networks. In the future, the complex interactions of global networks will increasingly influence the shape of urban life and urban development in Japanese cities.

Japan is one of the most highly urbanized countries in the world. The high level of urbanization has been mostly achieved in the last 50 years and is expected to continue, although at a reduced rate (table 2.1). However, the large city is not something new for Japan. There is a long tradition of urban life. During the eighteenth century, Tokyo, with an estimated one million inhabitants, was the largest city in the world, and in 1700 Osaka was probably third in the world urban hierarchy after London. Again today, with approximately 39 million people, the Tokyo Metropolitan Area, as opposed to the city of Tokyo, is the largest in the world (Masai,1990).

EARLY HISTORIC CITIES: NARA, HEIANKYO (KYOTO), AND KAMAKURA

The development of cities in Japan can be traced back to the Nara (710-794) and Heian (794-1185) periods, when the first permanent capitals of Heijokyo

Table 2.1. Urban Population in Japan, 1920-90

Year	National Population (millions)	Urban Population (millions) (percent)		DID Population (millions) (percent)		Percent Land Area in DID
1920	55.9	10.1	(18)	—		—
1930	64.4	15.4	(24)	—		—
1940	71.9	27.6	(38)	—		—
1950	83.2	31.4	(37)	—		—
1960	93.4	58.6	(63)	40.8	(43.7)	1.03
1970	103.7	74.2	(72)	55.5	(53.5)	1.71
1980	117.1	88.9	(76)	69.9	(59.7)	2.65
1990	123.6	94.4	(77)	78.1	(63.2)	3.11

Source: Japan Statistical Yearbook 1995 (Tokyo: Statistics Bureau, Management and Coordination Agency, Government of Japan, 1994)

Note: In 1960 Japan established Densely Inhabited Districts (DIDs) in the population census. Because of the expansion of city area by absorption of neighboring *machi* (towns) and *mura* (villages) and amalgamation into new *shi* (cities), the old definition of urban and rural areas had become unsatisfactory. A DID is defined as a group of contiguous census-enumeration districts with a high population density (4,000 inhabitants or more per square kilometer) within the boundary of a city, ward, town, or village constituting an agglomeration of 5,000 inhabitants or more. DIDs are actually built-up urban areas that should rightfully be called "urban."

(now Nara) and Heiankyo (now Kyoto) were established. Both of these old cities of Japan illustrate the detailed town planning in early Japan. Nara was built on a plain crossed by the Sahogawa and Akishinogawa. Empress Gemmei moved her court there in 710. The city was laid out on a grid pattern of square blocks modeled on that of the Chinese Tang Dynasty (618-907) capital of Chang'an. Major streets intersected to form 72 large blocks—8 rows running north to south and 9 rows running east to west. Each large block was subdivided into 16 smaller blocks. Later, 12 additional large blocks were added on the northeast side of the city and 3 partial blocks on the northwest. After the capital was moved from Nara in 784 by Emperor Kammu, the city continued as an important center and attracted pilgrims to its many Buddhist temples.

Heiankyo (literally "capital of peace and tranquility") was the original name of Kyoto, the capital of Japan from 794 to 1868. Heiankyo was located between the Rivers Kamogawa and Katsuragawa. Heiankyo was also patterned after Chang'an. The course of the Kamogawa was shifted to flow around the city, and canals were dug parallel to the major north-south avenues. The new capital city measured about 4.5 kilometers (2.8 miles) east to west and 5.2 kilometers (3.2 miles) north to south. With the exception of the state-sponsored Toji and Saiji, constructed near the Rajomon gate, no temples were allowed within Heiankyo. Among other reasons, the capital was moved to Heiankyo to eliminate the excessive political power of the Nara Buddhist priests. The residence of the emperor and imperial government offices were located in an area called the *daidairi* (outer palace grounds) in the northernmost part of the city. Also located there was the hall called the *daigokuden*, from which, initially, the emperor governed the country. The palace of the emperor stood at the right center of the daidairi within the dairi (inner palace grounds). Directly south of the daidairi was a large park, Shinsen'en.

Heiankyo was divided by the broad avenue Suzaku Oji (84 meters, or 276 feet, wide) into two districts, Sakyo to the east and Ukyo to the west. In each of these districts was an office called the *Kyoshiki.* Together they administered the affairs of the capital city. The two main districts were subdivided into large square sectors, called *bo,* by streets running east to west and avenues running north to south. The Shijo Oji area was the center of industry and commerce in the city. The Ukyo quarter was a damp lowland, and the city developed toward the east, straddling the Kamogawa, with its population center near the west bank of the river. During the Onin War (1467-77), more than half of the city was destroyed, but it was rebuilt in the sixteenth century. The palace was moved to the present site in the north-central section of modern Kyoto in the eighteenth century, but the present buildings, now known as the *Kyoto Imperial Palace,* date from the nineteenth century.

During the Nara and Heian periods, Japan fully emulated the elements of Chinese city planning and succeeded in creating a reasonable approximation of the city after a Chinese model, complete with detailed administrative areas and an impressive capital that demonstrated the transcendent magnificence of the emperor. While the Chinese influences never died out completely, the Japanese created indigenous urban architecture, style, and institutions later that bore only a slight resemblance to Chinese prototypes.

At the start of the Heian period, Kyoto had a population of at least 100,000. Soon, other cities were built, primarily for political and military purposes, although some, such as Naniwa (now Osaka), also was developed to serve the needs of travelers. In the seventh and eighth centuries, Osaka, now the third-largest city in Japan after Tokyo and Yokohama, was a port for trade with China and the site of several imperial residences. In 1583 Toyotomi Hideyoshi, the national unifier, built the Osaka castle. In the Edo period (1600-1868) Osaka served as the entrepôt for goods, especially rice, for the entire nation and was called *Japan's kitchen.*

By the thirteenth century, Kamakura, seat of the Kamakura shogunate (1192-1333), had a population of more than 10,000. Kamakura, overlooking

Sagami Bay, was a small seaside village when it was selected as the seat of the shogunate. The feudal bureaucracy that was created by the shogun to oversee the vassals made Kamakura the center of political power in the nation. As a capital city it offered two major advantages: it was far removed from the intrigues and refined influences of the imperial court in Kyoto, and it was a natural stronghold. Bordered by Sagami Bay to the south, Kamakura was protected on the other three sides by an unbroken crescent of hills. Easily defensible passes were cut through these hills at strategic points to enable overland travel to and from the town without jeopardizing its security. The leaders of the Kamakura shogunate began to patronize Buddhist temples. The vigorous urban culture of Kamakura—which stood in clear contrast to the cultivated delicacy of the aristocratic city culture evolved by the courtiers of Kyoto—sprang up in large measure from the affinity that developed between the warrior leaders and the Zen monks.

After the fall of the Kamakura shoguns early in the fourteenth century, a new shogunal government was established by the Ashikaga family in Kyoto, but Kamakura remained the center of administration of the Kanto region until the civil wars that preceded the rise of the Tokugawa family in the sixteenth century.

ORIGINS AND DEVELOPMENT OF CITIES IN FEUDAL JAPAN

As the central authority of the military government declined in the fifteenth and sixteenth centuries, towns increasingly evolved around castles built by regional warlords (*daimyo*) to defend their petty fiefdoms. The castle of the local fiefs—surrounded by the living quarters of a large group of professional warriors, the *samurai,* became propitious centers for the development of cities. These towns offered the advantages of a strategic market, a degree of protection in a period of internecine warfare, and opportunities for amusement and entertainment. Thus, most of the first large cities and towns of Japan had their origins as strategic political-economic centers of small feudal semi-independent territories. Artisans and traders flocked to these castle towns, and in several instances a town became so specialized because of some feature of trade or manufacture that it acquired national fame. So firmly established did these specializations become that, even now, certain Japanese cities have maintained their reputation for specific trades. During the Edo period (1600-1868) these castle towns continued to grow in size and stability (fig. 2.1). The castle town of Edo (now Tokyo) had a population of over one million by the mid-eighteenth century.

The castle town (*joka machi*) formed the administrative center of a *daimyo* domain and became the characteristic form of the Japanese city from the mid-sixteenth century until the Meiji Restoration of 1868. The antecedents of *joka machi* can be traced to the turbulent fourteenth and fifteenth centuries,

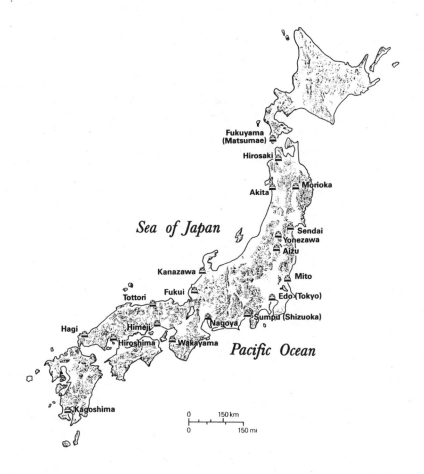

Figure 2.1 Major Castle Towns and Treaty Ports in Medieval and Feudal Japan, 1185-1869

when local magnates built wooden fortresses, often situated on bluffs and protected by walls or moats, to secure control over the surrounding territories. Full-fledged urban communities emerged in the sixteenth century with the enforced resettlement of the *samurai* around their lord's castle and the joining of market and castle in a single location.

Initially, castle towns were small, consisting of the castle complex and surrounding dwellings. The growing authority of the daimyo was increasingly mirrored in their imposing city plans. The relatively few daimyo who survived the internecine warfare of the sixteenth century converted their cities from defensive outposts to administrative and commercial headquarters for mobilizing the area's resources. After the advent of the Tokugawa rule, in 1600, separate

Photo 2.1 The castle at Aizu Wakamatsu, northern Honshu. Aizu Wakamatsu was established as a castle town of the Aizu domain in the late sixteenth century. Photo by P.P. Karan

branch-castle settlements were abolished by the rule "one domain, one castle." The number of joka machi stabilized at between 200 and 250. The preoccupation of the Japanese society of that time with social distinctions was reflected in the segregation of elite residences, the correspondence of the lot's size and proximity to the castle with the samurai resident's rank, and the designation of urban commoners' wards. The common people of the towns—other than the nobles, samurai, and priests—were called *chonin*. Although some of the chonin were wealthy merchants, the vast majority were poor artisans, peddlers, and day laborers. The function of the chonin was to serve the needs of the administration and of the samurai who staffed it. They were always subordinate to the samurai authorities. Guilds, groups, and other associations of townsmen existed for control purposes rather than for self-government. After the abolition of the feudal domains in 1871, the highly structured residential and social patterns of the castle town began to disappear abruptly.

The castle towns of Japan monopolized local and regional military and administrative functions and prevailed in commerce and crafts as well (Hall, 1934; Trewartha, 1934). Almost all of the large population concentrations occurred in joka machi, which generally contained about one tenth of a domain's population, including all or most of the samurai. By the early eighteenth century, most castle towns had reached their peak populations.

Other types of city origins in feudal Japan are post-station towns (*shukuba machi*), religious towns (*monzen machi*), port towns (*minato machi*), and market centers (*ichiba machi*). Post-station towns developed along the five radial roads, *gokaido,* which extended from the shogunate capital of Edo. These towns catered to the needs of travelers along the major roadways. The daimyo and their retainers stopped in special inns in shukuba machi, en route to fulfilling their obligation of alternate-year residence (*sankin kotai*) in Edo. Alternate-year residence in Edo was a device developed by the shogun to maintain control over more than 260 daimyos who were autonomous feudal rulers of four-fifths of Japan. The daimyo had to maintain residential estates in Edo, where their wives and children were permanently detained by the shogunate. Shukuba machi facilitated the national integration of Japan through an efficient regulation of movement across the country.

Monzen machi developed near popular temples or shrines. Establishments catering to the pilgrims developed along the roads leading to the shrine or temple. Inns and related facilities emerged near these centers such as Ise, Zenkoji (at Nagano), Kambara, Suwa shrines, and Mishima. Nara is one the major monzen machi of Japan. The town developed under the protection of the great temples. During the centuries of unrest, the merchants and country folk gathered about the great temples. Unlike the castle, which usually occupied a central position in the town, the temples and shrines most commonly occupied peripheral locations. Temples and shrines played a major role in the economy of these towns, influencing their growth and morphology.

Trading centers that developed along seaports are known as *minato machi*, or port towns. Many towns such as Hakata (now part of Fukuoka), Sakai (in Osaka Prefecture), Nagasaki, and Hyogo (now Kobe) flourished as minato machi. During the seclusion policy of the Tokugawa shogunate, when overseas trade was almost entirely forbidden, domestic trade continued at the port towns of Osaka, Shimonoseki, and Niigata on the major sea routes. Many of these free ports were under the control of the merchants who inhabited them.

Another group of Japanese towns developed as *ichiba machi*, or market centers. These market towns established a link with urban life for the merchants of nearby villages and served as their trading places. Most of these towns grew up where some unusual opportunity for trade existed, such as the intersection of two or more important roads. These towns held one-day fairs or outdoor markets and were named after the date of the first opening during the thirty-day lunar month. Examples include Mikkaichi, meaning "Third Day Market" (in Toyama Prefecture), Yokkaichi, "Fourth Day Market" (in Mie Prefecture), and Futsukaichi, "Second Day Market" (in northern Kyushu).

A number of towns have developed as *onsen machi*, or hot-springs towns or spas, which have been major popular attractions for the Japanese people since ancient times. Many of these towns have now developed into large-scale resort complexes. The town of Tamayu, Shimane Prefecture, is based on Tamatshukuri onsen, one of the best-known hot-springs spas in western Honshu. The development of Matsuyama, western Ehime Prefecture, Shikoku, is in part based on Dogo onsen, one of Japan's oldest spas. Beppu, a major spa town in Kyushu, receives nearly 12 million visitors annually. Atami, Shizuoka Prefecture, developed as a resort town around numerous hot springs in the area. Takarazuka, known for its hot springs since the eighth century, is now a residential satellite of Osaka and Kobe. Noboribetsu in Hokkaido is another example of spa town that has developed in recent times. These spa towns have many hotels, Japanese-style inns, restaurants, and recreational facilities.

With few exceptions, all of Japan's modern cities have grown from one of these origins. Many cities had more than one function in feudal times. For example, Shizuoka and Nagoya were both joka machi and shukuba machi. Osaka was both a joka machi and an ichiba machi. In general, towns that had strong locational advantages in feudal days have retained their site advantage in modern times and have become the great industrial and commercial cities. Castle towns such as Osaka, Tokyo, Nagoya, and Hiroshima have not only maintained their locational advantages but have improved their positions as centers of commerce and industry.

Although the city in Japan has ancient roots, the contemporary geographic framework of Japan's urban pattern was established during the feudal period. After 1868, many castle towns became prefectural or regional capitals and added educational, cultural, and service aspects, resulting in the functional transformation of historic cities. Smaller castle towns became centers of light

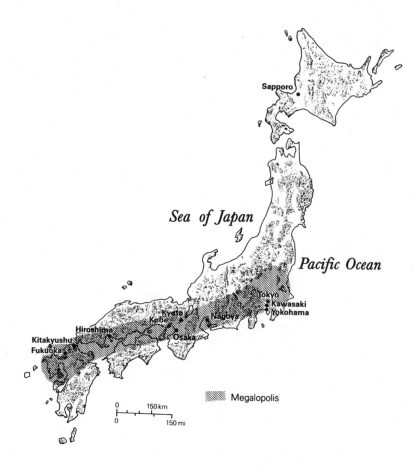

Figure 2.2 Japanese Megalopolis, 1995

industries such as food processing, textiles, brewing, and farm implements.
The larger castle towns attracted heavier industries such as metals and ship-
building and became foci of transportation networks.

   Castle-port cities such as Osaka, Niigata, Shimonoseki, and Nagoya have
continued their administrative-political functions and have added important
manufacturing and service functions. Japan's railroads follow the old feudal
highway network, and former stage towns such as Sendai, Kawasaki, Hama-
matsu, and Nagano have now become railroad centers with manufacturing and
commercial functions. Many religious centers, as well as resort towns, have
grown in importance during modern times along with the surging economy.

areas and the pace of subsequent land use changes to urban functions declined, but by 1975 four more cities—Kitakyushu, Sapporo, Kawasaki, and Fukuoka—joined the "million cities" group, and the population of the 10 "million cities" formed 20.8 percent of the country's population. This figure dropped slightly, to 19.9 percent, in 1980 mainly because of a decline in the populations of Tokyo and Osaka. In 1980 Yokohama, with a population of 2.8 million, was the second-largest city in Japan, while Osaka was third (Karan, 1994). In 1990 there were 209 cities with a population of 100,000, and more than 72 million people lived in these cities. The population of the 11 "million cities" of Japan in 1990 are given below (table 2.2). Except for Sapporo all the "million cities" are located in the Japanese Megalopolis.

The period between 1970 and 1990 was marked by the technological and industrial transformation of the nation, as it evolved into a postindustrial information-based society. By 1990, the population of the Tokyo metropolitan area (Tokyo and its surrounding seven Prefectures) had reached 39 million, a concentration of 32 percent of the nation's population in the Kanto plain and adjacent areas. The cities of Tokyo, Osaka, and Kitakyushu were losing population, but all the other "million cities" were growing. Particularly significant was the growth of population on the outskirts of major cities (Kuroda, 1990; Kuroda and Tsuya, 1989). In 1990 the built-up urban areas constituting the Densely Inhabited Districts contained 78 million inhabitants, or 63.2 percent of the urban population, on 3.11 percent of the total area of the country.

THE JAPANESE MEGALOPOLIS

The axis of the greatest concentration of cities in Japan extends from Kanto to Kinki and along the Inland Sea to northwest Kyushu. This belt forms the Japanese Megalopolis (fig. 2.2), with six great metropolitan areas—Tokyo, Yokohama, Nagoya, Kyoto, Osaka, and Kobe—and extends along the Inland Sea to include cities such as Himeji, Okayama, Fukuyama, Hiroshima, and across the Inland Sea the cities of Tokushima, Takamatsu, Niihama, Imabari, and Matsuyama on Shikoku, and Kitakyushu, Fukuoka, and Nagasaki in northern Kyushu, along with the constellation of their suburbs and satellites (Harris and Edmonds,1982; Kiuchi, 1963). The Japanese Megalopolis, similar to the urbanized northeastern seaboard of the United States, represents a new order in the organization of space with increasing dominance of the service sector of the labor force and the advent of the post-industrial, informational, and transactional era.

Compared with other parts of the country, the Japanese Megalopolis is a unique combination of great population numbers and density, history, wealth, physical diversity, and dynamism. When Japan took its census in 1990, the Megalopolis was home to 78 million people, or 63 percent of the nation's

Photo 2.2 A view of the urban landscape in the Japanese megalopolis at Nisshin, near Nagoya. Photo by Kohei Okamoto

Photo 2.3. New urban growth on the Nobi Plain section of the Megalopolis. Photo by Kohei Okamoto

population. Nearly two-thirds of all Japanese live here, occupying about 3 percent of the country's land. Residential densities in the region exceed 6,600 persons per square kilometer (Masai,1994). In some of the old urban cores, population densities are lower, but they generally exceed 11,000 per square kilometer in Tokyo.

Historically, the region has been the major center of population and economic activity in Japan since the feudal period. The historic Kinki District, where Japan emerged as a cohesive state in the late-fifth century, lies in this urbanized belt. It has been the gateway for virtually all of Japan's trade, and during the Meiji era it served as the launching pad for much of the nation's economic development and modernization. Today, along with the population, the Japanese Megalopolis has a disproportionately large share of the nation's wealth, personal income, commerce, and industry.

Physically, all cities of the Megalopolis are built on alluvial plains or are in part built upon hills or terraces bordering the alluvial plains. The size of the cities and the size of the plains on which they are located are highly correlated. Tokyo, the largest city, is on the large Kanto Plain, Osaka is on the Osaka Plain, Nagoya is on the Nobi Plain, Hiroshima is on the delta of Otagawa, and Fukuoka is on Hakata Bay. All the great cities, except Kyoto, are on the sea coast, and the Megalopolis occupies a narrow belt along the sea coast between Tokyo and Nagasaki. The region has an intricate shoreline of estuaries, deltas, capes and bays, tidal marshes, and many picturesque islands.

Today, the Japanese Megalopolis is a region of immense population concentration along the major railroads that follow the coastal belt, but auto-era dispersal and decentralization is beginning to occur. Here, on 3 percent of the nation's land, most of Japan's labor force commutes between home and work by rail, and therefore the Megalopolis also accounts for most of the country's rail and vehicle mileage. Daily activities in the Megalopolis consume the bulk of the energy used in Japan and generate an equally large share of all the nation's garbage, rubbish, waste gases, and other pollutants. The magnitude and complexity of this urbanized belt of Japan is overwhelming. While the modern features of Japanese cities—factories, smokestacks, wide streets, and noisy, motorized forms of transport—are similar to the features in Western cities, in most Japanese cities the ancient forms and structures are still recognizable despite rapid development.

Between the metropolitan built-up areas from Tokyo to Nagasaki, the Japanese Megalopolis contains hundreds of villages. Some of the most productive farming in the country thrives on the suburban edges of Tokyo, Osaka, Kyoto, Kobe, Hiroshima, and Nagasaki. However, only a very small percentage of people living in the villages are full-time farmers. The vast majority of village households comprise part-time farmers who are supported by urban-type jobs, and in every other aspect they are urban. Consumer electronics,

Photo 2.4 Elevated superhighways such as this one near Yokohama, high speed rail, and *Shinkkansen* (bullet trains) follow the narrow Pacific coastal belt of the Megalopolis from Tokyo to northern Kyushu carrying millions of passengers each day. Photo by P. P. Karan

Photo 2.5 Farm scene in Megalopolis, near Himeji. In addition to rice, farmers grow vegetables and flowers for the urban market. Farming here is part-time activity, with most people working full time in manufacturing and service industries. Photo by P.P. Karan

Photo 2.6 Nagasaki at the southwestern end of the Megalopolis is a major telecommunication hub in Kyushu. Photo by P.P. Karan

precision machinery, integrated circuits, construction, and government service are important parts of the economy of the Japanese countryside in the Megalopolis. Part-time farming provides extra pocket money.

Fundamentally, the Japanese Megalopolis is a vast, interlocking urban network of job trips, shopping and service trips, and social or recreational trips linking dwellings, nonresidential buildings, and recreational and farmland open space. The network is dramatized vividly from the air on a dark winter morning as one watches the lights come on as millions of people rise and begin their day. In a short time, the buildings, roads, and rail lines come alive with hundreds of millions of points of light, and millions of moving lights mark the streams of traffic from home to work. People converge from a multitude of dwelling places and diverge again in several million workplaces. The pattern of commuting is incredibly immense in the large metropolitan areas, but, beyond those high-intensity areas, the interconnected networks of the Japanese Megalopolis branch out to the farthest edges of the region, linking congested urban/industrial clusters that make up this great conurbation on the Pacific belt of Japan.

The last 25 years have witnessed remarkable changes in the economic, social, and geographical makeup of the cities in the Japanese Megalopolis and in their political and cultural dynamics. Comprehensive strategies blending urban, industrial, and telecommunication policies have been employed to create new futuristic cities and urban spaces (Edgington, 1989). In the 1970s, a large new town for public research and development was developed at Tsukuba near Tokyo, and in 1980s Kansai Science City was developed near Osaka (Castells and Hall, 1994). Several other towns and cities were also designated as "Technopolis" for the development of high-technology industry (Masser, 1990). Japan's Ministry of Posts and Telecommunications developed "Teletopia" program to assist public information services in sixty-three model cities. The Ministry of Construction has developed its "Intelligent City" program to encourage the hard-wiring of cities with fiber-optic systems and advanced urban-management networks (Terasaka, Wakabayashi, Nakabayashi, and Abe, 1988). These efforts represent the most important national approach to urban and regional development in Japan on the basis of technology.

Cities such as Tokyo, Yokohama, Osaka, Kobe, Kyoto, Hiroshima, Fukuoka, and Nagasaki are emerging as electronic hubs for telecommunications and telematics (services and infrastructures linking computer and digital media equipment over telecommunications link) networks. Cities of the megalopolis have become powerhouses of communications whose traffic floods across global telecommunications networks. This has started a process of transformation from an industrial, manufacturing–dominated urban society to one increasingly dominated by information, high-technology manufacturing, service, and leisure industries, forcing changes in urban labor markets and urban socioeconomic dynamics. A complex interaction between technologies and the social, economic, cultural, and political change is underway in the cities (Gottman, 1982). At stake here are industrial innovation and trade policy, which are crucially affected by the spatial and social development of telecommunications infrastructures and services, stimulating Japan, as well as Europe and the United States, to construct "information-superhighway" policies with which to boost their economic positions and their strength in the export markets for hardware, software, and support services. These policies have important implications for the Japanese Megalopolis because cities here are the centerpieces of the national and increasingly international telematics market place. Contemporary city economies of the megalopolis can be understood only through their relations to global economic and technological changes.

Increasing shifts toward liberalization and the growth of investment markets have led to a remarkable boom in financial services fueling the growth of larger cities of the megalopolis which are placed at the hub of global electronics and financial networks. As a result, economic activity involving processing and adding value to knowledge and information are now becoming a dominant aspect of the economies of many cities in the megalopolis, transforming them into "post-industrial information cities" (Hepworth, 1987). The world financial and corporate capitals such as Tokyo and Osaka (Sassen, 1991) have emerged as key command and control centers where the best jobs are located. They remain the economic powerhouses of the Japanese Megalopolis. Centralization is occurring here as well as decentralization. In particular, headquarters and control functions are centralizing further onto the elite group of command centers such as Tokyo, Osaka, and Nagoya. At the same time, decentralization of routine service functions from larger cities is leading to new processes of urbanization in other smaller cities. Certain cities, such as Hiroshima, Kumamoto, and Fukuoka, have managed to specialize in advanced manufacturing, research and development, or high-technology services. Some have strengthened their roles as centers for consumption, leisure, and tourism services for both their regional and national hinterland. In addition, many older industrial cities with weak service bases such as Kita Kyushu, are competing to sustain their socioeconomic fabric.

The urban landscape of cities in the megalopolis is being reshaped by global economic forces. Derelict or decaying old industrial spaces are being transformed in many cities into postmodern urban developments as foci of global consumption and culture. Office complexes, business and technology parks, and shopping malls are reshaping the urban areas. Core cities are being turned into extended urban regions that blend into the wider megalopolis. In some cities and regions of the megalopolis, new processes of innovation and manufacturing growth are having an important impact on urban economy. In Osaka and Tokyo, the teleports form the centerpieces of massive land-reclamation and property-development projects (Itoh, 1988). Tokyo's

Photo 2.7 Toyota City in the Megalopolis is the headquarters of Toyota Motor Manufacturing Company. Located in the Aichi Prefecture, the company manufactures automobiles, industrial vehicles, auto parts and components, and prefabricated housing units. Photo by P.P. Karan

Photo 2.8 Japanese cities are investing heavily in the development of suburban shopping centers such as this one outside Nagoya. Photo by Kohei Okamoto

Teleport Town is built on the reclaimed land in the Tokyo Bay. New urban settlements are planned for completion in the twenty-first century on Ariake and Daiba sites, which will include blocks of high-technology "intelligent buildings," sports and leisure activities, and international conference centers.

A range of new industrial spaces, linked into the global market involve key sectors such as semiconductors, electronics, biotechnology, and environmental technologies. Examples of such localized production complexes are spread all across the megalopolis in gleaming, state-of-the-art facilities with major clusters on Kyushu (Silicon Island), Osaka, Nagoya, and the Tokyo metropolitan area. Within these spaces, continuous intellectual and knowledge inputs are far more important than in the previous era of production in the megalopolis. Research and development are ongoing activity, since short product cycles require constant improvements in products. This means that links with academic research institutes and universities, good global transport, and telecommunication infrastructures are important to new emerging high-tech industries in the megalopolis.

Northern Kyushu region of the megalopolis has fared better than the rest of the urbanized belt in the 1990s. This is partly because land prices never rose as much in Kyushu as in Osaka or Tokyo. The relatively cheaper land—and cheaper labor—has drawn many companies. Toyota and Nissan, the country's biggest car makers, built factories in 1992. All the big electronic companies also have plants in Kyushu. A tenth of the world's semiconductors are made in the area. With a tenth of the country's population, this part of the megalopolis accounts for about 12 percent of its gross domestic product. Its economy is about the same size as those of Indonesia, Thailand, and Malaysia combined.

Fukuoka, with a population of more than one million, is the largest city in the Kyushu section of the Megalopolis. This is where the companies have their regional headquarters. One of Japan's largest shopping centers, Canal City, opened here in April 1996. Offices are being built in Fukuoka at a rapid pace. In 1995, about 75,000 square meters (800,000 square feet) of new office space was built in the city, compared with about 55,000 square meters for the whole of the Kansai region of the megalopolis around Osaka. A similar amount of office space is expected to be built in 1996.

About 40 miles to the east, in Kita Kyushu, the second-largest city in the Kyushu section of the Megalopolis, the most-conspicuous features are oil-storage tanks and smoking factory chimneys. Fukuoka is the model of a modern service-driven economy (service companies account for four-fifths of output); Kita Kyushu epitomizes old Japan—the industries that thrust the country into the modern era but whose competitive edge has been eroded by rivals abroad. Once Kyushu's biggest city, Kita Kyushu's fortunes were built on steel. At the heart of the economy is the Yawata steel works. Founded in 1901, the factory became, with Nippon Steel, the world's largest steel company.

Because of the wealth of coal in the area, other-energy-intensive companies, such as chemicals and glass, were also set up there. In 1950, Kita Kyushu's companies accounted for 5 percent of Japanese output. In its heyday in the 1970s, the Yawata works alone employed 46,000 people. Now it employs 8,000, and some of its land is used for a theme park. Kita Kyushu contributes just 0.7 percent of the country's gross domestic output.

But even in Kita Kyushu the economy is improving. Once a byword for pollution, the city has cleaned itself up. Fish have returned to its rivers. An energetic local government is striving for change. Its model is places such as Baltimore in the United States, an old industrial town that has managed to adapt and prosper. It is trying to attract conferences and sell technological know-how abroad. An offshore airport is being built; and its shipping channel will be deepened. It is too soon to say whether all these efforts will bear fruit, but beneath the bald statistics, change is afoot in the western end of the Japanese megalopolis.

With Japan's "internationalization" there has been an influx of foreign labor migrants into the cities of the megalopolis, adding another dimension of change to the urban centers of the region. Attracted by the economic prosperity and shortage of labor, particularly of young workers in construction and manufacturing, the foreign population in Japanese cities has been rapidly increasing. The number passed the one million mark in 1977, 2 million in 1984, 3 million in 1989, and almost 5 million in 1996. Aside from the legal permanent residents, there are illegal, undocumented migrants, mostly from Korea, China, the Philippines, Bangladesh, Pakistan, Sri Lanka, Iran, and Latin America. Brought up in a period of economic boom and faced with many employment options in highly paid jobs, young people in Japan tend to avoid employment in "3Ks"-type jobs—*kitanai* (dirty), *kiken* (hazardous), and *kitsui* (physically hard work). Such a feeling of disdain for 3Ks jobs creates a gap in the labor market, encouraging foreign labor to take up clandestine employment. These international migrants are changing the social geography of cities and towns in the megalopolis.

The economic and social shifts in the Japanese Megalopolis have led to a growing concern to address the environmental dimensions of the cities. Largest number of citizen's complaints concerning environmental pollution are concentrated in the Megalopolis (fig. 2.3).There is need to address the legacies of pollution and dereliction from the industrial era, as well as the sideeffects of burgeoning traffic congestion. The need to compete as an attractive business environment is joining with wider social awareness to force environmental issues to the fore front of urban development policy. Concern centers on the need for environmentally sustainable urban future.

To a large degree, the environmental problems that now characterize Japanese cities have arisen because, during the last 25 years, the Japanese have superimposed a vast industrial/urban economy on an already exceptionally

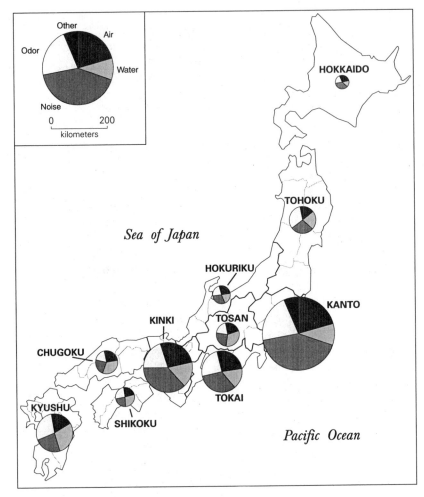

Figure 2.3 Regional Patterns of Environmental Pollution Complaints, 1995

intensive agricultural base in a country possessing an unusually low proportion of flat land. The exceptional congestion, arising from the juxtaposition of tightly concentrated industrial plants with no-less-crowded residential areas, has led to some of the most severe environmental stress in the urban areas. Land shortage may be regarded as the root cause of many of these problems. Demand for urban land greatly outstrips the supply, and, as a consequence, land prices are high. High land price in large cities of the Megalopolis has resulted in widening of commuting zones around these cities. The excessive overcrowding of Japanese commuter trains is also partly due to high land prices; the construction of additional railway tracks to relieve pressure during rush hours would involve purchase of expensive urban land.

Among the environmental issues, air pollution caused by emissions from vehicles remains a serious problem in most larger cities of the Japanese Megalopolis. In May 1996, patients suffering from air-pollution diseases filed suit in the Tokyo District Court against the central government, the Tokyo metropolitan government, the Metropolitan Expressway Public Corporation, and seven companies that manufacture diesel vehicles. The victims demand a ban on the emission of pollutants and compensation. This is the first lawsuit involving Tokyo's air pollution, which is getting worse every year, and the first lawsuit nationally to focus on traffic pollution from vehicle exhausts and to put the responsibility for such pollution on the vehicle manufacturers—Toyota, Nissan, Mitsubishi, Hino, Isuzu, Nissan Diesel, and Mazda. A ruling in 1995 recognized central government and the expressway public corporation, which construct and manage roads, as responsible for air pollution. According to research conducted in 1994 by the Tokyo Council for Air Pollution Monitoring Movement, the average concentration of nitrogen dioxide in Tokyo was 0.068 parts per million (ppm), far exceeding the government's standard of 0.060 ppm. In Tokyo, as well as the other cities of the Megalopolis, 70 percent of the nitrogen dioxide in the atmosphere is discharged by vehicles. Nitrogen oxides are a principal contributor to the photochemical smog which first appeared in Tokyo in July 1970. Since then, it has appeared in all the major cities of the Megalopolis.

In 1988 central government canceled the designation of Tokyo as a polluted area, which ended the recognition of patients suffering from the effects of environmental pollution. There are now 500,000 to 600,000 patients in Tokyo suffering from air-pollution diseases who are not recognized as such. The number of recognized patients, based on the metropolitan government's regulation, increased threefold between 1988 and 1994. In major lawsuits regarding pollution-related diseases, the rights of the victims to compensation has been established, and enterprises must accept financial responsibility for damages they inflict on the community. Even so, when environmental goals conflict with "stable" growth in the Japanese cities, the latter generally prevails.

URBAN DEVELOPMENT CHALLENGE

What are the future development challenges facing Japanese cities as they enter the twenty-first century? There are several major challenges: a realignment of the urban structure; the provision of better living environments; better disaster-proofing; supplying housing spaces in good residential districts, and provision of infrastructure.

There are, however, two urgent problems that Japan must tackle before these goals can be achieved. The first is the problem of residential redevelopment. It includes redevelopment to maintain a residential population in the inner-city area and to rebuild wooden houses and apartment buildings. The second urgent problem is disaster preparedness.

Many cities have poured tremendous energy into the relatively easy to develop suburbs but have done little about the old and congested industrial and residential districts of their inner cities. For example, Kobe became famous for the massive development project that began in the 1950s with the slicing off of part of the Rokko Mountains behind the port and using the earth to reclaim lands in the bay. There Kobe built a small offshore city that included homes, hotels, an international conference hall, and a hospital; on the site of the former mountain, Kobe started a new suburban residential development. At the same time, the city's densely populated inner core was neglected. Lack of inner-city development projects is a weakness of all Japan's major cities.

Dealing with the decline in the inner-city resident population has been an issue for major Japanese cities since the 1970s. Authorities in large cities have tried to turn back this "hollowing" with a "rezone of exclusive residential district" (replacing areas reserved for only one or two-storied houses with areas for multilevel buildings) and a "bonus housing system," which permits a larger building volume for buildings combining residences and offices. This sort of housing redevelopment has traditionally been handled as a local problem, but, in the middle of the 1980s, the central government tried to restore residential neighborhoods by rezoning areas of central Tokyo as "exclusive residential districts." Under this program, height restrictions that had kept buildings to a maximum of three stories were lifted and high-rise housing projects were encouraged. Unfortunately, the program did not lead to the increase in residential space envisioned. Developers were more interested in meeting the demand for offices elsewhere in the city.

During the five years from 1985 to 1990, the population of Tokyo's seven central wards declined by 9 percent. Recovery of residential areas has thus become an urgent challenge for the central wards. In 1992, the government revised the City Planning Law and increased the number of zoning areas from 8 to 12. Traditionally, there have been eight different zoning designations, including residential, commercial, industrial, and the like. The revisions added new types of residential zones and allowed for "exclusive high-rise residential districts" that would bring residential spaces back to downtown areas.

Redevelopment of wood-built houses and apartment buildings is another problem. Tokyo, for example, has about 800.000 of them and is pushing redevelopment in densely populated areas as a means of improving living standards and disaster preparedness.

Japanese cities, which have been engines for the nation's rapid economic growth, are not only cramped but also have had their share of major disasters, with earthquakes occurring frequently. Many redevelopment programs are at least in part attempts to prepare the cities for possible misfortune. In Tokyo's case, the Metropolitan Government takes the lead in designating places of shelter and building escape roads, and it also redevelops areas into what is called "disaster-prevention shelter bases." The Kobe earthquake of January 1995 drove home the need for preparedness. Roads, railways, and other lifelines collapsed, houses and buildings crumbled, and fires raged for days. In all, 6,200 lives were lost, and 420,000 households were affected. About 32 percent of greater Kobe was partially destroyed, and more than 50 percent of its central areas were obliterated. Kobe, which was considered a low-risk area, had only set its building code to resist earthquakes of 5 intensity, which was one of the reasons the damage was so great. Kobe earthquake registered 7 on the Japanese scale of intensity.

The majority of the burned or collapsed buildings were low wooden buildings. but 19 percent of housing structures six stories or higher were affected as well. The chief victims of the Kobe quake were the poor and elderly, who lived in low-rent, dilapidated housing demolished by tremors or fires. Fifty-three percent of those killed by the quake were 60 years of age or older. The mass-transit railway linking the small offshore city built on reclaimed land in Osaka Bay to the mainland was destroyed. The vitality of a city depends on social and public services—transportation, electricity, gas, water supply and sewage, communication, and medical services. The Kobe earthquake showed how the lives of citizens can be crippled by the breakdown of these services. No emergency relief centers or contingency disaster plan existed. The inadequacy of municipal welfare programs for the elderly became apparent in the relief effort.

Japanese cities, Kobe included, are now having to revise their earthquake-resistance standards, and redevelopment projects are being reviewed in terms of these new perspectives on disaster preparedness.

What shape should urban redevelopment take in Japan? First, it seems as if every city in Japan is adopting a cookie-cutter redevelopment program. Cities need to be more innovative and must take advantage of local strengths. Second, urban redevelopment needs to put more emphasis on cultural perspectives, with emphasis on distinctive local or regional personality. Japanese urban planning in this regard has been inadequate, and cultural perspective should be treated with more care in the twenty-first century. Third, Japanese cities must prepare for the coming "gray society." There are some housing projects for the elderly that are going up in Tokyo and other cities, but urban development must adapt the cities themselves to the needs and concerns of elderly people; for example, by constructing more parks and by replacing steps with slopes.

Finally, in addition to being economic spheres, Japanese cities must become amenity-equipped sustainable communities that can maintain vital functions and lifelines in emergencies. Every city in Japan needs to formulate urban policies incorporating several important concerns. Large-scale urban-development projects that entail destruction of the natural environment, especially the razing of forests and the building of artificial islands, should be avoided. Forests, agricultural lands, river beds, and coastlines should be preserved as open spaces or parks. In 1988, in order to bring more land into the housing market, the government increased taxes on the farmland within the areas designated for "urban promotion" to a level equal to those on residential land. The result was reduction of urban farmland, which were the only open space left in larger Japanese cities. The open space is a critical problem in Japanese cities; for example, the ratio of parks to inhabitants is 1 square meter per capita in Tokyo compared with 23 square meters in London and 12 square meters in New York. For open space, cities in Japan have relied on areas devastated by industrial activity, such as gravel pits in the Tama valley or reclamation sites around Tokyo Bay, which have been reconstructed for recreation at public expense. The urban agricultural land should be kept green as urban farms or wooded public parks.

REFERENCES

Castells, Manuel, and Peter Hall. 1994. *Technopoles of the World.* London and New York; Routledge.
Edgington, D.W. 1989. "New Strategies for Technology Development in Japanese Cities and Regions." *Town Planning Review* 60 (1):1-27.
Gottmann, J. 1982. "Urban Settlements and Telecommunications." *Ekistics* 302 (Sept/Oct): 411-16.
Hall, Robert B. 1934. "The Cities of Japan: Notes and Distribution and Inherited Forms." *Annals of the Association of American Geographers.* 24:175-200.
Harris, Chauncy D., and Richard L. Edmonds. 1982. "Urban Geography in Japan: A Survey of Recent Literature." *Urban Geography* 3:1-21.
Hepworth, M. 1987. "The Information City." *Cities.* August: 253-62.
Ito, Tatsuo, and Yoshio Watanabe. 1980. "Recent Trends in Urban Geography of Japan." In *Recent Trends of Geographical Study in Japan.* Tokyo: Science Council of Japan, pp. 89-98.
Itoh, S. 1988. "Urban Development by Teleport." In *Teleports and Regional Development.* Edited by K. Duncan and J. Ayers. North Holland: Elsevier, pp. 235-41.
Japanese Cities: A Geographical Approach. 1970. Tokyo: The Association of Japanese Geographers. Special Publication No. 2.
Karan, P. P. 1994. "The Distribution of City Sizes in Asian Countries." In, *The*

Asian City: Processes of Development, Characteristics and Planning. Edited by Ashok K. Dutt, Frank J. Costa, Surinder Aggarwal, and Allen G. Noble. Dordrecht, Boston and London: Kluwer Academic Publishers, pp. 53-70.

Kiuchi, Shinzo. 1963. "Recent Trends in Urban Geography in Japan." *Annals of the Association of American Geographers.* 53:93-102.

Kuroda, Toshio. 1990. "Urbanization and Population Distribution Policies in Japan." *Regional Development Dialogue.* 11:112-29.

Kuroda, Toshio, and N. Tsuya. 1989. *Urbanization and Counterurbanization in Japan: A National Case Study.* London: Edward Arnold.

Masai, Yasuo. 1990. "Tokyo: From a Feudal Million City to a Global Supercity." *Geographical Review of Japan.* 63:1-16.

Masai, Yasuo. 1994. "Metropolitization in Densely Populated Asia: The case of Tokyo." In, *The Asian City: Processes of Development, Characteristics and Planning.* Edited by Ashok K. Dutt, Frank J. Costa, Surinder Aggarwal, and Allen G. Noble. Dordrecht, Boston, and London: Kluwer Academic Publishers, pp. 119-26.

Masser, I. 1990. "Technology and Regional Development Policy: A Review of Japan's Technopolis Programme." *Regional Studies* 24:41-53.

Sassen, S. 1991. *The Global City: New York, London, Tokyo.* Princeton: Princeton University Press.

Scholler, Peter. 1984. "Urban Values: A Review of Japanese and German Attitudes." *Urban Geography* 5:43-48.

Terasaka, A., Y. Wakabayashi, I. Nakabayashi, and K. Abe. 1988. "The Transformation of Regional Systems in an Information-Oriented Society." *Geographical Review of Japan* 61(Series B)1:159-73.

Trewartha, Glenn T. 1934. "Japanese Cities: Distribution and Morphology." *Geographical Review.* 24:404-17.

Yamada, Hirohisa. 1992. "Regional Differences in the Land Price Decline in Three Metropolitan Areas, Japan. *Science Reports of the Tohoku University (Geography).* 42:21-37.

3   Urban Landscapes of Japan

Cotton Mather

Japan today is one of the most highly urbanized nations in the world. Four-fifths of its population now resides in urban areas, and the landscapes of the cities, towns, and villages are a vivid portrayal of both growth and modernity.

In the Edo Period (1603-1867), Japan's population was almost stable at 30 million. The country then was largely dependent on agriculture, and many scholars believed that this was the pinnacle population under this type of economy, but Japan's current population represents a quadrupling of that of the Edo Period and the transformation of a rural to an urban society. Japan now is one of the 10 most-populous nations in the world. Amazingly, this strikingly large population is on an area of just 1/26 the size of the United States, but the Japanese problem of living space is far more constraining than these figures imply.

Nearly 73 percent of the land of Japan is mountainous, and only 14 percent is arable. Moreover, the arable land is patchy in its distribution, and it is difficult to connect. In yesteryear, Japan was rural in nature and dependent on agriculture. The cities, towns, and villages grew on this base of relatively small parcels of flat land—flat land that is mostly the deltas of streams. These deltas are at the seaward end of stream courses, so most of Japan's population is urban and coastal oriented.

The challenge of modern and urban Japan is basically to organize compactly, three-dimensionally, efficiently, and interconnectedly. This Japan has done with great success. Japan now has the highest average life expectancy in the world, the world's largest source of investment capital, and the highest per capita income in Asia. Furthermore, Japan is now the second-largest economic power on the planet.

Contrasts in scale on the Japanese landscape are the rule. The areas of flat land are very small and are separated by large areas of rough topography. Mountains dominate the terrain of all the main islands. Indeed, Japan is mostly mountainous, mostly forested, and mostly sparsely inhabited. This is a stunning aspect of Japan, so populous and so urban a nation of such small area yet with much of the land essentially devoid of population.

The island aspect of Japan has thus evolved from a rural to an urban-oriented society, from one focused on its segmented areas of flat land and a rural life to one that is urban, compact, intricately organized, and with its urban sectors finely interlaced with its transportation system. One in five Japanese now resides in the eight largest cities: Tokyo, Osaka, Yokohama, Nagoya, Kyoto, Kobe, Fukuoka, and Sapporo. In contrast to the rural reality of the Edo Period, the present reality is one of most Japanese living in jammed urban environments where private space per person is drastically constricted.

The apex of this urbanization is *Tokaidopolis*, the spectacular metropolitan sprawl that stretches along southern Honshu from Kobe and Osaka through Kyoto and Nagoya to Yokohama and Tokyo. This amazing agglomeration, 300 miles long, is an urban system of gigantic dimensions and intricacy. Tokaidopolis, a part of Japan's megalopolis, embraces most of the nation's residences, all of the central government, the headquarters of most of the large industrial and financial institutions, most of the prestigious universities, and all of the great organizations of publication and communication. This concentration of human beings and their institutions has developed into a world-renowned complex famous for its unparalleled productivity, but one with stressful social and environmental aspects. Mainly these pertain to limitations of space for the individual and the family. So Japan's population is highly urbanized and is crowded on the nation's patchy distribution of flattish land, which in aggregate is only one-eighth of the entire country—an area smaller than Costa Rica.

Thousands of individual scenes in urban Japan catch the eye of the observer, but there are recurrent characteristics that represent the distinctive cultural impress of the Japanese people on their land. The Japanese landscape is a vivid portrayal of Japanese ideas and their value system of spatial organization. An identification of the urban landscape lends an understanding to the cultural refinements that have evolved on such a physical base.

PRIMARY CHARACTERISTICS OF THE JAPANESE URBAN LANDSCAPE

The primary characteristics of Japanese urban landscapes are (1) a paucity of idle land, (2) interdigitation, (3) compactness, (4) meticulous organization, and (5) immaculateness. These features of the urban landscape of Japan are related to the severely limited land and the endeavors to organize and maximize that land.

Paucity of Idle Land

The largest of Japan's lowlands is the Kanto (or Tokyo) Plain, which is only about 5,000 square miles in area—about the size of Connecticut. Yet on this single small lowland is a population equal to all of Canada! Small wonder that land in Japan is used intensively, sometimes being sold by the square meter, and that idle land in urban areas is virtually nonexistent (photo 3.1).

Land is precious throughout Japan, more so in the cities than in the towns, more so in the towns than in the country, and more so in old Japan than in Hokkaido, but nowhere is land more precious than in the large metropolitan

Photo 3.1 The renowned Ginza district of Tokyo, the world's most expensive retail shopping and restaurant district. Motor vehicles are excluded on the busiest weekend hours. Photo by Cotton Mather

centers. Not only are these centers without idle land, they are used so intensively that they are three dimensional. Empty lots in America's urban areas may exist for speculative reasons, but in Japan such lots will be used now though they are subject to higher economic use tomorrow. The Japanese do not *zone out* use as in America. They *zone in* multiple types of use and thus produce interdigitation on the landscape.

Interdigitation

The Japanese response to severe constriction in urban areas has been to leave no land vacant, even temporarily, and to have no exclusion of any major type of land use. This pattern evolved as the population increased and with the cultural progression of experience to manage the extraordinary shortfall of space.

Two significant aspects that evolved on the urban landscape should be borne in mind. One is that it is interdigitated, and the other is that the interdigitation pattern is finely textured. That is, the land is subdivided into relatively small parcels. What does this miniparcelization denote?

Japan is mainly a nation of minisized units. Most of the retailing, for example, is done in small shops. The nation does have huge apartment buildings, but most urban dwellers live in small houses or upstairs over shops or other

Photo 3.2 An open storefront in the Arakawa-ku section of Tokyo with the operator's residence on the second floor. The street accomodates pedestrians, bicycles, motor scooters, and children. Photo by Cotton Mather

commercial establishments (photo 3.2). Great corporations—such as Sony and Nissan—exist, but more than two thirds of all Japanese industrial workers are in companies with fewer than 300 employees. Over half of the Japanese factories have fewer than 10 employees, and Japan, on a per capita basis, has almost twice as many wholesalers and retailers as does the United States. The urban landscape mirrors this preponderance of minisized units, or fine texturization, and each type of land use is interdigitated with another type (photo 3.3). Also, there is almost no unused land awaiting speculative development. Although Japan does have land speculation, since the land is so extraordinarily expensive, it is already in some type of interim use.

Compactness

Compactness is another fundamental characteristic of Japanese culture whose impact is felt on the modern urban landscape. Individuals without an historical perspective may assume that this is simply the result of so many people on so little space. Let us bear in mind, however, that the Japanese population has quadrupled in the last 125 years. In 1870, Japan was not straining for space. Yet at that time the Japanese did venerate their long-established miniature verse form known as *haiku*, and they had their scaled-down garden, the bonsai,

Photo 3.3 An interdigitated landscape in the Saijo area of northern Shikoku. Note the vinyl greenhouses in the foreground, and houses, shops, and agricultural fields in the middle ground. In back are houses, a school, and a warehouse. The Japanese view this interdigitation as being well integrated. The residents know their neighbors and share a strong sense of community. Photo by Cotton Mather

their box within a box, their folding fan, their anesama doll, their tatami mat, which could be folded, and their tiny tea house. So the Japanese predilection for compactness is not simply a modern accommodation to so many people on so little space. While Hokkaido has more space per person than Honshu, Shikoku, and Kyushu, throughout the nation the Japanese have contracted their space in much more refined and confined terms than Americans would have done in similar circumstances.

The pressures of the Japanese people on place are most stringent in the huge metropolitan agglomerations such as Nagoya, Osaka, and Tokyo. Those three urban entities alone embrace 43 percent of the national population. Such an astonishing concentration of human beings on such limited space has been possible only with an extraordinary sense of compactness. Huge apartment buildings stack living unit atop living unit, and each of these units has internal space refinements that overwhelm the American mind. Americans do have large apartment complexes, but the individual units in the United States are

Photo 3.4 Modern apartments in northeastern metropolitan Tokyo. The average floor space per dwelling unit in Japan is just slightly over half that in the United States and is considerably smaller than that in western Europe. Photo by Cotton Mather

much larger and lack the internal niceties of confined space that typify the average Japanese apartment (photo 3.4).

Compactness also extends to the places where urban residents of Japan shop. Huge shopping complexes have been constructed, but much of the retailing occurs in the immediate neighborhood where each shop operator is a specialty retailer. These shops are small, varied, and numerous. Moreover, they are nearby. Sidewalks are absent, and the narrow street serves as a passageway for cyclists and pedestrians, so no parking space is needed. Thus, more compactness! Because their home refrigerators are necessarily small, for the Japanese contact with the shopkeeper and his family is frequent. The relationship is both commercial and social. Both they and the members of the shopkeeper family sleep in the same neighborhood and are members of the same community.

Many Japanese do not own an automobile. Those who do may park it in a multi-level, steel-girded structure with an elevator that maximizes space utilization. School grounds are confined. Residences are on minimal lots. In short, everywhere in urban Japan is exemplification of the premium of space. This compactness of the urban landscape is statistically manifested by much higher population densities than that characterizing the American urban scene.

Photo 3.5 Repairing a net along the clean waterfront of the fishing port of Nagahama-cho in western Shikoku. Debris or refuse is completely absent. Photo by Cotton Mather

Meticulous Organization

The urban landscapes are meticulously organized in terms of both time and area. This perhaps has been an outgrowth of a rural heritage where most Japanese farmers owned tiny plots of land. Land was precious even in the era of rural dominance. At that time, *multiple cropping*—the following of one crop after another in rapid succession so that two or more crops could be grown each year on the same piece of land—was practiced. And, long ago, the farmer practiced *interculture*—the growing of two or more crops on the same land at the same time. Thus, fast-maturing crops such as vegetables could be inter-planted among slower-growing tree crops, yet another type of meticulous organization of time and space as well as an illustration of spatial interdigitation on the landscape. These concepts from the rural era have in effect been transmit-ted into a meticulous organization of the modern urban scene, where it has evolved into an interculture or interdigitation of land use for the function of the urban neighborhood.

This meticulous organizational aspect of the Japanese as it pertains to the urban neighborhood is linked with their predilection for reduction; thus, the small Japanese rock garden, the pioneer development of the small automobile, the small transistor, and the small computer.

Americans, by contrast, ever generous with space, have focused on the simplicity of broad urban areas, each relegated to a single type of land use, thus zoning space into industrial, wholesale, retail, or residential areas. Unlike its Japanese counterpart, the American urban landscape focuses on functional economic zones rather than the social concept of the neighborhood.

Immaculateness

No modern industrial nation seems more immaculate than Japan. The clean waterfronts, the neat machine yards, the litter-free factory grounds, the spick-and-span public areas, the swept streets, and the debris-free homes (both back and front) set Japan far apart from the trash-laden lands and those with gaudy billboard-lined thoroughfares, ugly back alleys, and sprawling zones of urban shacks (photo 3.5). Americans, especially, may well maintain that immaculateness is a fundamental characteristic of the Japanese landscape.

Yet there is a curse, a dark and somber side, one common to all industrial nations—severe pollution. *Kogai,* or pollution, is menacing in absolutely every Japanese city. A yellow pall overhangs all Japanese urban centers, and the streams, lakes, bays, and the surrounding areas are laden with poisonous liquids and solids. Japan is an advanced industrial nation, one with an advanced stage of toxicity.

SECONDARY CHARACTERISTICS OF THE JAPANESE URBAN LANDSCAPE

Secondary aspects of the urban landscape of Japan are (1) gardens with sculptured plants, (2) lack of lawns, (3) profusion of aerial utility lines, (4) walled areas with gates, and (5) waning of traditional architecture.

Gardens with Sculptured Plants

The public gardens of Japan are internationally renowned. The public garden is the model, the idolized representation of the aesthetic element from which the economic and spatial compromises must be made for the home. The public garden is a subjugation of nature in which the scale and form of spacious panoramas are miniaturized. Nature in the public garden is in a controlled setting with paths that proffer ever new and glorious perspectives. At its best, the public garden soothes the soul, invites inspiration, and leads to meditation. It is indeed an exultation of nature and the human spirit.

The home garden constitutes a ubiquitous landscape element of Japanese culture. Unlike the public garden, the home garden is typically in a very confined space, separated from the public thoroughfare by a masonry enclosure (photo 3.6). It is arranged with meticulous attention to perspectives gained

Photo 3.6 Home and garden in town of Onoe, Aomori Prefecture of northern Honshu. Masonry encloses the small lot with controlled plant forms. Large windows of the house afford expanded and enriched visual space from the interior. Photo by Cotton Mather

through the fenestration of the home. This represents visual integration of the interior and the exterior so often lacking in the Occidental world. Space is ever precious in Japan; it can be reduced, enriched, and controlled by the sculpturing of plants. Home gardens in Japan are a careful endeavor to enhance the esthetics of the home environment, and they are very private.

The Japanese garden emphasizes nature controlled by the human hand, whereas the English garden is one of studied naturalness, and the French garden represents a rational order with a geometric aspect that is imposed on disorderly nature.

Lack of Lawns

A striking aspect of the Japanese urban landscape is the absence of lawns. This is simply because, in Japan, the lawn is viewed as bland, undeveloped space. Even in Hokkaido, where space is least crucial, lawns are lacking. The lawn is not a feature of the private residence or the great public garden, nor is it even a component of the Japanese cemetery (photo 3.7). Every parcel of flattish land

Photo 3.7 A cemetery in Kita-ku area of Tokyo that is surrounded by residential-commercial land. This quiet island of stone memorials, with surfaced walkways amid trees and shrubs, is without even a patch of grass. Photo by Cotton Mather

in the nation is prized; it is not to be squandered on a monotonous sward. In the Japanese garden, the ultimate objective is to produce a contrived, constricted, controlled, and inspired interplay of rock, water, plants, and light for every minute parcel which in Japan is truly the finest manifestation of "landscape architecture." It is verily an absolute rejection of filling in empty areas with splotches of grass.

This lack of lawns in Japan is to Americans an especially intriguing landscape characteristic. On reflection, Americans may wonder why we merely fill in our open space with just grass. It is certainly noteworthy that for most of the regions in America imported types of grass are planted, that our lawns occupy more land than any single crop, that our 26 million acres of turf grass is an area larger than the state of Indiana, that most of the water in our western cities is used for watering lawns, that our urban householders use far more chemicals than do our farmers, that most of the pesticides used on our lawns have been untested for long-term effects on humans, that our compelling preoccupation with lawns is not an American custom but an offshoot from England, that we expend most of our lawn-time just cutting the growth that we stimulated with fertilizers, and that the most common lawn scene in our country is working the lawn, not enjoying it! Seemingly stuck in our cultural craw are the 1872 words

Photo 3.8 A street in a residential-commercial sector of Tokyo with narrow vehicular lanes, difficult pedestrian walkways, and an absolute maze of transmission wires and cables. Photo by Cotton Mather

of Senator John James Ingalls (1948) that "grass is the forgiveness of nature—her constant benediction."

Profusion of Aerial Utility Lines

Among the most conspicuous elements on the urban landscape of Japan are the utility lines. They are strikingly noticeable for four main reasons: they are so numerous; they are above ground; they spread in every conceivable direction; and they are at many elevational levels. The Japanese are fascinated by technology and employ power and communication lines in myriad ways; hence their extreme dependence on these wired connections. But why are the Japanese utility lines so profuse, so complex in pattern, at so many elevational levels, and why are they solely above ground?

The Japanese are a frugal people. They do not waste space, they are slow to discard what is still useful, they are quick to add and adapt, and, lastly, they have an "inside," not a flamboyant "outside," perspective.

Japan's utility line system evolved with one more wire or one more cable for every new line needed. Old lines were retained, and new lines were added, but they were neither combined nor buried (photo 3.8). If they were serving different elevational needs, so they were placed, and they ran in new directions wherever they were to be used. The appearance of this awesome maze by-passes the Japanese perspective. Their system was not based on appearance or on one grand organization. Rather, it just grew.

The "outside" perspective ranks high in the Occidental world, where cities favor broad boulevards, grand traffic circles, and heroic monuments and statues. So, in the Occidental realm, we find such examples of grand exterior display as the Champs Élysées of Paris, leading from the Place de la Concorde to the Arc de Triomphe, celebrated for its impressive breadth, its tree-lined beauty, and the fountain display at its center. Vienna has its imposing Ringstrasse, a magnificent 150-foot-wide boulevard planted with four rows of trees and lined with splendid edifices and enormous monuments. Rome has its St. Peter's Basilica, with its ellipitical piazza bounded by quadruple colon-nades and the monumental avenue leading to the piazza. In Buenos Aires there is the Avenida de Mayo and the Avenida 9 de Julio, the latter reputed to be the world's broadest boulevard. Even Washington, D.C., has its magnificent mall flanked by great avenues and dominated by the Capitol, the Washington Monument, and the Lincoln Memorial.

Tokyo and the other Japanese metropolitan centers have no counterpart. The Imperial Palace has an "inside," not a flamboyant "outside," perspective. Indeed, the actual palace is walled and surrounded by moats.

So the streets of Japan have one main characteristic, be they the ordinary thoroughfare in a residential-commercial sector or in a major downtown area: they are functional. They are thoroughfares, along and across which are utility lines and pedestrian and vehicular traffic, whereas the Occidental streets have an "outside," or display, aspect, which is of major significance to their cultural psyche.

Walled Areas with Gates

Residential life in Japan in the twentiethth century underwent enormous changes, and during this period the idealized was far from the realized. In the early part of the century, most of the population was rural, although the settle-ment form was in a *strassendorf,* or street village, pattern, where neighborly social relations were strong. The houses were usually flimsy, one-storied struc-tures with only three or four rooms, no basement, no attic, and no continuous foundation. The building was framed on wooden poles and roofed with thatch or tile. Unlike the Chinese preference for clay, brick, or stone, the Japanese were partial to wood. They appreciated the patina of weathered wooden exteri-ors and the mellow tones of hand-rubbed wood on the interior.

The homes were much adapted to a subtropical clime, with sliding panels on the south side that opened to the southern breezes of summer and to the sun in winter. Sliding panels with translucent panes facilitated the multifunctional use of rooms and the passage of light. The broad roof overhang beyond the walls

Photo 3.9 A prefectural road, on the northwestern part of the Kanto Plain, with no shoulders. This narrow road, designed before the advent of the automobile, is a thoroughfare for pedestrians, bicyclists, and motorists. Photo by Cotton Mather

added shelter to the open rooms and related to the changing angle of the sun from winter to summer. A fire pit was used for cooking. Room heating was inadequate, so during cold periods the occupants hovered near the fire. This was the realized.

The homes of the wealthy were in bold contrast. These houses had roofs of tile, metal, or composition. They were larger, often two-storied, and were set back from the street behind a walled area with a locked gate for privacy. Behind the wall was a garden with weathered rocks, sculptured plants, and a pond arranged meticulously to make it an integral component of the home. These relatively spacious residences, with their walled-in gardens, represented the substance and style of the idealized. They still do.

Most of Japan's population resides now in a new reality. They live largely in crowded urban areas with drastically confined private space per individual. The culmination of this is in Tokaidopolis. This world-renowned, massive urban complex, so famous for its productivity, has produced extremely stressful social and environmental consequences. They pertain mainly to the long daily commute via public transportation from residence to work and to the limitations of space for the individual and the family. So the residential unit is compact, children go to parks or commercial playgrounds, automobiles are a luxury, and much of daily life takes place in public and semipublic places. Lacking a guest room in the house, most urban Japanese entertain not in the

Photo 3.10 A multilayered rail landscape at Oji, in northeast Tokyo. Teeming commuter crowds converge on this terminal by foot, bicycle, motorbike, and automobile, then proceed on the surface or upper level by fast passenger trains or travel underground on subways. Photo by Cotton Mather

Photo 3.11 A small Shinto shrine in Kyoto. The city, a major tourist attraction, has more than two hundred Shinto shrines and fifteen hundred Buddhist temples as well as other national treasures. Civil wars and fires, however, have destroyed many cultural gems. Photo by Cotton Mather

home but at restaurants and coffee shops. The idealized home for the majority is just a dream, but one that embodies both the space and style of an elegant and refined tradition.

Waning of Traditional Architecture

Linking the urban centers together and constituting a vital part of the landscape within the urban areas are the road and railway systems. The road system is of poor quality and quantity compared to those in other major industrial nations (photo 3.9). Japan does have a superhighway system, but it has limited outreach, and the right-of-ways are mostly shoulderless and strikingly narrow. About 84 percent of Japanese roads are classified as "other roads," which are suitable only for slow-moving traffic; a third of them are unpaved. Japan has far fewer cars per 1,000 population than any other leading industrialized nation.

Japan, however, has one of the world's most efficient and intricately organized railway systems (photo 3.10). Significant are the *Shinkansen,* known as "bullet trains," in addition to the Limited Express Trains and the local trains. The nation's railways carry more than 22 billion passengers annually, most of whom are daily commuters. The high price of space does not accomodate huge movement by automobile, so the railway is a vital landscape element in both rural and urban Japan.

The nation has precious jewels from the past on the urban landscape, such as the renowned historic buildings in Nara and Kyoto (photo 3.11), but most of the constructs on the present landscape are similar to those found throughout the modern industrial world. Traditional architecture has been waning, and the loss of old displaced structures has been hastened by both natural and human disasters. In the past half century alone, typhoons, tsunamis, earthquakes, and fires have exacted a dreadful and recurrent toll on the nation of Japan. Indeed, few old societies have so few structures from bygone eras. This has been accentuated not only from disasters, but also by Japan's striking pace of economic development. The capital city of Tokyo, for example, rightfully places high regard on and takes pride in its Imperial Palace, but few primary cities in the world are so overwhelmed by modern edifices and with so few symbols of the past. It is conspicuous even in the small outlying urban nodes of Japan that most of the buildings are modern in age, form, and function.

The primary characteristics of the Japanese cities portray the macro aspects of their urban landscapes. In the Japanese psyche, these characteristics represent a neat, well-organized, and full utilization of specific areal resources. The secondary characteristics are refinements of both time and space that place a premium on the cultural privacy of the Japanese that is such an enigma to the Occidental mind.

REFERENCES

Arnold, Edwin. 1892. *Japonica.* New York: Charles Scribner's Sons.

Association of Japanese Geographers. 1980. *Geography of Japan.* Tokyo: Teikoku-Shoin.

Christopher, Robert C. 1983. *The Japanese Mind.* New York: Fawcett Columbine, Ballantine Books.

Collcut, Martin, Marius Jansen, and Isso Kumakura. 1988. *Cultural Atlas of Japan.* Oxford: Phaidon.

Henderson, Harold G. 1958. *An Introduction to Haiku: An Anthology of Poems and Poets from Baho to Shiki.* Garden City, N.Y.: Doubleday.

Ingalls, John James. 1948. In Praise of Blue Grass. In *Grass, The Yearbook of Agriculture 1948* Washington: U.S. Department of Agriculture. p. 7. Reprinted from an address in 1872 by Senator John James Ingalls (1833-1900).

Itoh, Teiji. 1984. *The Gardens of Japan.* Tokyo: Kodansha International.

Keene, Donald. 1971. *Landscapes and Portraits: Associations of Japanese Culture.* Tokyo and Palo Alto, Calif.: Kodansha International. Reprinted as *Appreciation of Japanese Culture.* Tokyo and New York: Kodansha International, 1981.

Kornhauser, David. 1982. *Japan: Geographical Background to Urban-Industrial Development.* New York: John Wiley.

Lee, O-Young. 1982. *The Compact Culture: The Japanese Tradition of "Smaller is Better."* Trans. by Robert N. Huey. Tokyo: Kodansha International.

Minear, Richard H. 1994. *Through Japanese Eyes.* New York: Apex Press.

Noh, Toshio and John C. Kimura, eds. 1989. *Japan: A Regional Geography of an Island Nation.* Tokyo: Teikoku-Shoin.

Reischauer, Edwin O. 1988. *The Japanese Today: Continuity and Change.* Cambridge, Mass.: Harvard University Press.

Statistical Handbook of Japan. 1996. Tokyo: Statistics Bureau, Management and Coordination Agency.

Trewartha, Glenn T. 1965. *Japan: A Geography.* Madison: University of Wisconsin Press.

4 From Castle Town To Manhattan Town with Suburbs

A Geographical Account of Tokyo's Changing Landmarks and Symbolic Landscapes

ROMAN CYBRIWSKY

Many large cities around the world employ landmarks such as prominent buildings and other structures as symbols and use them to shape a favorable image. More often than not, the image they seek is about the city's great size, political or economic power, or sophistication. Examples of well-known symbols range from the World Trade Center, Empire State Building, and Statue of Liberty in New York to the Golden Gate Bridge in San Francisco, and the Sears Tower in Chicago. Abroad, we have the Eiffel Tower in Paris, Big Ben and the Houses of Parliament in London, the Kremlin in Moscow, the Gate of Heavenly Peace at Tiananmen Square in Beijing, and the Opera House in Sydney Harbor. Some landmarks have been around for a long time and have evolved as symbols of their respective cities (e.g., the pyramids outside Cairo), while others were constructed explicitly to be symbols and to give the city wider recognition (e.g., the Pyramid Sports Arena in Memphis, Tennessee).

Tokyo is an especially interesting study in urban symbolism and image. Its symbols have changed with different chapters of history, as the city has remade itself at different junctures and has presented a new public face. Moreover, the city has had more than its share of bad luck with symbols, which have had comparatively short lives because of fires and other disasters. Therefore, more than most cities, and certainly more than any truly large and globally important city, Tokyo is continually creating and constructing new symbols. Furthermore, in Tokyo, as opposed to other cities, urban symbols tend to copy those elsewhere. This is an unusual characteristic worthy of elaboration.

In this chapter, Tokyo's symbols at different times are examined along with comments about future symbols. The study of symbols is a vehicle for understanding how a city has developed and changed, and for dealing with its complexity. Collectively, a city's landmarks can be a summary of a city's biography and can be read to learn about its social history, values, relations with other places, and more. This kind of approach is popular in academic geography, and it relates to the discipline's time-honored tradition of landscape interpretation (Ford, 1994; Lewis, 1976; Relph, 1987).

However, this paper is not just about the symbols of a city. It is also about the symbolic landscapes. The difference between the two is explained in an excellent essay by Donald Meinig that was published in 1979 in a collection called *The Interpretation of Ordinary Landscapes.* As opposed to landmarks, which are specific, named structures or localities, symbolic landscapes are particular *kinds* of places. They are fondly regarded, evoke positive images about the places where they are set, and often are part of the iconography of a nation. In Meinig's words, they reflect the "shared set of ideas and memories and feelings which bind a people together" (1979:164). Examples that Meinig identified for the United States include the typical New England village, "Main Street" from the Midwest, and idyllic suburbia, all of which say things about America that Americans like to hear.

This chapter begins with a discussion of the Edo Period, (1600-1868), when Tokyo was called *Edo* and was the seat of power of the Tokugawa line of shoguns. It is followed by a chronological discussion of the landmarks of the Meiji and Taisho periods (1868-1912 and 1912-26, respectively), the post–World War II era (1945-60), and the present day. The essay will conclude with comments about evolving landmarks and proposals for the future, which are intended to give Tokyo the landmark of all landmarks. Comments on symbolic landscapes are interspersed throughout the text. Because they are much more complicated than landmarks, comments about them will be exploratory. It will not be possible to go through all of the many structures that might qualify as symbols of Tokyo (past, present, or future) in this limited space; consequently, the focus is on the most important landmarks and symbolic landscapes, with a sampling of others.

Edo-Period Landmarks

Let us start with Edo Castle. This is the castle that was ordered constructed in 1603 by Tokugawa Ieyasu (1543-1616), the powerful first shogun of the Tokugawa line. It replaced a run-of-the mill castle, also called Edo Castle, that had been erected in 1457 by Ōta Dōkan (1432-86), a minor warlord. Ieyasu's castle was to be the biggest in the land, indeed in the whole world, and would be a symbol of his great power and authority. The outer defensive perimeter was 16 kilometers (10 miles) in length, while the inner defenses, consisting of a complex pattern of walls and moats, had a length of 6.4 kilometers (4 miles). It dominated Edo. All the provinces in Japan were made to contribute materials and labor for construction, and much of the life of Edo itself was necessarily devoted to the project and to providing for the happiness of the shogun and his inner circle.

In 1651, after nearly a half century of building, the project was completed. Given its size, it must have been an effective symbol of the shogun's authority and of the capital city itself. However, in 1657, barely six years after

Figure 4.1 Landmarks of Tokyo

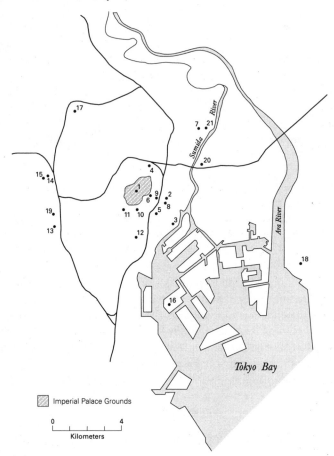

Imperial Palace Grounds

0   4
Kilometers

Edo Period Landmarks
1. Edo Castle *
2. Nihombashi (bridge)

Meiji Period Landmarks
3. Tsukiji Hoterukan *
4. Nikoraido
5. Ginza BrickTown *
6. Mitsubishi Londontown *
7. Asakusa
8. Gaisenhōshukumon *

Taishō Period Landmarks
9. Tokyo Station
10. Imperial Hotel *

No Longer Standing

Post-Earthquake and Post-War Periods
11. National Diet Building
12. Tokyo Tower
13. Yoyogi National Gymnasium
14. New Shinjuku City Center
15. Tokyo Metropolitan Government Headquarters

Other Mentioned Landmarks
16. Telecom Center
17. Sunshine City
18. Tokyo Disneyland
19. Meiji Shrine
20. Edo-Tokyo Museum
21. Sensōji

completion, a devastating fire, called the *Great Meireki Fire,* swept across Edo, found its way past the walls and moats, and burned most of what was inside. Its *donjon,* the central keep, far and away the tallest structure in Edo, was lost forever. Other buildings were rebuilt, but the castle was never the same, even though the shogunate held tightly to power for nearly two centuries more. By the time the Tokugawa line finally fell (1868), and the Emperor Meiji (1852-1912) located his capital on the site, Edo Castle was little more than a dilapidated shell, the last damage having been done by a series of fires in the 1860s.

The site of Edo Castle is still the symbolic heart of Tokyo. The Imperial Palace, where Japan's emperor lives with his family, is there now. Not really a palace, it is instead a very private and ample house that is rarely shown in photographs or other depictions. The grounds are quite large. Some stretches of stone wall and moat remain, as well as some reconstructed guard towers. Mostly, however, the grounds are an oversized empty place where something big once stood. The anthropologist Roland Barthes referred to it nearly a generation ago as Tokyo's "empty center," a "sacred nothing" around which this great and unusual city turns (Barthes, 1982:30-32). If we should go to one of the few observatories that look into the grounds, we would find that there is not much to see. A visit to the East Imperial Garden (*Kokyo Higashi Gyoen*), a sector of the Imperial Palace grounds that is open to the public, reveals foundation stones from the old castle and its massive central keep; the fact that the donjon foundation is set in an open field underscores the emptiness of the site

An Edo Period symbol of a different sort is the bridge called *Nihombashi,* or "Japan Bridge." The first version was erected in 1603, also under Ieyasu's orders. It became the nucleus of the first commercial district in Edo and Japan's "0 marker" for measuring road distances. It is not known whether it was originally meant to be a symbol, because it was a fairly modest bridge over a small river or canal, but it became a symbol, regardless, and has remained an important Tokyo landmark ever since. The bridge was a popular theme for artists of the Edo Period, particularly masters of *ukiyo-e,* the woodblock print. Katsuskika Hokusai (1760-1849), Torii Kiyonaga (1752-1815), and Ando Hiroshige (1797-1858), among others, depicted the bridge as a symbol of Edo life and spirit, especially among the commoners (*chōnin*) who resided in *shitamachi,* the low-lying quarters at the foot of the castle. The degree to which these artists' efforts helped to make Nihombashi a symbol of Edo, versus the degree to which they depicted the bridge because it was already important, is uncertain. It is probably some of both.

Nihombashi still stands, although not the original span. The current bridge is a later incarnation, one erected in 1910-11 during a time when Japan was fascinated with western architecture. The bridge looks like something in Vienna or Prague. It is hard to photograph, because it is in a crowded section with no clear sight lines. What is worse, in the early 1960s, during the rush to prepare Tokyo for the 1964 Olympics, an elevated expressway was built over

Photo 4.1 Remains of the Edo castle. Photo by Roman Cybriwsky

the Nihombashi River, from then on putting the old bridge under a giant shadow. The word *Nihombashi* lives as the name of the important commercial district at the same location.

In terms of *symbolic landscapes* from the Edo Period, the first and foremost scenes are from shitamachi. The word means "low city" and refers to the crowded neighborhoods of ordinary people at the foot of Edo Castle. The *ukiyo-e* artists popularized this district with their bright prints showing the various ingredients of Edo's symbolic landscapes: crowds on the streets, busy canals and bridges, festivals, lively pleasure quarters, theaters, actors, musicians, prostitutes, bath houses, shops, artisans, cherry blossoms, fresh snow, rain, temples, and shrines. These prints often depicted Mount Fuji in the background, for orientation. *Shitamachi* was the true spirit of Edo, the hearth for a distinctive townspeople's culture, and a very special place where the moral and aesthetic ideals referred to as *iki* prevailed. It did not matter which street was shown; Edo's low city was shown in a positive light.

Also within the world of Edo, the pleasure quarter named *Yoshiwara* was especially highly esteemed (Longstreet and Longstreet, 1988). It was depicted frequently by artists and writers of the time. Yoshiwara can be regarded as one of the symbolic landscapes of Edo, if not a landmark, too.

MEIJI-PERIOD LANDMARKS

The Meiji Era was a time of great change in Japan. The feudal order fell, and a wave of rapid modernization and learning from the West set in. Things Western became popular, but they were also strategic, as Japan's new leadership adopted an intelligent strategy of defending the country by showing to foreign powers and its own citizens alike, that Japan could do anything that the foreigners could do. And so began a period of mimicking the West. Edo, now renamed Tokyo, was the place to show the Western face; it was refashioned accordingly (Barr, 1968; Meech-Pekarik, 1986; Seidensticker, 1983).

The first landmark in this category was the Tsukiji Hoterukan. This was a showpiece hotel completed in 1868 near the foreigners' quarter at Tsukiji, near Tokyo Bay. It was a striking brick building that combined curious Western accretions on a traditional Japanese timber-frame base. In doing so, it reflected Japan's first awkward encounters with the world beyond Japan after nearly two and a half centuries of isolation. Even the word *hoterukan* was a strange new blend: the first syllables correspond to the Japanese pronunciation of "hotel," while *kan* is from the Japanese for "inn." In true Tokyo fashion, the "Hotel-inn" lasted only about four years: it was destroyed in a great fire in 1872.

Another landmark hotel came a few years later. This was the Rokumeikan, completed in 1883 in Hibiya, close to the government center. It was the work of an English architect, Josiah Conder (1852-1920), who was brought to Japan at the request of the Ministry of Technology specifically to lend Tokyo a Western look. This building, too, was unusual. It was covered with stucco and combined Moorish, Mediterranean, and other European styles. Here, cosmopolitan Japanese could mix with foreigners at dinner parties, society balls, and musical performances and could learn Western ways. The so-called Rokumeikan Era is remembered for its great splendor and is often romanticized in Japanese films and dramas, but it lasted only seven years. As politics and fashions changed, the building was put to a new use in 1890. It deteriorated and was bulldozed in 1941.

Conder is also responsible for *Nikoraido,* or the Nikolai Cathedral. This is the cathedral of the Russian Orthodox Church in Japan and is associated with Nikolai (Ioann Dmitrievich Kasatkin; 1836-1912), a Russian Orthodox missionary who worked in Japan during this period of extreme foreign influence. The building still stands on its hilltop site in the Kanda area (photo 4.2).

The same fire that had destroyed the first hotel, the Hoterukan, also destroyed Ginza, which until then was only a modest commercial district. The Ginza that followed, however, was a showpiece and a new symbol of the new fangled city. Under the direction of another English architect, Thomas Waters (1830-?), and at enormous expense to the government, the district was fashioned into *Ginza renga gai,* "Ginza Brick Town," a supposedly fire-proof and deliberately European-looking business quarter. Its two-story buildings were made of brick and had colonnades, balconies, and windows that opened up and down. The gas lights along the streets were the country's first. There was some initial resistance by the public to brick buildings in Tokyo's heat and humidity.

Photo 4.2 Nikolai Cathedral, Tokyo. Photo by Roman Cybriwsky

With government subsidies and superior transportation advantages, however, the Ginza soon caught on and became quite a popular district. By the second decade of the twentieth century it was where *mo-bo* and *mo-ga* (modern boys and modern girls) congregated in sophisticated cafes and trendy shops. Their practice was called *gim-bura,* "killing time in Ginza."

Not far away, at the foot of the old Edo Castle (now the Imperial Palace), leaders of the Iwasaki family, founders of the Mitsubishi fortune, began developing a large vacant tract (an old parade ground) into Tokyo's first office district in the 1890s. Josiah Conder had a hand in this project, as did his students. The result was Mitsubishi Londontown, a district of red-brick buildings reminiscent of London's Kensington. However, instead of trolleys and carriages the streets were served by rickshaws. Today the commercial district in the same location is still an important office center called *Marunouchi.*

Meanwhile, in Asakusa, a lively temple town and pleasure quarter to the north of the developing business center, entertainment functions were taking on a new twist. A strange type of building, the cloud-scraping pavilion, *Ryōunkaku,* or simply the "Asakusa 12 Stories," was erected and opened to the public in 1890. It had an octagonal shape and, at about 220 feet (and 12 stories), was Japan's first high-rise. It was also the first building in the country with an elevator. If the Rokumeikan was the great symbol of the elites during the Meiji Period, the Twelve Stories in late Meiji was the symbol of the masses and their pleasures (Seidensticker, 1983: 71). It had a shop with goods from around the world and observation levels equipped with telescopes. However, the elevator did not work well and was quickly closed by authorities. After that, the people walked.

A landmark event of the Meiji Period was the Russo-Japanese War (1904-05). Victory over a European power and the acquisition of new territories in Korea and Manchuria was a symbol to the Japanese of their independence and superiority. In celebration, still another landmark was constructed, *Gaisenhoshukumon,* "the gate of triumphal return." It spanned the main street in the Nihombashi commercial district and looked much like its Parisian counterpart, the Arc de Triomphe built in the early nineteenth century.

On September 1, 1923, all of these Meiji landmarks—Ginza Bricktown, Mitsubishi Londontown, the Twelve Stories, the Orthodox cathedral, and the victory arch—either collapsed or were badly damaged. September 1, 1923, was the date of the Great Kanto Earthquake. The Twelve Stories lost its top four floors. Even though the remaining eight stories stood strong amid the rubble, they were dynamited and removed in the postearthquake clean-up. *Nikoraido* survived, but barely so; today's cathedral is a reconstructed version smaller than the original and with less ornamentation. With the exception of *Nikoraido,* no trace of these landmarks remains today.

A CURIOUS PROPOSAL

Perhaps it is time to note that, precisely because of the exceedingly strong foreign influence on Japan during the Meiji Period, there was at least one proposal made at that time to construct a truly Japanese landmark. The proposal was made in April 1873 by Mishima Michitsune, a bureaucrat who served as governor of several prefectures and who later (in 1885) became superintendent-general of the Tokyo Metropolitan Police. His idea was to construct a high mountain in central Tokyo beside the Imperial Palace and to build a golden Shinto shrine atop the summit. He would then move Ise Jingu, the sacred shrine dedicated to Amaterasu Omikami, the mythical ancestor of the imperial family, from it historic location in what is now Mie Prefecture to the inside of that new shrine. He argued that this would be appropriate because the Emperor now resided in Tokyo and the city was the country's new capital. Furthermore, he insisted that Japan needed a dramatic affirmation of its national identity because of the excessive foreign look that Tokyo was taking on. For better or worse, Mishima's idea was never adopted (Inoue, 1984).

TOKYO STATION AND THE IMPERIAL HOTEL:
TWO LANDMARKS FROM THE TAISHO PERIOD

Tokyo Station, built next to the office district right after the Meiji Period, also survived the earthquake and continues to serve the city today. Designed by

Tatsuno Kingo (1854-1919), this landmark has been described as a copy of the central station in Amsterdam (Wurman, 1984:25). In a continuation of the Tokyo tradition of landmark troubles, however, Tokyo Station was bombed in World War II and came out much shorter; it is missing its two upper floors and its once-prominent cupolas. Nevertheless, it is a treasured landmark. Not long ago, a developer (the Mitsubishi Estate Company) proposed to rearrange things. To make better use of the land, the developers argued, a cluster of high-rises should be build on the site, and the rail tracks should go below the ground, like at the World Trade Center. The old red brick building should be saved, however, in spectacular fashion: it would be lifted to the top of the high-rises as their crown (Matsuda, 1988).

Another Taishō-Period landmark was Frank Lloyd Wright's Imperial Hotel, completed in 1922 after six years of construction (James, 1988). It replaced an earlier Imperial Hotel ("the old Imperial Hotel," or "the first Imperial Hotel"), which conveniently burned just as the finishing touches were being put on the second Imperial. Wright's structure survived the earthquake the next year, and even World War II, but was taken apart in 1967 to make room for the present Imperial Hotel (the third one), a high-rise. The facade and lobby of the building are on display at Meiji Mura, a theme park near Nagoya, while other bits and pieces of the famous hotel are scattered around Tokyo in places such as the Foreign Correspondents' Club and the newest Imperial Hotel.

SYMBOLIC LANDSCAPES FROM THE MEIJI AND TAISHO PERIODS

Both Ginza Brick Town and Mitsubishi Londontown may be viewed as symbolic landscapes, in addition to being landmarks. The Western look of the streets in these two areas was something that made the Japanese feel good about themselves; it did not matter which street or which building you looked at. On the other hand, symbolic landscapes are supposed to have permanence, at least for a while, if not through the ages. On this count, these two districts were not symbolic landscapes, because they were transitory; the earthquake and fires took both of them away, but both areas were also faddish to begin with.

A strong argument can be made that the real symbolic landscapes of Meiji and Taishō were the same as those of the Edo Period: the city's bridges, canals, and rivers and the activity on them; the crowded streets of *shitamachi;* unchanged places such as shrines and temples and their precincts; traditional pleasure quarters such as Yoshiwara; and other pockets of the city that retained Edo identity. These were all places that were painted with high regard by the next generation of *ukiyo-e* artists and that were romanticized in song and literature. The 1937 novel *Bokuto kidan,* by Nagai Kafu (1972), translated in 1958 as *A Strange Tale from East of the River,* is an example from shortly after our period. The novel tells the story of Oe Tadasu, an aging writer who enjoys escaping

Photo 4.3 Tokyo Tower. Photo by Roman Cybriwsky

from the modern city and immersing himself in one of Tokyo's traditional pleasure districts. In a city that was changing rapidly with industrial growth, new
technologies, and floods of migrants from the countryside prefectures,
Tokyoites held tightly to the memories of how their city used to be and looked
fondly at old neighborhoods that were repositories of Edo life and culture.

THE POST-EARTHQUAKE AND POSTWAR PERIODS

The earthquake of 1923 and World War II put a temporary stop to the building
of new landmarks. The National Diet Building, completed in 1936 after nearly
two decades of work, was an exception for the time and was an imposing edi-
fice constructed during the period before World War II. The landmarks that
came with postwar reconstruction were symbols of Tokyo's return to the world
community.

    First was Tokyo Tower (photo 4.3). This instantly famous landmark
opened to considerable fanfare in 1958. Its formal purpose had to do with the
reception and transmission of communication waves, but its greater role was to
stand tall and be seen, Godzilla notwithstanding. Its height, 333 meters (1,093
feet), was a calculated 33 meters taller than the Eiffel Tower was at that time;
its form, although not exactly the same, is similar enough to the structure in
Paris to be called a copy. For its designer, a Japanese university professor
named Dr. Naitō Tachu, it was a crowning achievement: his thirtieth tower and

the biggest by far. The Japanese public called him Dr. Steel Tower. In the book *Tokyo Rising*, Seiedensticker relates a description of Tokyo Tower as a monument to Japanese lack of originality (1990: 251). However, Naito insisted until the end that any similarities between Tokyo Tower and the tower in Paris were coincidental.

In 1964 Tokyo hosted the Summer Olympics. They were held in place of the games that were not played in 1940 and were a chance for Tokyo to welcome international visitors and to show off reconstruction less than 20 years after World War II ended. There were many spectacular building projects, including new roads, rail lines, the monorail to Tokyo International Airport (Haneda), international hotels, and the games facilities themselves. Perhaps the most recognizable symbol of the Olympics was the Yoyogi National Gymnasium, a striking building distinguished by a blend of modern shapes and Japanese traditions. This building, the work of Tange Kenzo, Tokyo's master designer and most influential architect, is still standing.

SHINJUKU

Today, the leading symbol of Tokyo is the skyline of high-rise office and hotel buildings at Shinjuku, the biggest of several "commercial subcenters" of the city. It is Tokyo's answer to the Manhattan skyline and the place where comparisons begin between the "Big Apple" and the "Big Mikan." The high-rise section of Shinjuku is an ongoing redevelopment project that was first announced in 1960; it is formally called *Shin Toshin Shinjuku* (New Shinjuku City Center). The first of the high-rises, the Keio Plaza Hotel, opened in 1971. The Keio Plaza Hotel ended the short reign of the Kasumigaseki Building, which had opened three years earlier in the government buildings district of Tokyo near the Imperial Palace, as *the* high-rise of Japan. Now more than a dozen of Tokyo's tallest buildings are in Shinjuku. Its skyline is the frequent backdrop for a great many movies, television dramas, commercials, and magazine ads. It is also a frequent prop for news reports, both Japanese and international, about Japan's modern economy. Everyone in Japan recognizes Shinjuku, perhaps to the same degree that Mt. Fuji is a well-known form.

There is no shortage of references in Shinjuku to Manhattan. Not only is the area sometimes referred to specifically as Tokyo's Manhattan, it also has its own Central Park (*Shinjuku Chūō Kōen*) and within the park (taking certain liberties with geography) a waterfall fountain named *Niagara Falls* (photo 4.4). There are also some Statue of Liberty replicas in Shinjuku, as there are in many other places in Japan; they usually signal either a pachinko parlor or a love hotel. Other examples of Manhattan-in-Shinjuku are seen on Christmas cards; one shows a nighttime view of the Shinjuku skyline, Christmas snow, Santa and his reindeer in flight above the tall buildings, and, on the glass sur-

Photo 4.4 Niagara Falls in Central Park, Shinjuku, Tokyo. Photo by Roman Cybriwsky

Photo 4.5 Holiday card showing Shinjuku-New York confusion. Photo by Roman Cybriwsky

face of one of the high-rises, the unmistakable reflection of the Statue of Liberty (photo 4.5). The author has a souvenir key chain that reads "Tokyo Megalopolis" and shows Tokyo Tower, some nondescript, Manhattan-like tall buildings, and the clear form of New York's Chrysler Building (photo 4. 6)! (There are no buildings in Tokyo that resemble the Chrysler Building.)

This is actually a very complicated topic that is worthy of detailed attention. Peter Popham, author of a highly regarded book about Tokyo, has thought about Tokyo–New York comparisons, too, and observed that Shinjuku's dramatic skyline is "very eagerly modern" and represents "the embodiment of [Tokyo's] Manhattan fantasies." Yet, on closer inspection, he noted

> . . . it's not like Manhattan at all; it's just like Japan, only fifty stories high. That most venerable Japanese magic trick, in frequent use since at least the eighth century, by which they solemnly and meticulously copy some product of another culture and wind up with something that is unmistakably Japanese is at work again (Popham, 1985: 101-102).

Tokyo's newest and largest landmark is the headquarters of the Tokyo Metropolitan Government, or simply "City Hall" (photo 4.7). It is a complex of three interconnected buildings located in Shinjuku's area of high-rises, directly across from Central Park, which was opened in 1991. The tallest building of the complex is the tallest in Tokyo—48 stories and 243 meters (797 feet). For about two years it was the tallest building in Japan, until Yokohama opened its appropriately named new high-rise on the waterfront, "Landmark Tower." Tokyo's City Hall is touted as the city's landmark for the twenty-first century: it is supposed to look like the future and resemble a computer chip or semiconductor. The designer was Tange Kenzo. It is interesting to note that it was Tange who designed the previous City Hall, the one in downtown Tokyo that was no longer adequate and had to be abandoned.

Because of the enormous size of the project, critics say that the new City Hall is Tange's monument to himself, or perhaps a monument to long-time Tokyo Governor Suzuki Shunichi or his Liberal Democratic Party. It has also been described as "Tax Tower" (because of its luxurious appointments and high cost) and, by a rival architect, the "Tower of Bubble," referring to the buoyant economy that made the building possible (Tabata, 1991: 18). The new City Hall can be seen for miles across Tokyo's western suburbs. In this way, it is a return to Edo Castle, the imposing monument to authority that no one could ignore. City Hall is also supposed to be an echo of Notre Dame Cathedral in Paris. Tange has said this himself, in explaining the twin towers configuration above the 150-meter level (Tokyo Metropolitan Government, 1993: 96).

Photo 4.6 Souvenir key chain with Shinjuku-New York confusion. Photo by Roman Cybriwsky

Photo 4.7 New city hall, Tokyo. Photo by Roman Cybriwsky

Photo 4.8 Ancient and "high-tech" defenses at the base of the new city hall. Photo by Roman Cybriwsky

Tange designed City Hall as a symbol of Tokyo's entry into the twenty-first century, and also as a symbol of Japan's past. Both dimensions are shown in photo 4.8. At the street level and below, the stone facing of City Hall is meant to resemble the stones of Edo Castle. There is a kind of moat as well. That is, the architect's intention was to have the modern building rise out of a traditional Japanese foundation. There are also various other aspects of the design that are meant to reflect the building traditions in old Edo (Kenzo Tange Associates, 1991-93:31). Unfortunately, it seems that most people do not notice these historical aspects and are not particularly impressed when the architect's intentions are explained to them. They see the building as modern (or postmodern), period. What many people do notice, and comment about, is that Citizens' Plaza, the formal entry plaza, is adorned with numerous statues of nude or seminude young women. City Hall, it seems, is a fine symbol of the Japanese tradition of sexism (Shimizu, 1994).

TODAY'S SYMBOLIC LANDSCAPES

The most important symbolic landscapes in Tokyo today are still those that represent old Edo: historic shops, houses, or street scenes that have survived from the past, or that are reminiscent of earlier days, evoke nice thoughts about the city and are highly prized. So, too, are scenes of traditional religious architecture and associated festivals or celebrations. In fact, there has been a nostalgia boom underway in Tokyo, and walking explorations of old Edo, particularly remnant neighborhoods of shitamachi, are quite popular (Enbutsu, 1993; Moriyama, 1993).

A different kind of symbolic landscape is a scene of idyllic suburbia. In this regard, every society greatly values high-quality residential environments and takes pride in its accomplishments. Unfortunately, Tokyo has long lacked good housing and open space for most residents and has had to live with crowding, pollution, a lack of greenery, and other shortcomings. There have been significant gains in these areas in recent years, however, particularly since Japan has achieved its great wealth, and major plans and efforts have been instituted to construct healthful and pleasing residential environments. The results of these efforts are symbolic landscapes that represent Japan's economic success and high quality of life (Robertson, 1991).

Idyllic suburban landscapes are popularized on television as settings for various soap operas and dramas, as well as on TV commercials for new products for the home. They are also seen on countless posters and flyers that advertise houses for sale or the services of builders. These ads are especially numerous on trains and subways, where they hang next to advertisements for wedding halls, English language schools, and Fuji-view burial sites (Nussbaum, 1985). We also see idyllic suburbia presented in the publications of the planning profession. For example, consider the cover of the "3rd Long-Term Plan for the Tokyo Metropolis," which has been reproduced elsewhere (Cybriwsky, 1991: 204-206). It is an artist's rendition that contrasts suburban and central city spaces and reveals quite clearly widely held biases about what the two environments should be like. Suburbia is presented as a green, clean, and spacious environment in which children play wholesome outdoor games, mothers watch attentively over their babies, dogs frolic, and the elderly sit on benches. The central city is in the distant background, marked off from suburbia by a rigid frame and represented by a Shinjuku-type skyline, Tokyo Tower, and some religious architecture that suggests the old city. Presumably, the working-age men of this community are in the office towers of this other environment or taking off for business abroad on the futuristic jet that is shown.

It would be a fascinating study to analyze in detail the design elements of Tokyo's new suburban landscapes. Various themes would emerge. One of these themes would be various international borrowings, much like the international borrowings that we have already seen in Shinjuku and other parts of the city itself. For example, there is a stylized "Parthenon" on a hilltop overlooking the business center of Tama New Town, a planned bedroom community in the western suburbs. The street that leads to this structure is *Parutenon-dōri* or

"Parthenon Street." A second theme would be various manipulations of nature, combined with re-creations of a fabled Japanese past. Such landscapes were discussed by Jennifer Robertson, another urban anthropologist, in her book about Kodaira, a suburban town on the west side of Tokyo (Robertson, 1991). She focused on *furusato-zukuri,* the making of hometowns, and explained how modern Kodaira was designed in a way that enhances new residents' sense of belonging to the community by allowing them to identify with the nostalgic aspects of local history and to imagine unspoiled local natural environments they had never known.

EVOLVING LANDMARKS AND LANDMARKS FOR THE FUTURE

Tokyo is preparing landmarks for the future (Crowell, 1994). The focus is Tokyo Bay, where large new islands are being created on landfill to enlarge the city. A specific plan is Tokyo Teleport Town, a high-technology business center that would keep Tokyo in close touch with commercial centers around the world. This district would be a model residential community for 100,000 inhabitants. The World City Exposition was scheduled to be held there in 1996 to demonstrate advances in urban design, technology, and amenities, but the show was called off in the spring of 1995 by newly elected Tokyo Governor Aoshima Yukio to save costs.

One building within Tokyo Teleport Town is being singled out as the major landmark, Telecom Center. As the name suggests, this will be the hub of the sophisticated global communications system. In the promotional literature about Telecom Center, there are references to this building as Tokyo's answer (for the second time in history; see *Gaisenhōshukumon* above) to the Arc de Triomphe. It has a shining glass surface like so many other of today's buildings, but the form is clearly that of a very large arch. Other parts of Tokyo's waterfront planning suggest that the city is also emulating riverfronts in both Baltimore and Memphis, or some similar recreation-oriented urban waterfront in a North American city. Furthermore, the new long bridge to the reclaimed land in Tokyo Bay has the English-language name Rainbow Bridge, just like the bridge at Niagara Falls connecting New York and Ontario. It, too, has been referred to as Tokyo's new symbol.

Further down the line, there are other proposals. Architect Ojima Toshio has written the following call to action:

> With the recent internationalization of society, people now gather in Tokyo from everywhere in the world, and it seems to me that they now need a city **landmark**. . . . I believe that there is a need to build a landmark in Tokyo which stands above the pyramids, the Colosseum in Rome, the Houses of Parliament in London, the Arc

de Triomphe in Paris, the Empire State Building in New York, and
Red Square in Moscow . . . (Ojima, 1991:6-7).

And so, Ojima has proposed the mother of all landmarks: he wants to
build a giant *torii* (Shinto gateway) over Uraga Channel, the entrance to Tokyo
Bay. This will symbolize Tokyo's "launching-out" (as he calls it) into the world
(8). "Just as Greece lived off the Mediterranean and worshipped Poseidon," he
wrote, this giant *torii* will be a landmark that looks out over the Pacific (8). What
is more, there will be six other gates at each of the major ports of Tokyo Bay, and
seven gates of a different sort in Ginza and Nihombashi, to "symbolize the
status of the area in the tertiary industries of fashion and distribution" (8).

Finally, there is Millennium Tower. The brainchild of the Obayashi
Corporation, a construction company that wants the construction contract, and
British architect Norman Foster, Millennium Tower would stand in Tokyo Bay
and be 840 meters high, almost twice the height of Chicago's Sears Tower.
Some 50,000 people would live there and enjoy the full range of urban services
and amenities. They would have a nice view, too. The proposal also calls for
Millennium Tower be an employment center and, of course, an attraction for
visitors. It might also be a tempting target for that giant, restless catfish under the
sea that is said to cause Japan's many earthquakes. As a summary of the project,
the journal *Japan Architect* concludes, "This extraordinary presentation has attracted great attention from all quarters as a concrete indication of the imminent
arrival of the age of the super high-rise tower" (Foster Associates, Ltd., and
Obayashi Corporation, 1991-93: 120).

SOME FINAL THOUGHTS

There are many landmarks that are not discussed in this essay. For example,
someone might ask about the high-rise office building in Ikebukuro named
Sunshine City, or places as different from each other as Tokyo Disneyland or
the Meiji Shrine. All of these places are also identified strongly with Tokyo, in
addition to the landmarks mentioned earlier. A brand-new, very important landmark is the Edo-Tokyo Museum, which opened in 1993 and is operated by the
Tokyo Metropolitan Government. This is a large and informative museum
about the history of the city. It has a distinctive profile that makes it instantly
recognizable (photo 4.9) and a prominent location across the historic Sumida
River bridge from central Tokyo, right next to the city's main sumo stadium.
The museum (and the sumo stadium) are wonderful places.

Yet, even without discussing all these additional buildings, the main
point is that Tokyo has had an interesting series of landmarks; individually and
collectively they give useful insights into the city's history. A related point is
that landmarks in general, as well as symbolic landscapes, can be helpful in the

Photo 4.9 Edo-Tokyo Museum. Photo by Roman Cybriwsky

study of a particular city, as well as devices for writers who want to tell that city's story.

Tokyo is unusual among cities in having so many landmarks that copy those from a abroad. This is a fascinating characteristic: here is an extremely powerful and influential city—indeed, one of the greatest urban centers in the world—yet, many of its most visible public identity symbols are taken from other cultures. More than that, they copy directly the very identity symbols of famous cities far away. This makes Tokyo appear to be a "wanna-be" city and suggests that some sort of urban inferiority complex is at work. When applied to Tokyo, urban studies might be the province of not just urban geographers, urban historians, sociologists, anthropologists, economists, and the like but also a subject for "urban psychologists" or "urban psychoanalysts."

The pattern of copying Western styles began in the Meiji Era. This is well understood in the literature and is explained as a rational response by Japan to the threats to its security that came with the uninvited arrival on its shores, starting in 1854 after a long isolation, of technologically and militarily superior Western powers. However, the copying continues, even in this age when Japan is on top in the world. Particularly in its capital city, Japan is making efforts to put forward a sophisticated, international, or cosmopolitan face: sometimes the results look a bit awkward.

Photo 4.10 Gate to *Senso-ji,* Tokyo. Photo by Roman Cybriwsky

However, what we are seeing here is just one aspect of Tokyo. In studying urban symbols, we are focusing on a city's most public face—that face which is presented precisely for global consumption. There is a contrasting, private side to the city as well. Exaggerated public symbols call the world's attention away from what is private and personal in Tokyo and keep the private and personal intact. In this respect, many of the landmarks that have been mentioned here, as well as symbolic landscapes, have important political functions. In a world of rapid and confusing changes, and of many negative influences, this arrangement in Tokyo is quite intelligent.

There are other kinds of landmarks in Tokyo, as well, some of them very historic and traditional. They are not publicized as much as others but are treasured more personally by the citizenry and play important roles in people's lives. *Senso-ji,* the temple at Asakusa, is a very special example of such a place. This temple has been around for a long time, even longer than Edo itself, and has religious significance; it also attracts a good number of foreign visitors. Like some of the other landmarks, it has been celebrated in traditional art. The temple's Gate of the Thunder God (shown in photo 4.10) is an especially famous landmark of the city and qualifies as a symbol of Tokyo (or Edo). Because of various convulsions over the city's history, there are not many such places left. Senso-ji has been treated separately, because, in part, the hoopla about all of the other landmarks—the copycat landmarks, if you will—and all of their various changes have worked to keep and protect the Asakusa Temple (and select other places) safe from change.

ACKNOWLEDGMENTS

Thanks to Nobuko Ikue for her generous assistance with this paper and to Professor Toshiake Ohji of Kyoto University for sending me a copy of the paper by Inoue.

REFERENCES

Barr, P., 1968. *The Deer Cry Pavilion: A Story of Westerners in Japan, 1868-1905*. New York: Harcourt, Brace & World.

Barthes, R., 1982. *Empire of Signs*. London: Jonathan Cape.

Crowell, T., 1994. "Tokyo of the Future: Dazzling Ideas that Will Reshape City Life," *Asia Week*, May 1, cover and pp. 34-35, 38, 40-44.

Cybriwsky, R. 1991. *Tokyo: The Changing Profile of an Urban Giant*. London: Belhaven, and Boston: G. K. Hall.

Enbutsu, S. 1993. *Old Tokyo: Walks in the City of the Shogun*. Rutland, Vermont, and Tokyo: Charles E. Tuttle Company.

Foster Associates, Ltd., and Obayashi Corporation. 1991-93. "Millenium Tower," *Japan Architect*, 3 (Summer): 120-25.

Ford, L. R. 1994. *Cities and Buildings: Skyscrapers, Skid Rows, and Suburbs*. Baltimore: The Johns Hopkins University Press.

Inoue, S. 1984. "*Mishima Michitsune to kokka no zokei: Shocho to shiteno toshi to kenchiku*." In *Kokuminbunka no Keisei*. Edited by M. Asukai. Tokyo: Chikuma Shobo, pp. 319-358.

James, C. 1988. *Frank Lloyd Wright's Imperial Hotel*. Toronto: General Publishing Co.

Kenzo Tange Associates. 1991-3. "The New Tokyo City Hall Complex," *Japan Architect*, 3 (Summer): 16-43.

Lewis, P.F. 1976. *New Orleans: The Making of an Urban Landscape*. Cambridge, Mass.: Ballinger Publishing.

Longstreet, S., and E. Longstreet. 1988. *Yoshiwara: The Pleasure Quarters of Old Tokyo*. Rutland, Vermont, and Tokyo: Yenbooks.

Meech-Pekarik, J. 1986. *The World of the Meiji Print: Impressions of a New Civilization*. New York and Tokyo: Weatherhill.

Matsuda, K. 1988. "A Bold Plan to Remodel Tokyo's Business Center," *Japan Echo*, XV, (2):28-30.

Meinig, D.W. 1979. "Symbolic Landscapes: Models of American Community," In *The Interpretation of Ordinary Landscapes: Geographical Essays*. Edited by D.W. Meinig. New York and Oxford:Oxford University Press, pp. 164-92.

Moriyama, T. 1993. *Tokyo Adventures: Glimpses of the City in Bygone Eras.* Trans. by B. and R. Gavey. Tokyo: Shufunotomo Co., Ltd.

Nagai, K. 1972. *A Strange Tale from East of the River and Other Stories.* Trans. by E. Seidensticker. Rutland, Vermont, and Tokyo: Charles E. Tuttle.

Nussbaum, S. P. 1985. "The Residential Community in Modern Japan: An Analysis of a Tokyo Suburban Development." Ph.D. dissertation, Cornell University.

Ojima, T. 1991. *Imageable Tokyo: Projects by Toshio Ojima* Tokyo: Process: Architecture No. 99,.

Popham, P. 1985. *Tokyo: The City at the End of the World.* Tokyo: Kodansha International.

Relph, E. 1987. *The Modern Urban Landscape.* Baltimore: The Johns Hopkins University Press.

Robertson, J. 1991. *Native and Newcomer: Making and Remaking a Japanese City.* Berkeley, Los Angeles, and London: University of California Press.

Seidensticker, E. 1983. *Low City, High City: Tokyo from Edo to the Earthquake.* Rutland, Vermont and Tokyo: Charles E. Tuttle.

————. 1990. *Tokyo Rising: The City Since the Great Earthquake.* New York: Alfred A. Knopf.

Shimizu, A. 1994. "Sexism in Tokyo's New Public Art: Results from Field Research and Opinion Surveys." M.A. thesis, Temple University.

Tabata, M. 1991. "Symbol of a Capital City," *The Japan Times,* April 10, p. 18.

Tokyo Metropolitan Government. 1993. *Tokyo: The Making of a Metropolis.* Tokyo: Tokyo Metropolitan Government.

Wurman, R.S. 1984. *Tokyo Access.* Los Angeles: Access Press, Ltd.

5   Suburbanization of Tokyo and the Daily Lives of Suburban People

KOHEI OKAMOTO

In 1990, 43 percent of Japan's population was concentrated within a 50-kilometer (31-mile) radius of the three large metropolises: Tokyo, Osaka, and Nagoya. The majority of this population lived in the metropolitan suburbs. The suburban residents of these three large metropolitan areas number 41 million, which corresponds to one third of the total population of Japan.

The metropolitan suburbs expanded rapidly during the period of high economic growth in the 1960s. During this period, Japan experienced a major internal migration, as large numbers of people moved into the urban areas from the rural countryside and settled in the metropolitan suburbs. This massive migration tapered off in the late 1970s, and the increase in population of the suburbs has now slowed down considerably. Today, the suburbs are populated by second-generation migrants who were born and grew up in the suburbs. Many Japanese will spend their entire lives in the suburban areas of large cities, so it is very important to study the metropolitan suburbs and suburbanites when considering Japan's society of today and the future.

This chapter consists of two parts. The first part describes the process of urbanization and suburbanization in Japan after World War II. A recent structural transformation of the Tokyo metropolitan area will be examined closely. The second part, based on data on Kawagoe (a suburb of Tokyo), evaluates the quality of life in Japan's metropolitan suburbs. The analysis will focus on time-space constraints among suburbanites, centering on their working activities from the time-geographic perspective.

URBANIZATION AND SUBURBANIZATION OF JAPAN'S MAJOR METROPOLITAN AREAS

In the course of Japan's postwar recovery and period of high economic growth, there have been major employment shifts away from primary industries and toward secondary and tertiary industries. These changes were accompanied by a massive migration from the rural areas to urban areas because of the income differentials and unbalanced labor demands of both areas. In 1950, 38 percent of Japan's total population lived in cities; by 1970, this figure had risen to 72 percent. Many migrants flowed into the industrial belt along the Pacific Ocean and concentrated especially on three major metropolitan areas of Tokyo, Osaka, and Nagoya.

In Japan, a "metropolitan area" is an urbanized area with a large central city. Japan's Statistics Bureau defines 11 metropolitan areas with central cities of a half million or more population. The central cities of the three major metropolitan areas have an especially large population: the Tokyo Ward area, 8.2 million; Osaka City, 2.6 million; and Nagoya City, 2.2 million. The geographic spheres of metropolitan areas have been defined in various ways. The Tokyo metropolitan area, as defined by the National Capital Region Development Law of 1956, consists of Tokyo and seven prefectures within 150 kilometers (93 miles) of central Tokyo. However, most often only Tokyo, Saitama, Chiba, and Kanagawa Prefectures are considered to be part of the Tokyo metropolitan area. Here, data on the commuting distance published by Japan's Statistics Bureau, which defines a metropolitan area as a region within 50 kilometers (31 miles) radius of the municipal office of a central city, is used. Tokyo's commuting zone exceeds 50 kilometers and is over 70 kilometers from central Tokyo.

The rate of population growth in the three major metropolitan areas for every five-year period since 1955 is shown in table 5.1. Until the 1950s, the population influx concentrated on the central cities of the metropolitan areas. However, the rate of population growth in central cities declined after the 1960s because of rising land prices, housing shortages, and environmental deterioration in the central cities. The population of the Tokyo Ward area and Osaka City has been falling since the latter half of the 1960s. On the other hand, the population of areas surrounding the central cities expanded in the 1960s. Many migrants from rural areas moved into the metropolitan suburbs during this period. In addition, the population dispersed from the central cities to the suburbs within the metropolitan areas. The oil crisis of 1973 marked the end of the period of rapid growth in the Japanese economy, and the pace of urbanization also began to slow in the 1970s. Nevertheless, the growth of metropolitan suburbs has continued.

As for the development process of a metropolitan area, the three-step model based on the European experience is well known (Klaassen and Paelinck, 1979). In the first step—urbanization—the population of a central city increases rapidly and is followed by the growth of the surrounding areas. When the rate of population increase in the surrounding areas exceeds that of a central city, the process enters the second stage—suburbanization. Although this stage can be divided into the early phase, in which the population of a central city still increases (the phase of relative decentralization), and the latter phase, in which it declines (the phase of absolute decentralization), the total population of a metropolitan area continues to increase in both phases. When the total population begins to decrease, a metropolitan area enters the third stage— deurbanization. According to Klaassen and Paelinck (1979), some large cities in Europe, including London, were in the stage of deurbanization in 1970. The

Table 5.1. Population Increase in Central City and Surrounding Areas in Three Major Metropolitan Areas of Japan, 1955-1960 to 1985-1990 (percent)

Metropolitan Area	1955-60	1960-65	1965-70	1970-75	1975-80	1980-85	1985-90
Tokyo	19.2	20.3	15.9	12.8	6.4	5.6	4.9
Central City	19.2	7.0	-0.6	-2.2	-3.4	0.0	-2.3
Surrounding Area	19.2	35.2	30.5	22.9	11.6	8.2	8.0
Osaka	14.0	20.8	13.0	9.1	3.6	3.0	2.0
Central City	18.2	4.8	-5.6	-6.8	-4.7	-0.5	-0.5
Surrounding Area	12.3	27.7	19.6	13.5	5.6	3.8	2.5
Nagoya	10.9	12.9	11.1	9.7	5.4	4.0	3.6
Central City	19.5	14.0	5.2	2.1	0.4	1.4	1.8
Surrounding Area	7.3	12.4	13.9	12.9	7.3	4.9	4.2
Three Metropolitan Areas	16.0	19.2	14.2	11.1	5.4	4.6	3.8
Remaining Areas	-0.1	-1.7	0.3	4.1	4.0	2.6	0.8
Japan Total	4.7	5.2	5.5	7.0	4.6	3.4	2.1

Source: Population Census

Note: Metropolitan area is the region within 50 kilometers (31 mile) radius of each central city. The central city is, respectively the Tokyo Ward area, Osaka City, and Nagoya City. Surrounding area (suburbs) is all but the central city in a metropolitan area.

New York metropolitan area also declined in population during this decade. Berry (1976) found that U.S. metropolitan areas grew less rapidly than nonmetropolitan areas in the 1970s, and he named this phenomena "counterurbanization."

The three major metropolitan areas of Japan shifted from the stage of urbanization to the stage of suburbanization in the 1960s, as shown in table 5.1. Since 1965, Tokyo and Osaka have experienced "absolute decentralization." However, since the 1970s, the population increase rate of the three metropolitan areas has been consistently higher than the rate of the remaining areas of Japan, and the symptoms of deurbanization or counterurbanization have not appeared so far. Thus, Japanese metropolitan areas have remained in the stage of suburbanization and maintained their growth.

CONCENTRATION IN THE TOKYO METROPOLITAN AREA
IN RECENT YEARS

As the 1980s began, the growth of the Tokyo metropolitan area became very evident. Although the population growth rate of the Tokyo metropolitan area slowed after the late 1970s, the overall population growth in Japan slowed even more. As a result, the proportion of people living in the Tokyo metropolitan area kept increasing. In contrast, the growth rate of the Osaka metropolitan area, which is the second-largest metropolitan area, has fallen below the overall population growth in Japan since the late 1970s (table 5.1).

The concentration of the population in the Tokyo metropolitan area after the 1980s is closely connected to the fact that Tokyo has grown into a major international financial center. The proportion of all large businesses with 300 or more employees headquartered in the Tokyo area rose from 33.8 percent to 36.2 percent between 1978 and 1989, while the nationwide share of Osaka has decreased from 17.7 percent to 16.6 percent during this period (Economic Planning Agency, 1991:.63). The larger companies tend to concentrate in Tokyo. This trend relates strongly to the progress of an information-dependent society. Although the rapid development of communication networks has increased the accessibility of public information, the greater dependence on information has also increased the business value of informal information obtained through face-to-face contact with government agencies, financial institutions, and clients, thus encouraging the concentration of business headquarters in Tokyo (Economic Planning Agency, 1991: 250).

The current concentration of population and economic activity in the Tokyo metropolitan area is therefore different in character from that occurring during the high-economic-growth period in the 1960s. During that period, the concentration characterized all metropolitan areas including the Tokyo metropolitan area. There was a large-scale transfer of population into metropolitan areas in general. In contrast, the current concentration is limited to the Tokyo metropolitan area.

The promotion of Tokyo as a "world city" and major international financial center has led businesses to locate their offices in Tokyo, which has generated a great demand for office space in central Tokyo in particular. This concentration of offices downtown has pushed residential areas out into the suburbs. In the late 1980s, especially, the "bubble economy" of Japan increased the speculative demand for land, causing the price of commercial land to rise dramatically, which in turn affected the price of residential land. The high land prices spread from central Tokyo to its metropolitan suburbs. As a result, it became more difficult to obtain reasonable housing within Tokyo's neighboring suburbs, and the residential areas were pushed further and further away from central Tokyo.

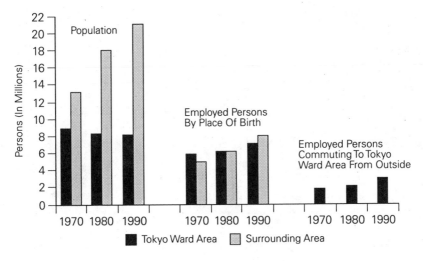

Source: Population Census 1990
See Note in Table 5.1 for Definition of Surrounding Area

Figure 5.1 Resident Population and Employed Population in the Tokyo wards and surrounding area

GROWTH AND SELF-DEPENDENCE OF SUBURBS

In general, the growth of suburbs is accompanied by an increase of economic activities or jobs in the suburbs, but early suburbanization in Japan took place without this type of growth. This led to the development and expansion of the so-called bed towns (dormitory suburbs). Figure 5.1 shows this phenomenon in the Tokyo metropolitan area, which illustrates the change after 1970 in the residential population and the employed population in the Tokyo Ward area and vicinity. The employed population of the suburbs is increasing more rapidly than that in the Tokyo Ward area. However, its pace is slower in comparison with the population increase in the suburbs. As a result, the population living in the suburbs and working in the central city is increasing every year. Workers commuting to the Tokyo Ward area doubled, from 1.6 million in 1970 to 3.1 million in 1990. The current Tokyo Ward area has lost its residential population but increased its working population.

Let us consider the employed population in the Tokyo Ward area and suburbs in terms of the kind of work. Jobs here were classified largely into three groups (excluding agriculture, forestry, and fishery occupations) according to the occupational classifications used in the Population Census (fig. 5.2). The number of persons engaged in production and transport occupations in the

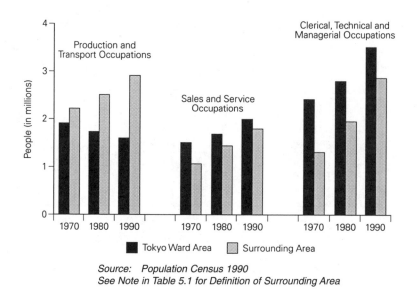

Figure 5.2 Employed Persons by Place of Work and Occupation

suburbs already exceeded the number in the Tokyo Ward area in the 1970s, and the difference between these two areas has widened ever since. As for sales and service and clerical, technical, and managerial occupations, more persons work in the Tokyo Ward area than in the suburbs. However, the employed population of the suburbs is increasing more rapidly than that in the Tokyo Ward area.

Figure 5.2 suggests the decentralization process of the economic activity that each occupational group represents (Kawaguchi, 1990). First, the manufacturing industries shifted from an overcrowded central city to the suburbs, which increased the number of blue-collar jobs there. Next, retail shops and businesses related to individual consumption located in the suburbs in expectation of the increased demand caused by the population increase, which led to more employees in the sales and service sectors in the suburbs. Finally, the managerial functions represented by white-collar jobs have become suburbanized because the central city cannot control the multiplier effects of the suburbs any longer. Thus, the employment opportunities in the suburbs have expanded overall to a greater or lesser degree for each of the occupational groups.

In addition, shopping opportunities have expanded rapidly in the suburban areas in recent years. Many huge shopping centers, even department stores, have located in the suburbs. Suburbanites tend to purchase high-priced

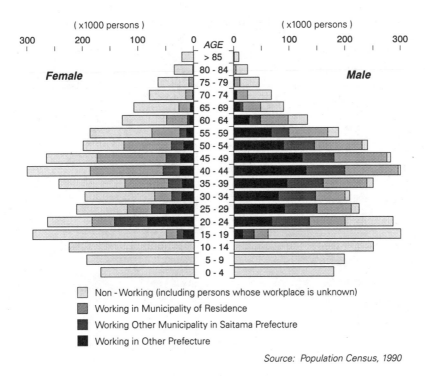

(x1000 persons)   (x1000 persons)

300   200   100   0   AGE   0   100   200   300

Female   Male

> 85
80 - 84
75 - 79
70 - 74
65 - 69
60 - 64
55 - 59
50 - 54
45 - 49
40 - 44
35 - 39
30 - 34
25 - 29
20 - 24
15 - 19
10 - 14
5 - 9
0 - 4

☐ Non - Working (including persons whose workplace is unknown)
▨ Working in Municipality of Residence
▨ Working Other Municipality in Saitama Prefecture
■ Working in Other Prefecture

Source: Population Census, 1990

Figure 5.3 Age Structure and Workplace of Residents in Saitama Prefecture

goods in the suburbs without going to the central city. They seldom visit commercial centers such as Ginza and Shinjuku in the central city. The suburbs are being enhanced as a place for daily life, and dependence on the central city is decreasing (Kawaguchi, 1992).

In spite of these trends, it is also true that the number of commuters to the Tokyo Ward area from the suburbs has been increasing. Examining the age and sex of commuters helps clarify who stays in the suburbs and who goes to the central city. Figure 5.3 is the population pyramid of Saitama Prefecture, one of the suburban prefectures of Tokyo. The diagram also shows where the inhabitants are working in each age/sex group, not just the age/sex structure of Saitama Prefecture. The main workplace for working females is within the municipality of residence, which means they work near their homes. Few women over 30 years old commute outside Saitama Prefecture. In contrast, about 30 percent of working males work outside Saitama Prefecture. We can also regard most of them as commuters to the Tokyo Ward area because 87 percent of commuters to other prefectures commute to the Tokyo Ward area, according to the Population Census of 1990. Thus, the location of the workplace is very

Photo 5.1 Morning rush hour at Kawagoe Railway Station. A large number of commuters board trains at all stops during the thirty- to forty-minute ride between Kawagoe and Ikebukuro station, until they are packed like sardines as the trains approach Tokyo. Most commuters change at Ikebukuro to other railways or subways to get to their workplaces in central Tokyo. Photo by Kohei Okamoto

different for the suburban females and males: the female works close to home, the male at some distance.

The typical commuters to the central city from the suburbs are white-collar males, and their numbers are increasing. Today, the metropolitan suburbs provide increasing employment opportunities as well as daily necessities and services. For many suburbanites, the suburban areas suffice for their daily lives; they need not visit the central city often. However, the central city has recently improved as the business center, where professional people are increasing in number. Many are commuters from the suburbs who must live far from the central city because of the high residential land prices. As they move farther from the central city in search of affordable housing, they require more time for commuting. According to the Metropolitan Area Transportation Census, the average one-way commuting time to the Tokyo Ward area from the suburbs was 1 hour and 20 minutes in 1990. The long journey to work is a great burden on commuters in terms of time and fatigue, because of the extreme crowding of commuter trains, but the financial burden is light, since the transportation fares are paid largely by employers.

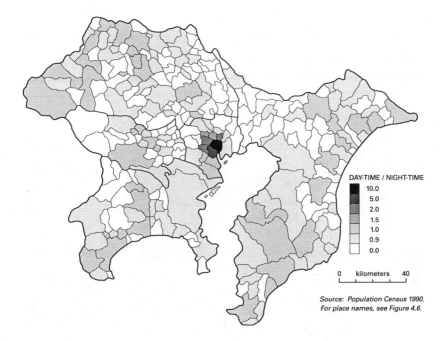

Figure 5.4 Ratio between Daytime and Nighttime Population in the Tokyo Metropolitan Area

Figure 5.3 also indicates the typical age structure of the metropolitan sub-urbs. Populations ranging from 40 to 45 and 15 to 19 years of age predominate. The age groups of 40 to 45 years are those of the baby-boomer generation, who were born just after World War II, and the age groups of 15 to 19 years are their children. The former are mainly the people who immigrated to the Tokyo met-ropolitan area from outside in the great migration period of the 1960s, while the latter were by and large born and brought up in the Tokyo metropolitan area. With applied cohort analysis, Nakagawa (1990) found that the recent segrega-tion of the 1966-70 birth cohort (the age 20-24 group in fig. 5.3) in the suburbs of Tokyo was caused by members of the Tokyo-born younger generation who also moved to the suburbs with their parents in the past.

Today, the percentage of the suburban-born population is growing in the suburban areas. The pyramid in figure 5.3 has a narrow base, which suggests a low birth rate in the suburban area. However, the suburbs are expected to have a higher birth rate in the near future because greater numbers of younger people are living there. The higher growth potential of the metropolitan sub-urbs in Japan requires an assessment of the suburbanites' quality of life.

Photo 5.2 Residential districts in Kawagoe consisting of both single family homes and apartment buildings housing commuters. Photo by Kohei Okamoto

WORKING ACTIVITIES AND TIME-SPACE CONSTRAINTS AMONG SUBURBAN PEOPLE

In Japan's urban areas, many suburbanites commute to metropolitan centers every weekday. In the Tokyo metropolitan area in 1990, for example, 3.6 million workers and students commuted daily to the Tokyo Ward area from the suburbs. The number of these commuters has increased 20 percent over the past five years. Commuters tend to travel mostly to the central part of Tokyo, which has become more and more specialized as a business center and has lost its residential population in recent years. It is notable that the daytime population is now more than 10 times the nighttime population of central Tokyo (fig. 5.4).

Thus, in major cities in Japan, large numbers of people concentrate in the metropolitan center in the daytime and return home to the suburbs at night. Japanese geographers call this phenomena "urban daily rhythm." The enormous commuter flow that causes this phenomenon has produced a variety of problems. Rush-hour congestion is, of course, the best known of these problems. The scene of Tokyo commuters "jammed inside trains like canned sardines, and pushed in even tighter by white-gloved platform attendants" (Cybriwsky, 1991: 94) during the morning rush hour is familiar around the world.

Photo 5.3 On the periphery of Kawagoe, large residential districts have developed housing commuters to Tokyo. Photo by Kohei Okamoto

Routine overcrowding on commuter trains is clearly a serious problem, but another problem arising from working and commuting activities and the urban daily rhythm should be pointed out: constraints on the individual time-space schedule of suburbanites. Recently, residential housing has spread further from the metropolitan centers. Long-distance commutes clearly impose strong constraints on the working people's time-space schedule on weekdays. They leave home early in the morning and get home late in the evening. They have little time to be with their family on weekdays. Such conditions not only makes it difficult for them to deepen their family relationships but also weakens human relationships in the community. This problem is examined in the light of research findings in Kawagoe.

In the time-geographic approach developed by the Swedish geographer Torsten Hagerstrand, space and time are regarded as resources on which individuals have to draw in order to realize projects, while the realization of any project is subject to various constraints in space and time (Hagerstrand,1970; Arai et al., 1989; Arai, 1993; Okamoto, 1995*b*). Modern society after the industrial revolution has needed a synchronization of activities, or a coordination of activities in time and space, in order to accomplish "production project" efficiently (Pred, 1981). As a result, workers have been compelled to act according to "time discipline" and "space discipline."

Photo 5.4 A view of Kawagoe from the city hall. On the few smog-free days during the year, Mount Fuji may be seen in the distance, but not on this day in November 1996. Photo by Kohei Okamoto

Photo 5.5 Kawagoe Railway Station is surrounded by new commercial buildings. The ticket counter is upstairs; the bus terminal is downstairs. Photo by Kohei Okamoto

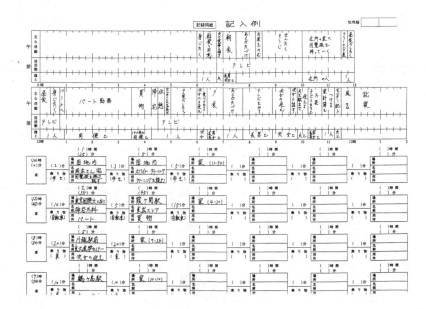

Figure 5.5 Format of the Activity Diary

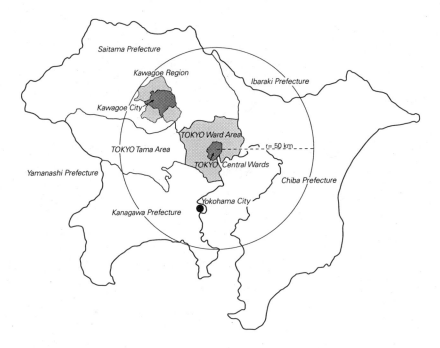

Figure 5.6 Kawagoe Study Area

Photo 5.6 Old commercial core of Kawagoe. Although the old core area is declining, some old store buildings have been preserved. Photo by Kohei Okamoto

Table 5.2. Respondents Performing Various Activities (percent)

Activity	Day			
	Monday		Sunday	
	Husbands	Wives	Husbands	Wives
Work	91.4	50.7	13.2	9.5
Shopping	8.6	71.9	48.9	82.1
Eating out	18.8	10.3	14.8	14.4
Leisure	8.6	9.9	38.5	18.4
Escorting	3.2	26.1	5.5	10.0
Social	2.2	19.7	24.9	40.3
Other	9.1	27.1	11.5	14.4

The dominance of the factory mode of production and the popularization of the clock and the watch have generated time discipline, while the introduction of zoning in planning and the development of mass transport have generated space discipline. Time discipline has brought a division between working hours and nonworking hours, while space discipline has divided the daily activity of people into work-related space and home-related space. Consequently, time discipline and space discipline together produce the urban daily rhythm, in which a large population concentrates in the metropolitan center in the daytime and disperses to the suburbs at night. Suburban residents strengthen this spatiotemporal system by synchronizing their individual activity routine with the urban daily rhythm every day. On the other hand, their daily activities are strongly constrained in this system. Suburban residents are active, as well as reactive, in the relationship with the urban daily rhythm. Here we will try to clarify how the suburban people use space-time as a resource and how they receive the constraints from the "urban daily rhythm" as a societal space-time system.

THE KAWAGOE SURVEY

To examine the quality of suburban life, the author and three colleagues selected two metropolitan suburbs and investigated the daily lives of suburban residents in Kawagoe, a metropolitan suburb of Tokyo, and Nisshin, a suburb of Nagoya, on 1990. Data were taken from an activity diary survey (Jones et al., 1983) of households in the two suburban cities. In this survey, the space-time budgets on Sunday and Monday for both husbands and wives were scrutinized in detail, that is, what activity was done at what time, in what place, and with whom. Figure 5.5 shows the format of the activity diary. The time-budget survey described various activities of the persons participating in the survey along time. At the same time, the travel survey collected data on details of each trip. The crosscheck of the time budget and travel surveys and interviews provided accurate information about these activities. Besides the space-time budgets, the survey obtained supplementary information on the households, including household structure, private automobile ownership, and dwelling history (Okamoto, 1993). About 200 households were investigated in each suburban city, but this paper deals mainly with the data from the Kawagoe survey.

Kawagoe, in Saitama Prefecture, is located about 35 kilometers (20 miles) northwest of Tokyo (fig. 5.6). Kawagoe developed as a castle town and an old commercial center in the prefecture. Recently, Kawagoe has become a commuter suburb of Tokyo. Some 23 percent of its working-aged people commute to Tokyo, according to the Census of 1990. From Kawagoe Station, it takes more than half an hour to travel to Ikebukuro Station and about one hour to Tokyo Station.

The Kawagoe residents surveyed engaged in various out-of-home activities on the Monday and Sunday of the survey. Table 5.2 shows the ratios of the

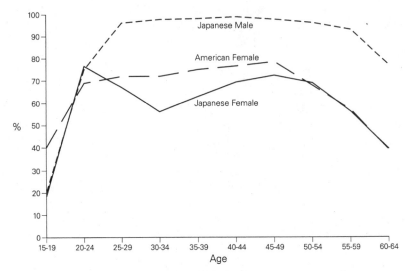

Source: ILO "Yearbook of Labor Statistics 1992"

Figure 5.7 Ratio of Working Persons by Age

respondents who performed each out-of-home activity. On Monday, almost all husbands worked, and the number of nonworking activities was very low, except for eating out. About 70 percent of the wives shopped on Monday. Working and "escorting" were the other significant activities for wives. In Japan, "escorting" means taking a family member to and from anywhere and mainly involves taking children to and from child-care facilities like day nurseries and kindergartens. The proportion of wives engaged in these escorting activities was closely related to their stage in life. The ratio was highest in wives with preschool-age children. Some 74 percent of wives with children from 3 to 5 years old performed this activity on the Monday of the survey.

On Sunday, the husbands' activities varied. Shopping, leisure, and social activities ranked high. Shopping was the most important activity for wives on Sunday, as well as Monday, and the ratio was even higher than on Monday.

Here, one should explain the nature of women's employment in Japan (Kamiya and Ikeya, 1994). Although the percentage of wives who worked on Monday was only 50 percent (table 4.2), this ratio varies according to their stage in life. Figure 5.7 shows the ratio of working women by age group throughout Japan. The age profile of Japanese working females peaked at ages 20-24 years, dropped off, and then rose again as they reached their forties, producing an *M* shape. This profile is rather different not only from that of Japanese males but also women from other countries, including Americans. In Japan, women's careers are often interrupted by childbirth and child rearing.

Photo 5.7 Kindergarten school. Children are driven to school by car or school bus.
Photo by Kohei Okamoto

This has also been the tendency in Kawagoe, although the ratio of working females in the metropolitan suburbs is even lower than the Japanese average in
general (figure 5.3).

INFLUENCE OF WORKING ACTIVITIES ON OTHER ACTIVITIES

Examining the influence of suburban people's work on their daily life first involves the influence of their work on other activities. Table 5.3 shows the geographical distribution of work locations of the Kawagoe residents surveyed.
One half of the husbands commuted to the Tokyo Ward area, about 20 percent
worked in the Tokyo Central Wards (Chiyoda, Chuo, and Minato), and about
30 percent worked in other Tokyo wards. On the other hand, the workplaces of
the wives were usually relatively near their homes. About 70 percent of the
women working full time and about 80 percent of the part timers worked in
and around Kawagoe City, which is called the "Kawagoe region" (fig. 5.6).

Husbands worked for more than 10 hours on the Monday of the survey.
The average working time for husbands was 10 hours 18 minutes. Because of
the long working hours and lengthy commuting time, husbands have little time
for other activities on weekdays. It is not true, however, that the longer time

Table 5.3. Geographical Distribution of Workplaces of Respondents

Location	Husband		Wife			
			Full Timer		Part Timer	
Saitama Prefecture						
Kawagoe Region	47	(24.5)	43	(71.7)	44	(81.5)
Other	37	(19.3)	6	(10.0)	4	(7.4)
Tokyo Ward Area						
Central Wards	34	(17.7)	5	(8.3)	2	(3.7)
Other Wards	67	(34.9)	6	(10.0)	4	(7.4)
Tokyo Tama Area	6	(3.1)	0	(0.0)	0	(0.0)
Kanagawa Prefecture	1	(0.5)	0	(0.0)	0	(0.0)
Total	192	(100.0)	60	(100.0)	54	(100.0)

Note: Numbers in parentheses are percentages.

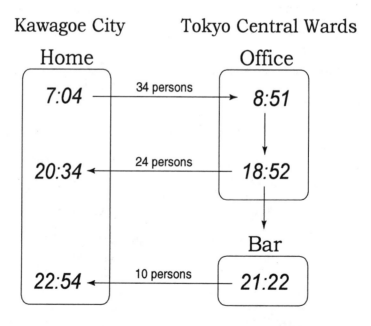

Figure 5.8 Average Monday Schedule of Husbands Commuting to Tokyo Central Wards

Table 5.4. Wives Who Shopped on Monday and Sunday, by Working Status (percent)

Status	Day	
	Monday	Sunday
Full Time	55.0	93.1
Part Time	82.1	75.0
Nonworking	77.0	79.3

they spend commuting, the fewer nonwork activities they perform. About one third of the husbands performed some nonwork activities, regardless of commuting time. In other words, job location did not affect the frequency of nonworking activities as much as the kind of nonworking activity itself. Husbands working in the Kawagoe region did various nonworking activities at various times on the Monday of the survey. Some took a walk before leaving for work, and some drove their wives to the train station on their way to work in the morning; others shopped or stopped for a drink on their way home in the evening; and some went out again after returning home from work. On the other hand, the nonworking activities of husbands working in the Tokyo Central Wards did not show much variety. It consisted of stopping for a drink on their way home from work. They tended to eat and drink with coworkers near their office after hours. Joining coworkers at a bar or a small Japanese-style drinking place after work is popular among Japanese business people. People sometimes eat and drink as part of their business; this is called *settai,* or entertaining business clients, which typically consists of having a meal at a high-quality restaurant and visiting Japanese-style hostess bars. On the Monday of the survey, 10 of the 34 husbands working in the Tokyo Central Wards did this. The ratio of husbands who stopped on the way home to perform nonworking activities was highest for commuters to the Tokyo Central Wards, despite the fact that their commute was the longest in the survey.

Figure 5.8 indicates the average Monday schedule of husbands commuting to Tokyo Central Wards. They left their homes in Kawagoe at about 7:00 A.M., began work at their offices in the Tokyo Central Wards at about 9:00 A.M., and worked until 7:00 P.M. The husbands going straight home arrived there around 8:30 P.M., but husbands stopping on the way home to eat and drink until around 9:30 P.M. got home around 11:00 P.M. Thus, the commuters to the metropolitan center, who have the longest commuting time, usually left home very early and got home very late. For them, home was little more than a place to sleep. They had little time to spend with their families on weekdays.

The average workday for full-time working wives was 8 hours 32 minutes, which is about 2 hours shorter than that for husbands. The commuting time of the wives was also shorter than that of the husbands, because the wives' places of work were relatively near their homes. Therefore, the temporal constraints for nonworking activities were less for the wives than their husbands. Most of the wives, however, went shopping on Monday, as shown in table 5.2, which means that both working and shopping are necessary for working wives, and they must coordinate these two activities. Shopping is more discretionary in terms of time and location than working, so the working wives gave precedence to working and used their spare time for shopping. They tended to shop on weekends and after office hours on weekdays. Table 5.4 indicates the ratios of wives who shopped on Monday and Sunday by working status. The ratio for full-time working wives was low on Monday and high on Sunday, in comparison with the ratio for part-timers and nonworking wives. Full-time workers tended to avoid shopping on busy weekdays. Nevertheless, more than half of the wives working full-time still shopped on Monday, and this percentage was much higher than that of husbands who shopped on Monday, which was less than 10 percent (table 5.2). The responsibilities of housekeeping tasks like shopping weighed on the wives even in the double-income families.

Escorting was the third-most-common activity wives performed on Monday (table 5.2). This ratio was especially high for the wives with young children, as mentioned before. Escorting is an activity fixed in space and time, like work activity, because the place and the service hours of child care facilities are fixed, so the influence of escorting activity on the wives' time-space scheduling is greater than their shopping activity. If both husband and wife with young children work full time, how do they coordinate their activities? This is our next topic.

Sharing and Coordinating of Spouses' Activities in a Two-Career Family with Young Children

Metropolitan suburbanites use public transportation to commute to metropolitan centers because access is difficult by car. Yet, it is almost impossible to escort young children to child- care facilities via jam-packed trains or buses during rush hours. Thus, suburban people cannot use child-care services near their places of work in metropolitan centers. However, a care facility in a suburb distant from the workplace is not an option for them either, because they would get to work too late after leaving their children at the facility and after leaving work they could not get back to the facility before closing time. Consequently, a husband and wife with young children cannot both work in a metropolitan center; one of them has to stay in the suburbs to care for or escort their children. The survey data support this hypothesis.

Table 5.5. Geographical Distribution of Workplaces of Wives, by Life Stage

Life Stage	Saitama Prefecture		Tokyo Ward Area		Total	Percentage Full Time
	Kawagoe Region	Other	Other Wards	Central Wards		
Younger wives without children	9	2	1	3	15	80
Wives with pre-school children	8	1	0	1	10	30
Wives with young school children	35	4	3	1	43	44
Wives with children of high-school age or above	29	3	4	1	37	57
Older wives without children	6	0	2	1	9	56

Table 5.5 shows the geographic distribution of the workplaces of wives by life stage. The workplaces of the younger wives without children extend from the local area to the metropolitan center. A few wives commute to the Tokyo Central Wards. Not surprisingly, the percentage of wives working full time is relatively high at this stage of life. It is safe to say that they have far greater options in terms of work location and type of work (notice in fig. 5.3 that females age 20-25 years work at various locations).

On the other hand, the options for wives with preschool children seem to be restricted. Most of their workplaces were within the Kawagoe Region, and only 1 in 10 wives commuted to Tokyo. The working ratio is low for women in this stage of life in Japan, as noted before. If a family lives with either the husband's or the wife's parents, the grandparents can help care for the children, which would enable the wife to work outside the home. However, this type of household is rare in the metropolitan areas. Therefore, almost all working wives with young children must use child-care services, and they are faced with the difficult problem of how to coordinate working with escorting their children to and from the child-care facilities.

Table 5.6 summarizes how each of 10 surveyed households dealt with the problem of working wives and preschool children. Here the focus is on the location of the wives' workplace. In all the households where the wife worked within the Kawagoe region, it was the wife who escorted children to and from the day-care facilities, except one household, where information on this subject

Table 5.6. Escorting of Children and Wives' Commuting in Households with Preschool Children

Household No.	Wife's Workplace	Husband's Workplace	Wife's Working Status	Age of Children	Person Who Escorts the Youngest Child	
					To the Facility	From the Facility
1	Kawagoe region	Kawagoe region	Full time	2, 6	wife	wife
2	Kawagoe region	Kawagoe region	Part time	5, 9, 10	wife	wife
3	Kawagoe region	Kawagoe region	Part time	4, 8	wife	wife
4	Kawagoe region	Kawagoe region	Part time	4, 6, 9	wife	wife
5	Kawagoe region	Tokyo/Other	Part time	5, 11, 15	wife	wife
6	Kawagoe region	Tokyo/Other	Part time	5, 9	wife	wife
7	Kawagoe region	Tokyo Central	Part time	4, 6	wife	wife
8	Kawagoe region	Tama area	Part time	1, 6	unknown	unknown
9	Saitama/Other	Saitama/Other	Full time	2	husband	wife
10	Tokyo Central	Kawagoe region	Full time	1	husband	neighbor

was unavailable because the wife took off work on the Monday of the survey. The wife of the first household worked full time and used a private car to travel to and from home, the workplace, and the day nursery. The other seven wives were part-time employees who used bicycles for commuting and escorting. Having a second car is not easy for households in the Tokyo metropolitan area, because of high parking costs. In a one-car household, if the husband drives to work, the wife is left without a car. This condition usually restricts her to working part time near her home, because a car is necessary for a full-time worker to move efficiently between home, workplace, and the all-day child-care facility (Okamoto,1995a).

As the distance between home and the workplace increases, it becomes difficult for a wife to escort children by herself. In the ninth household, both the husband and wife drove to their workplaces located between Kawagoe and Tokyo. The husband drove the child to day care on his way to work in the morning, and the wife picked up the child on her way home in the evening. In general, husbands' working hours were somewhat longer than those of the full-time working wives, so that husbands could not be expected to get to the day-care facility before closing time.

In a family where the wife worked full time in the metropolitan center, she was also unable to reach the child care facility before closing time, because of her long commute. The tenth household was such a family. The husband worked in the Kawagoe region, while the wife commuted to an office in the Tokyo Central Wards. In the morning, the husband drove his one year old to the care facility and his wife to the Kawagoe railway station on his way to work. In the evening, however, the husband could not pick up his child, because his usual finishing time at work was 7:30 P.M. and the service hours of the day care facility ended at 6:30 P.M. The wife also could not pick up the child time, because it takes her more than one and a half hours to get to the facility after she finishes work at 5:30 P.M., so the couple must ask others for help. They asked a neighboring woman who used the same day nursery for her own child to look after their child in her home after the nursery closed. Then the wife picked up her child at the neighbor's home after 7:00 P.M. Their coordination of commuting and escorting activities was like walking a tightrope. Even this method would not be feasible without the husband's flexibility in the morning. He could use a car in his commuting and escorting activities in the morning because his workplace was located in the Kawagoe region. If the husband had to commute to Tokyo, however, there would be almost no way to resolve the conflict. In fact, of the surveyed households with preschool children, there were no couples where both commuted to Tokyo.

Thus, our hypothesis was corroborated by the research data. A suburban couple can maintain their working status if they have no children. After childbirth, however, one of them must give up full-time work at a distant metropolitan center. Generally, this role falls to the wife. She is apt to stay home or work

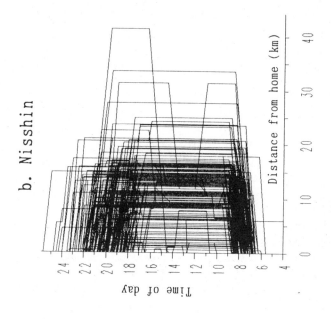

b. Nisshin

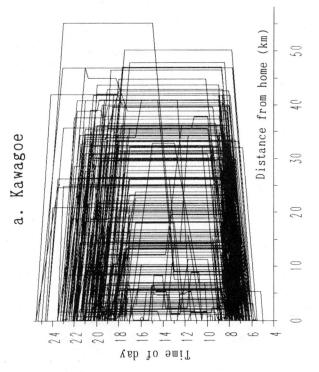

a. Kawagoe

Figure 5.9. Aggregated Paths of Husbands on Monday

part-time near her home. If the husband works locally, the wife could continue to work at the metropolitan center, assuming her husband's indispensable cooperation, but their commuting and escorting schedule would be a juggling feat, as with the sample household (Kamiya, Okamoto, Arai, and Kawaguchi, 1990).

In Japan's present labor market, once a wife retires from a full-time job in the metropolitan center, it is difficult for her to return to similar work after her children grow up. The working options for wives with children of school age or above would be even more limited. Nevertheless, most of the wives' jobs are located within the Kawagoe Region; there are relatively few who commute to Tokyo (table 5.5). In this later stage in life, part-time workers are most prevalent. Part-time work does not offer the wife many good prospects. If the couple wishes to maintain both their jobs in the metropolitan center, they may have no choice but to migrate to a place nearer their workplaces or to forego having children.

Recently, the drop in the birthrate has become an issue in Japan. Although various factors cause the declining birthrate, one of the most important is the problems women face trying to work and raise children at the same time (Economic Planning Agency, 1992). This difficulty involves not only the length of the workday but also the fixed time and space of work. In the Japanese metropolitan areas, people indeed work and commute on the urban daily rhythm.

Figure 5.9a shows the aggregated orbiting-paths of Kawagoe husbands on Monday, in which the time-space movement of each husband is arranged. The ordinate indicates the time of day, while the abscissa is the distance from each home. Between 6 and 8 A.M. paths leave home to work, which shows the density of paths during the morning rush hour. Before 9 A.M. each path changes to a vertical line and work starts. Although the vertical lines are more scattered, we can see the crowd of paths developing from around 30 to 40 kilometers from home where the Tokyo Central Wards are located. In the evening, the paths become slanted lines again for the return home, although this grouping of paths is less condensed than the morning bundle. This is the urban daily rhythm, common in Japanese metropolitan areas. In another area studied, Nisshin, a metropolitan suburb of Nagoya, the grouping of the husbands' paths was even clearer (fig. 5.9b). Suburban residents strengthen this spatiotemporal system by means of synchronizing their individual activities with the urban daily rhythm every day. On the other hand, their daily activities are strongly constrained in this system.

If a female wants to work in the same manner as a male, she has to synchronize her daily activity with the ebb and flow of this system. When both the husband and the wife are involved in the urban daily rhythm, the couple can hardly raise children. To improve this condition, making the time and space of work more flexible is imperative.

ACKNOWLEDGMENTS

I wish to thank Professor P. P. Karan for giving me the wonderful opportunity to participate in the conference on Japanese cities at the University of Kentucky. I also wish to thank Yoshio Arai of University of Tokyo, Taro Kawaguchi of Meiji University, and Hiroo Kamiya of Kanazawa University, who are comembers of the survey team in Kawagoe and Nisshin and who made a number of helpful suggestions on this paper. The Kawagoe survey was supported by the Housing Research and Advancement Foundation of Japan, and the Nisshin survey by the Fukutake Science and Culture Foundation.

REFERENCES

Arai, Y. 1993. *Seikatsu-katsudou-kuukan no kouzou to henyou nikansuru kenkyu* (A study on Human Activity Spaces). Doctoral thesis. Department of Urban Engineering, University of Tokyo.

Arai, Y., T. Kawaguchi, K. Okamoto, and H. Kamiya. 1989. *Seikatsu no kuukan, Toshi no jikan* (Anthology of Time Geography). Tokyo: Kokonshoin.

Berry, B. 1976. "The Counterurbanization Process: Urban America since 1970." In *Urbanization and Counterurbanization: Urban Affairs Annual Review.* Vol.11. Edited by B. Berry. Beverly Hills: Sage, pp.17-30.

Cybriwsky, R. 1991. *Tokyo: The Changing Profile of an Urban Giant.* London: Belhaven Press.

Economic Planning Agency, Japanese Government.1991. *Tokyo and Regional Areas: Diverse Choices for Affluence* (Annual Report on the National Life for Fiscal 1991). Tokyo: Printing Bureau, Ministry of Finance.

Economic Planning Agency, Japanese Government.1992. *The Arrival of the Society with a Small Number of Children* (Annual Report on the National Life for Fiscal 1992). Tokyo Printing Bureau, Ministry of Finance.

Hagerstrand, T.1970. "What about people in regional science?" *Paper and Proceedings of the Regional Science Association.* 24:7-21.

Jones, P.M., M.C. Dix, M.I. Clarke, and I.G. Heggie, 1983. *Understanding Travel Behavior.* Aldershot, U.K.: Gower Publishing Company.

Kamiya, H., K. Okamoto, Y. Arai, and T. Kawaguchi. 1990. *"Nagano-ken shimosuwa-cho niokeru kikon-josei no syuugyou nikansuru jikan-chirigakuteki bunseki"* (A time-geographic analysis of married women's participation in the labor market in Shimosuwa Town, Nagano Prefecture). *Geographical Review of Japan.* 63A:766-83.

Kamiya, H., and E. Ikeya. 1994. "Women's Participation in the Labour Force in Japan: Trends and Regional Patterns." *Geographical Review of Japan.* 67B:15-35.

Kawaguchi, T. 1990. *"Daitoshi-ken no kouzou-henka to kougai"* (Changing greater metropolitan area and suburban activity). *Regional Views* (Institute for Applied Geography, Komazawa University). 3:101-13.

———. 1992. *"Kougai-chiiki niokeru seikatsu-koudou-ken nikansuru kousatsu"* (A study on activity space of suburban residents in Japan). *Regional Views* (Institute for Applied Geography, Komazawa University). 5:83-99.

Klaassen, L., and J. Paelinck. 1979. "The Future of Large Towns." *Environment and Planning* A (11):1095-1104.

Nakagawa, S.1990. "Changing Segregation Pattern by Age Group in the Tokyo Metropolitan Area: From the Viewpoint of Migration with Cohort Analysis." *Geographical Review of Japan.* 63B:34-47.

Okamoto, K.1993. *"Nihon no toshi-jumin no seikatsu-kuukan to seikatsu-jikan: shiryo"* (The living space and time use of urban residents in Japan: a data book). *The Bulletin of Faculty of Sociology, Toyo University.* 30(3):50-119.

———. 1995*a*. "The Quality of Life in Metropolitan Suburbs of Japan: The Availability of Private Cars and the Daily Activities of Married Women." *The Journal of the Faculty of Letters, Nagoya University,* 122:155-65.

———. 1995*b*. "Daitoshi-ken kougai jumin no nichijo-katsudou to toshi no deirii-rizumu" (The daily activities of metropolitan suburbanites and the urban daily rhythm: the case of Kawagoe, a suburb of Tokyo, and Nisshin, a suburb of Nagoya). *Geographical Review of Japan.* 68A:1-26.

Pred, A. 1981. "Production, Family, and Free-Time Projects: A Time-Geographic Perspective on the Individual and Societal Change in Nineteenth-Century U.S. Cities." *Journal of Historical Geography.* 7:3-36.

6 Together and Equal: Place Stratification in Osaka

Kuniko Fujita and Richard Child Hill

The founder of a direct-mail company in the United States once remarked, "Tell me someone's zip code and I can predict what they eat, drink, drive, even what they think" (Reich, 1991: 277). The executive's boast rested on a truism about American urban life: social classes reproduce themselves by controlling territory.

Residential location provides differential access to valued resources in the United States. Neighbors have similar incomes and educational backgrounds. They indulge in the same consumer impulses. They pay roughly the same taxes for the same quality public services. Urban growth stratifies because privileged groups wield jurisdictional powers to exclude others from their tax-revenue and job-rich suburban enclaves. Indeed, the authors of an influential text on urban political economy go so far as to assert that, "geography is destiny" in the United States (Logan and Molotch, 1987: 194).

If "separate and unequal" best characterizes the political and social ecology of U.S. urbanization (Hill, 1974), then, by contrast, "together and equal" best characterizes urban form in Japan. Control over territory is not a means of class reproduction in Japanese cities. Our field research in Osaka[1] indicates that class-organized place stratification is practically nonexistent in Japan's second-most-powerful metropolis.

The spatial mixing of social classes in the Japanese city is the subject of this chapter. In the pages that follow, we explore several reasons why class segregation is so much lower in Japanese than in American cities. For one thing, Japan has much lower income inequality among occupational groups to begin with (Fahnzylber, 1990: 329-32; Ozaki, 1991: 189-92). For another, zoning is less strict, and land use is more mixed in the Japanese city.

The dampening of class inequality and the spatial mixing of classes can be traced to state development policies meant to mobilize the population to catch up with the West during the Meiji era and again during reconstruction after World War II. For example, Japan's nationally organized educational system is well known for standardizing the curriculum among schools, but it also standardizes educational facilities, thereby removing one of the main incentives for balkanization among local jurisdictions.[2]

Osaka Prefecture and the Kansai Region

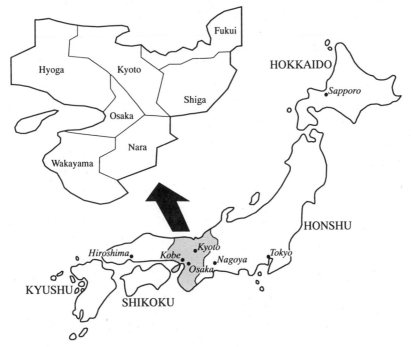

Figure 6.1. Osaka Prefecture and the Kansai Region

The continuing centrality of Osaka's urban core and the absence of po-larized central city/suburban relations departs significantly from the inner-city decay and vast inequalities between central city and suburbs in older U.S. urban areas (Rusk, 1993). Osaka is a 24-hour city. Crime is low. Population and employment are stable. Industry has been decentralizing, but the center city has retained high-value manufacturing, central coordinating, and service functions. The edge-city phenomenon—dynamic economic growth centers on the periphery of metropolitan areas—so much discussed among urban planners in the United States, has not taken hold in Japan.[3]

In Japan, the absence of class segregation facilitates urban intergovern-mental coordination. Osakans are making huge social investments in regional infrastructure—transportation, communication, research and development—to connect their production systems more firmly with the rest of Japan, Asia, and the world economy (Osaka Prefecture, 1994), and local governments cooperate in spreading public projects among subareas of the central city and urban area.[4]

While slums are negligible in Osaka, housing quality is low and prices high by the standards of Western developed countries. Japan's home ownership

OSAKA PREFECTURE

SETTSU

1 Toyonaka City
2 Ikeda City
3 Minoo City
4 Toyono Town
5 Nose Town
6 Settsu City
7 Suita City
8 Ibarki City
9 Takatsuki City
10 Shimamoto Town

KAWACHI

11 Moriguchi City
12 Kadoma City
13 Neyagawa City
14 Hirakata City
15 Katano City
16 Shijonawate City
17 Daito City
18 Higashi-Osaka City
19 Yao City
20 Kashiwara City

MINAMI KAWACHI

21 Matsubara City
22 Fujiidera City
23 Habikino City
24 Mihara Town
25 Taishi Town
26 Osaka-Sayama City
27 Tondabayashi City
28 Kanan Town
29 Kawachi-Nagano City
30 Chihaya-Akasaka Village

SENSHU

31 Sakai City
32 Takaishi City
33 Izumi-Otsu City
34 Tadaoka Town
35 Izumi City
36 Kishiwada City
37 Kaizuka City
38 Izumi-Sano City
39 Kumatori Town
40 Tajiri Town
41 Sennan City
42 Hannan Town
43 Misaki Town

Figure 6.2. Osaka Prefecture

rate is comparable to that of the United States, but 67 percent of American house owners have more than four rooms, while 72 percent of Japanese have fewer than three (Kodama, 1990; Osaka City, 1991).

In sum, the spatial mixing of classes in Osaka is rooted in a development model that has emphasized economic production over individual consumption, the diffusion of social investments among places, and "burden sharing" of high consumer prices and low social consumption outlays among the population.

Osaka in Profile

Osaka faces the Pacific Ocean and the Inland Sea and sits on a delta formed by the confluence of rivers entering Osaka Bay (see fig. 6.1). Centrally located,

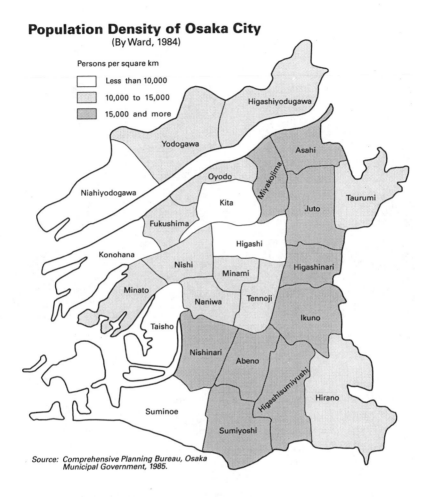

Population Density of Osaka City
(By Ward, 1984)

Persons per square km

- [ ] Less than 10,000
- [ ] 10,000 to 15,000
- [ ] 15,000 and more

Higashiyodugawa

Yodogawa

Asahi

Oyodo

Niahiyodogawa

Kita

Miyakojima

Taurumi

Juto

Fukushima

Higashi

Konohana

Nishi

Minami

Higashinari

Minato

Naniwa

Tennoji

Taisho

Ikuno

Nishinari

Abeno

Higashisumiyushi

Hirano

Suminoe

Sumiyoshi

Source: *Comprehensive Planning Bureau, Osaka Municipal Government, 1985.*

Figure 6.3. Osaka City Wards, Population Density

the city is a natural crossroad between eastern and western Japan. Osaka is the historical gateway to Kyoto via the Yodo River and to western Japan through the Inland Sea.

Japan's early emperors gravitated to Osaka as a geographically advantageous site for administrative affairs. Shotoku Taishi (578-622), regent to the Empress Suiko (554-628), located the nation's first major Buddhist temple, Shitennoji, near Osaka's present downtown. Toyotomi Hideyoshi, the shogun who unified sixteenth century Japan, constructed his government headquarters in Osaka and began building Osaka Castle in 1583. As the seat of central power, Osaka attracted merchants and craftsmen from all over Japan. River

Photo 6.1. Osaka's business park seen from Osaka Castle. Osaka is the business and financial center of western Japan. Photo by Richard Child Hill

and harbor development crisscrossed Osaka with canals during the feudal era. Local shipping firms organized river trade with Edo (present-day Tokyo), and Osaka became the center of commodity distribution for the nation (Nakamura, 1993). By the middle of the eighteenth century, Osaka's population numbered nearly 400,000, second only to Edo (Okugawa and Ueda, 1986:48).

Osakans reestablished their city as Japan's center of international trade after the Meiji Restoration in 1868. By the 1880s, Osaka's textile industry (cotton spinning and woolen and knitted goods) was leading Japan's industrial revolution (Gordon, 1988). Osaka lost her number-one industrial standing to Tokyo during the 1930s, when, as military expenditures came to dominate the economy, the business connection with government grew tighter, drawing companies to Tokyo, an attraction that has persisted to the present day (Morishima, 1982: chaps. 3-4; 53; Miyamoto, 1993; Hill and Fujita, 1995).

Osaka's economy boomed after World War II, with capital-intensive heavy manufacturing in coastal factory complexes. Since the mid 1970s, the city has emphasized knowledge-intensive manufacturing and services organized in the interior as well as in the coastal zones (Ueda, 1986). Seventeen million people now reside within a 60-kilometer radius of central Osaka, as many as live in Australia or Canada. The metropolitan area has three urban nodes—Osaka, Kobe, and Kyoto—each anchoring a prefecture. Osaka Prefecture numbers 8.7 million inhabitants and encompasses 43 cities and towns. Osaka City has a population of 2.6 million divided into 24 wards (figs. 6.2 and 6.3).

PLACE STRATIFICATION

There is a large and growing income gap between central cities and suburbs in the United States. The city of Detroit, for example, has a per capita income barely half that of the rest of the metropolitan area, as does Cleveland, and Milwaukee's income is just 62 percent of that of its surrounding suburbs (Rusk, 1993: 33). By contrast, Osaka City's per capita income (1,223,000 yen) is essentially the same as Osaka Prefecture's (1,268,000 yen). By a second measure of economic well-being, the average taxpayer's income, the gap between Osaka city (3,094,000 yen) and Osaka Prefecture (3,334,000 yen) is only 7 percent (table 6.1).

The income of the richest jurisdiction in a large American metropolis usually exceeds the poorest by a factor of 10 or more. Per capita income among cities and towns in Osaka Prefecture ranges from a low of 1,006,000 yen in the south-shore steel town of Kaizuka to a high of 1,723,000 yen in northern Minoh City, an attractive hamlet with a striking view of the mountains. Thus, the per capita income of the poorest city in Osaka Prefecture is 58 percent of that of the richest; measured by taxrolls, the ratio is 61 percent. As many Osaka suburbs are below as are above the central city's income level, but most hover around the average for the Prefecture.

The mixing of social classes among jurisdictions in Osaka Prefecture also characterizes wards in the central city. The distribution of occupational groups in each ward tends to replicate the social composition of the city as a whole (table 6.2). Only 3 of Osaka's 24 wards are exceptions to this rule: Chuo and Tennoji wards in the downtown financial district have a disproportionate number of professional, technical, and managerial residents. The Nishinari ward, home to Osaka's day laborers, is place of residence for an exceptionally large number of construction workers.

Our interviews suggest that Japanese choose their residence according to commuting distance from work, family networks, and stage in the life cycle, not according to the class and status characteristics of the neighborhood.[5] For example, the extended family of a university professor whom we interviewed includes government officials, teachers, factory workers, wholesale merchants and secretaries; all live near one another in a south-side quarter of Osaka City. And as shown in table 6.3, there is virtually no difference in the occupational distribution among residents in Osaka City and Osaka Prefecture as a whole. High-priced condominiums, middle-income private family housing, public housing for low- to middle-income families, and old, wooden low-income housing intermix in the city and metro area.

Table 6.1. Per Capita Income, Osaka Prefecture, Cities and Towns, 1989
(1,000 Yen)

Location	Per capita income	Average tax payer income
Osaka Prefecture	1,268	3,334
Osaka City	1,223	3,094
Sakai City	1,222	3,362
Kishiwada City	1,088	3,023
Toyonaka City	1,558	3,976
Ikeda City	1,542	3,939
Suita City	1,555	3,982
Izumiotsu	1,104	3,025
Takatsuki City	1,380	3,538
Kaizuka City	1,006	2,777
Moriguchi City	1,127	2,891
Hirakata City	1,371	3,705
Ibaraki City	1,419	3,623
Yao City	1,242	3,265
Izumisano City	1,106	3,072
Tondabayashi City	1,246	3,576
Neyagawa City	1,191	3,208
Kawachinagano City	1,361	3,889
Matsubara City	1,080	3,029
Daito City	1,129	2,990
Izumi City	1,156	3,342
Minoh City	1,723	4,553
Kashiwara City	1,215	3,235
Habikino City	1,223	3,424
Kadoma City	1,098	2,869
Settsu City	1,226	3,068
Takaishi City	1,283	3,456
Fujiidera City	1,287	3,441
Higashiosaka City	1,217	3,092
Sennan City	1,033	3,209
Shijonawate Cit y	1,133	3,070
Katano City	1,385	3,800
Osakasayama City	1,477	3,981

Source: Nihon Marketing Kyoiku Center, *Kojin shotoku shihyo* (Per Capita Income Index), Tokyo, 1990, 669

Table 6.2. Occupational Distribution among Residents of Osaka City Wards, 1990 (percent)

Region and Ward	Professional, Technical, Managerial	Clerical, Sales, Service	Skilled, Unskilled, Production, Labor	Others[a]	Total	(Total No. Employed Residents)
North:						
Nishiyodogawa	11.9	42.6	39.3	6.2	100	(48,508)
Yodogawa	14.2	52.2	28.6	5.0	100	(85,900)
Higashiyodogawa	13.9	47.9	31.5	6.7	100	(91,285)
East:						
Asahi	15.9	52.2	30.3	5.6	100	(53,368)
Miyakojima	16.0	48.8	28.3	6.9	100	(49,150)
Joto	14.7	48.2	31.7	5.4	100	(79,924)
Tsurumi	11.2	42.0	39.1	7.7	100	(47,039)
Higashinari	12.9	48.1	35.4	3.6	100	(42,891)
Ikuno	11.3	44.5	40.4	3.8	100	(79,576)
Central:						
Kita	16.6	54.9	21.7	6.8	100	(48,734)
Fukushima	14.6	53.9	27.2	4.6	100	(30,458)
Nishi	18.4	59.2	18.1	4.3	100	(32,365)
Chuo	20.7	64.0	14.4	1.9	100	(33,758)
Naniwa	11.9	56.6	25.6	5.9	100	(24,648)
Tennoji	23.0	54.1	19.4	3.5	100	(28,609)
West Bay:						
Konohana	10.1	43.0	39.1	7.8	100	(35,277)
Minato	10.7	46.0	34.1	9.1	100	(46,107)
Taisho	10.0	44.0	37.5	8.5	100	(40,062)
Suminoe	13.0	50.1	29.8	7.0	100	(65,619)
South:						
Nishinari	7.7	39.5	48.1[b]	4.7	100	(77,339)
Abeno	20.6	54.8	21.2	3.4	100	(51,582)
Sumiyoshi	16.9	52.5	25.4	5.2	100	(80,120)
Higashsisumiyoshi	14.9	49.5	30.4	5.2	100	(72,584)
Hirano	11.2	43.0	39.5	6.5	100	(100,502)
Osaka City	13.9	48.5	31.9	5.7	100	(1,345,405)

Source: Statistics Bureau, Management and Coordination Agency, *Population Census of Japan 1990*

[a] Protection, transport and communication, farming and fishery, and unclassified
[b] About 60% in construction and the rest in manufacturing

Photo 6.2 Osaka's "wedge" buildings indicating density of residential and work life in Osaka's Tennoji Ward and the zoning flexibility that permits it. Photo by Richard Child Hill

Mixed Land Use

Osaka City is a patchy mosaic of land uses (fig. 6.4). Japanese planning laws categorize land into eight zones, including residential, commercial, and industrial (Callies, 1994). The scope of land use is most restricted in residential areas where factories are prohibited, less so in commercial areas where small scale factories are allowed, and least of all in industrial zones where factories are approved. Because land-use zones gradually increase in scope, they encroach on one another, and land use is mixed. The kind of strict land-use zoning found in many cities in the United States is absent in Japan (Naruse, 1990: 131).

Several factors converge to explain Japan's mixed land-use system. The Japanese value land highly and strongly protect the rights of land owners. In Western cities, land is typically viewed as the receptacle for the structures built on it and the right to hold and monopolize land is constrained. Individual rights to land are mainly legitimated as a means to protect the use of the buildings attached to it.

The Japanese Civil Code regards land and the buildings on it as separate real estate. Land ownership is permanent and sacred, regardless of how land is used.[6] Land, even in the city, is often owned by families for generations. Consequently, the growth of Japanese cities is more negotiated and less systematically planned than in the West.

Land prices are very high in Japan. The land coefficient—total land assets divided by gross national product—has long been stable in the United States at 0.8 to 0.9. Japan's land coefficient exceeded 5.0 in 1988. Japan's land price per unit of area is about 100 times that of the United States. Osaka's ratio of rent to land price is about 1 percent, much lower than major cities in other countries (Naruse, 1990: 128).

Because private land ownership rights and high land prices make urban planning difficult, the city of Osaka takes a flexible and pragmatic approach to land use. City officials change zoning to meet immediate needs, and they accommodate mixed land use while attempting to make zoning stricter in smaller microunits within mixed areas.

The city's pragmatic approach to land use was especially evident during Japan's postwar economic boom. The city expanded industrial zones in the 1950s and 1960s, increasing the spatial mix of industry and housing. The east side, including the Higashinari and Ikuno Wards, is Osaka's major industrial district. The east side was a nonspecified land-use zone (where any use was allowable) in the 1920s. As industrial expansion flowed into housing zones and blurred the already obscure land-use differences in the 1950s, the city turned surrounding nonspecified and housing zones into subindustrial and industrial areas (Taguchi and Hojo, 1992). The city has often changed land-use zoning on the east side but always with mixed land-use results.

Table 6.3. Percent Change in Occupation among Residents in Osaka
Prefecture and Osaka City, 1970–1990

Occupation	Prefecture			City		
	1970	1990	Change	1970	1990	Change
Professional, technical	6.4	11.2	+4.8	5.2	9.8	+4.6
Managerial	5.6	4.3	-1.3	5.1	4.1	-1.0
Clerical	17.4	20.6	+3.2	16.7	19.8	+3.1
Craftsmen, production workers and laborers	39.9	31.7	-8.2	40.3	31.9	-8.4
Sales	15.0	18.0	+3.0	16.8	19.0	+2.2
Transport and communication	4.5	3.7	-0.8	4.5	3.9	-0.6
Protective service	1.0	1.1	+0.1	0.8	0.8	0.0
Service	8.0	7.7	-0.3	10.3	9.8	+0.5
Farmers, fishermen, and miners	2.2	0.7	-1.5	0.2	0.1	-0.1
Unclassified	0.0	1.0	+1.0	0.0	0.8	+0.8
Total	100.0	100.0		100.0	100.0	
Total No. Jobs	3,669,310	4,236,759		1,508,380	1,345,405	

Source: Bureau of Statistics, Management and Coordination Agency, *Population Census of Japan 1970 and 1990*

Mixed land use also stems from an acute shortage of housing. A much smaller percentage of land is available for housing in Osaka (53 percent) than in Tokyo (72 percent), and a much higher percentage is devoted to manufacturing and commercial uses (table 6.4). As land prices shot higher and higher in the 1980s, affordable housing in the central city became difficult to find.

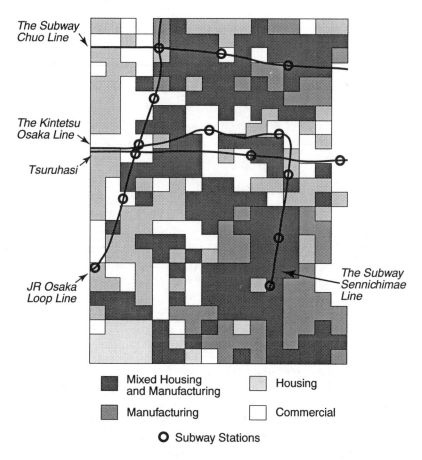

The Subway
Chuo Line

The Kintetsu
Osaka Line

Tsuruhasi

JR Osaka
Loop Line

The Subway
Sennichimae
Line

■ Mixed Housing
and Manufacturing

▓ Manufacturing

▢ Housing

□ Commercial

○ Subway Stations

Source: Yoshiaki Taguchi, "Daitoshi no Restructuring to Kogyo
Kasseika Mondai" (Restructuring of Big Cities and Industrial
Revitalization). In Masataka Ueda, ed., **Gendai Daitoshi No
Restructuring (Restructuring of Contemporary Big Cities)**,
Tokyo: University of Tokyo Press, 1992, p. 81.

Figure 6.4 Land-use Patterns in Osaka City's Eastern Part: Higashinari and Ikuno
Wards

The western bay area—covering the Konohana, Taisho, Suminoe, and
Nishiyodogawa Wards—is a mix of factories, warehouses, and port facilities,
without much housing. Big factories have moved out, vacant land is plentiful,
and land prices are low, but the area is currently zoned exclusively for industrial use, preventing housing development. The city recognizes a need to
change zoning in the area but is reluctant to do, so for fear that speculation

Table 6.4. Changing Land Use in Osaka City (percent)

Year	Commercial	Manufacturing	Housing	Agriculture	Others
1960	8.9	16.9	44.7	20.4	9.1
1970	12.2	25.1	50.4	8.2	4.1
1980	13.6	28.5	50.5	3.3	4.1
1990	13.9	25.6	52.6	2.5	5.4
Tokyo 1990	9.7	8.9	72.1	4.8	4.5

Source: Osaka City Economic Bureau, *The Outline of Osaka Economy,* 1992, p. 11

will send the land price skyrocketing. The issue is how to keep the land price down while managing to convert the factory abandoned area to housing. It is a salient political matter, since this area is a vital part of the city's future housing plan.[7]

INDUSTRIAL DISTRICTS

City efforts to retain small factories and housing in Osaka's traditional industrial district also contribute to the spatial mixing of classes. Osaka's east side and the neighboring suburb of Higashi-Osaka have the region's highest percentage of employment in manufacturing and the largest concentration of small, independent producers in the metal and machinery industry. Together, they constitute Osaka's traditional industrial district (table 6.5).

City officials, wishing to reduce pollution and attract corporate headquarter functions, intended to move small manufacturing plants to land reclaimed from Osaka Bay, but they reversed course as they came to recognize the industrial district's dynamic role in the Osaka economy. Like Tokyo's Ota area, Osaka's east side is an incubator for new products and businesses. Local firms exploit their strategic location in the center of the metropolitan economy to fuse with other industries. Today, the city protects small manufacturing firms from rising land prices and provides public services and infrastructure to help them restructure and upgrade their technologies.

There is a debate about how best to arrange housing and factories within Osaka's industrial district. The city is attempting to combine dwellings and industry in the larger zone and separate them in smaller subzones through factory apartments, urban-industrial parks, and city industrial towns.[8]

The city began building factory apartments in 1974 as part of a national policy to upgrade small industrial enterprises. The national government's Small

Table 6.5 Percent Weight in Manufacturing among Employed Residents and Employed Persons in Osaka City's Industrial District, 1990

Ward	Residents Employed in Manufacturing Among Total No. Employed Residents	Total No. Employed Residents	Persons Employed in Manufacturing Among Total No. Employed Persons	Total No. Employed Persons
Joto	30.7	79,924	35.1	73,034
Higashinari	36.1	43,891	43.6	58,262
Ikuno	39.6	79,576	44.3	74,960
Hirano	33.8	100,502	39.6	82,115
Osaka City	25.5	1,345,405	22.7	2,455,334
Osaka Prefecture	26.9	4,236,759	26.4	4,731,506
Higashi-Osaka City	35.8	260,696	39.1	267,240

Source: Population Census of Japan 1990

Business Corporation provided a group of small enterprises with low-interest loans to build jointly a factory apartment complex. The Osaka City and Prefecture governments provided additional loans. Osaka City Development Corporation coordinated the purchase of land, the building of factory apartments, and the sale of factory space to small enterprises. One such factory apartment is the Osaka Eastern Metal Work Center, a cooperative of six machine and metal-working enterprises, with 5 to 20 employees each, in Hirano ward. Others include the Osaka Rubber-Sandal Center, a cooperative of five rubber sandal companies in Hirano ward, and the Suminoe Machine Metal Center, a cooperative of seven machine and metal-working companies in Suminoe Ward (Osaka City, 1992).

Osaka commenced the City Industrial Town (CIT) program in the early 1980s. CITs are efforts to blend industrial parks into the surrounding urban environment. Osaka's Economic Bureau bought abandoned factory land. The Osaka City Land Development Corporation subdivided the land and allotted parcels to small enterprises. The firms then built their own small-scale factories. The city has created three CITs so far: Kami Industrial Park in Hirano Ward, Technopark Tsuneyoshi in Konohana Ward, and Technopark Yashima in Konohana-ku. The city began work on four more CITs in 1992—in the Taisho, Nishiyodogawa, Suminoe, and Konohana Wards. Each CIT accommodates 20 to 30 small enterprises. Some CITs include business incubators and parking structures (Osaka City, 1992).

Western advocates for industrial retention usually emphasize the deleterious effects of the loss of manufacturing jobs on income distribution. Relatively well-paid blue-collar jobs vanish, and the occupational structure polarizes into high-income professionals and low-wage service workers (Blue-stone and Harrison, 1992). Osaka is attempting to restructure and retain its industrial district, not through any intrinsic desire to keep manufacturing jobs, but because of the strategic role the district plays in the local economy. None-theless, retention of manufacturing no doubt works against class polarization in the city.

There are many occupational layers in Osaka's industrial district— production workers, independent producers, small-business owners, and a new middle class of professionals and managers. Considerable individual mobility occurs among these social categories. Many small-plant owners were once white-collar employees who came to Osaka in the 1950s and 1960s to work in large corporations. Often from farm families, their ultimate dream was not salaried employment but independent business ownership. When opportunities arose, they became independent producers, taking advantage of Osaka's industrial district to rent small factories on recently transformed farm land.[9]

Social mobility of a more traditional sort also occurs in the industrial district. Small machine-shop owners typically start as low-skill apprentices at low wages. Over time many become highly skilled master craftsmen earning moderate incomes, and some open their own machine shops after acquiring network management capabilities and make high incomes. This kind of social mobility has declined because the children and grandchildren of machinists are inclined to go to college and choose nonmanufacturing jobs. Osaka's industrial district, like those in the rest of Japan and abroad, faces a serious successor problem and the number of small producers is steadily dwindling (Taguchi and Hojo, 1992; Seki, 1994).[10]

A growing percentage of the small manufacturers who remain in the district are engaging in higher value, flexible production and services. Many own design shops or produce prototypes, activities which blur the distinction between manufacturing and services and add more layers to the industrial district.[11] In sum, individual mobility across a wide and flexible network of jobs blurs class distinctions in Osaka's industrial district and counteracts class segregation (Narita, 1986, 1990; Taguchi and Hojo, 1992).

CITY HOUSING POLICIES

Osaka combats its population decline with housing policies that help people remain in their neighborhoods, attract young couples to the central city, and spur mixed-income housing complexes. The city's housing policies also contribute to the spatial mixing of classes.

Low-income groups live in densely packed wooden housing built before and just after World War II. Blighted areas suffer from the pollution created by nearby factories and from a shortage of parks and open space. The vacancy rate is high, despite the scarcity of low-cost housing (Osaka City, 1991: 61). Elderly people predominate in these neighborhoods, their children having moved to the suburbs. Shop and office construction is driving up housing prices. Rather than encouraging gentrification, the city is redeveloping these areas with public housing under its Blighted Residential Area Renewal Project.

Renewal is very slow. Osaka has built 6,483 public housing units in 55 central city locations since 1960, and the city estimates 200,000 units still need renovation (Osaka City, 1991: 75). Private builders can participate in the program but seldom do because they have to build at market prices, making private apartments prohibitively expensive. The city is now redeveloping a blighted residential area on the east side, beyond the downtown JR Loop Line, and has plans to extend renewal to another 37 places.

The city has integrated some blighted residential areas into larger urban redevelopment projects under the 1976 Comprehensive Improvement Promotion Project for Specific Urban Housing Districts. Five urban redevelopment projects, under public/private management, are currently underway. The projects mix housing, retail shops, and offices, and one, the Sakuranomiyanakano Project, also includes factories.

The Sakuranomiyanakano project started in 1985. It is located about 3 kilometers east of the JR Loop Line/Osaka Station and north of the JR Loop Line/Sakuranomiyanakano Station. The project combines public and privately owned land. Forty-three percent of the land is targeted for housing, 2 percent for retail shops and offices, 16 percent for public facilities, and 4 percent for factories. Housing is sold or rented by the City Housing Corporation, national Housing and Urban Development Corporation (HUDC), the Japan Working People's Housing Association, and the private sector (Osaka City, 1991:18-20).[12]

Osaka City has experienced population decline but not nearly to the degree found in most older U.S. central cities. Many couples of child-rearing age prefer to live in the suburbs or countryside. Land prices are lower 30 to 40 kilometers from the central city, housing is more affordable, and house space is sufficient for children to have their own rooms. Flats in the central core are prized for their proximity to work but are too expensive for the average Japanese worker. The government provides mortgage loans for as much as 5-years income, but Osaka's downtown flats cost 6 to 7 years average annual income.[13]

The city is combating market-driven suburbanization with various inducements for middle-income families—especially young couples—to live in the central city, including long-term, low-interest loans for the purchase of public housing and condominiums (Osaka City, 1991). To increase supply, the city builds middle-income housing for rent or sale by the HUDC and the City Housing Corporation. The central government combats the effect of rising inner-city land prices with construction and rent subsidies under the Local Special Rented Housing System program.

The city also gives long-term, low-interest loans to private land owners who wish to construct high-quality rental housing on their property. Turning landowners into builders saves land-acquisition costs and helps reduce rents. The city provides especially favorable terms for rebuilding wooden rental housing and for joint construction of buildings by neighboring landowners.

THE DEVELOPMENTAL STATE

Under Japan's highly centralized administrative system, the national government controls the bulk of the nation's fiscal resources and allocates public goods to prefecture and city governments. Central state policies emphasizing uniform treatment of the citizenry countered peasant discontent and helped mobilize the population for rapid development during the Meiji era. The centralized intergovernmental system, despite persistent and sometimes intense conflicts over the distribution of power, has narrowed uneven development among localities, dampened class inequality within cities, and garnered popular support.

In spite of the success of centralization, local governments have long struggled for greater decentralization. Reform is belatedly under way. The central government still plays the role of developmental state but now consults more with local governments. National standards are more flexible, and local governments have more discretion to change them.

Central standards govern the distribution of education, housing, and infrastructure expenditures to cities and regions. The centralized education system sets local standards for school buildings, equipment, and facilities as well as teacher salaries and curriculum. There are 55,000 teachers in Osaka Prefecture, and education accounts for about 32 percent of the budget. Fifty percent of teachers's salaries are paid at the national level (the other 50 percent is negotiated at the prefecture level), so salaries are uniform among schools within Osaka prefecture. Cities are responsible for elementary and junior high schools; the prefecture for senior high schools.[14]

Osaka's housing policies also follow the lead of the central government as detailed in national 5-year housing plans. Osaka prefecture planned to build a half million housing units under the nation's sixth 5-year housing plan, which began in 1991, and a million by the year 2000 (Osaka Prefecture, 1991). Housing projects are allocated to subareas of the prefecture according to population size and growth rate[15] (table 6.5). Public housing is scattered among all wards in the central city (tables 6.6 and 6.7).

The allocation of public infrastructure projects is also made according to the central government's comprehensive national development plan. The central government implements projects after consultation and negotiation with Osaka prefecture, while the prefecture implements projects after consultation and negotiation with local governments (Osaka Prefecture, 1991a, 1991b). As a result of these negotiations, Osaka's big public projects are parceled out rather evenly across the region (Narita, 1990). The Kansai Science City Project is in the west, the International Cultural Park project is in the north, and the Kansai International Airport and Cosmopolis projects are in the south. The Airport and Cosmopolis were allocated to the South Bay area to counteract declining employment in heavy, chemical, and textile industries.[16]

MINORITIES: THE KOREAN EXPERIENCE

Japan has three minority groups: the Ainu living in the northern island of Hokkaido, the Burakumin living mainly in the Kansai area, and the Koreans. The Burakumin, strictly speaking, are not an ethnic minority. They are Japanese who came to be seen as occupational outcasts during the feudal era. They still experience discrimination in employment and marriage when their family origin is disclosed. The Burakumin live in various parts of the prefecture, including blighted residential areas in the central city.

Most Koreans register as foreigners and live as permanent residents in Japan.[17] Koreans were 58 percent of the 1.2 million foreigners living in Japan in 1991. Half of the Koreans in Japan live in the Kansai area, 27 percent in Osaka Prefecture.

Japan colonized Korea from 1910 to 1945; Koreans originally came to Japan during that time. The number of Koreans in Japan rapidly increased between 1920 and 1930 as a result of Japan's colonial policy and surged again just before and during World War II, when Koreans were brought to Japan as war hostages and forced labor.[18] By the end of the war, more than two million Koreans resided in Japan. Two thirds returned to Korea after the war; those who stayed were the forerunners of Koreans in Japan today (Kimbara, 1986).

Koreans constituted 80 percent of the foreign population until 1985, when Japan changed immigration laws. The 1985 immigration law permitted foreign contract labor for semiskilled production work and has been accompanied by an influx of Brazilian and Chinese workers to Japan. By 1991, the proportion of Koreans to all foreigners had declined to 57 percent (table 6.8).

More Koreans lived in Osaka in 1922 than in any city in the world outside of Seoul. Before World War II, Koreans in Japan mainly worked in mining areas, on dam and tunnel construction projects, and in Osaka's small factories. When a direct sea route between Osaka and Korea's southern-most island, Saishu, opened up in 1923, many Koreans came to Osaka in search of a better life.

Koreans settled on the east side in the Osaka city area called *Ikaino,* (meaning "Korea in Japan"), including the Ikuno and the Higashinari wards. Hoping to become craftsmen in Osaka's small factories, Koreans suffered the

Table 6.6. Osaka Prefecture's Distribution of Housing Projects, by Subarea, 1991-2000

Area	No. Housing Units	Expected Population by 2001 (millions)
1. North	170,000	1.85
2. East	280,000	2.15
3. Southeast	80,000	0.75
4. Southwest	170,000	1.80
5. Osaka City	300,000	2.80

Source: Osaka Prefecture, *Sumaizukuri Osaka 21* (Osaka's Housing Toward the 21st Century), Osaka, 1992

worst working and housing conditions the city had to offer. They labored in glass, plate, and rubber factories and lived in barracks on the outskirts of the city and along the river. Treated as outsiders and social problems, Koreans organized to fight for better working and housing conditions. By the early 1920s, Osaka and Tokyo were the centers of the Korean labor and rent-control movements.

More Koreans live in Osaka City than anywhere else in Japan. About half the Koreans in the Kansai area, including Kyoto and Kobe, live in Osaka (see table 6.9). Within the Osaka metropolitan area, 80 percent live in Osaka City and adjacent Higashi-Osaka, Sakai, and Yao. Within Osaka City, Koreans are concentrated on the eastside, especially in the Ikuno ward. Like the rest of Osaka's population, Koreans are moving to other parts of the Kansai region and beyond. As a result, the number of Koreans in the Osaka metropolitan area is declining while rising in Japan as a whole.

Korean culture is highly visible in Ikuno, where one in every five residents is Korean. The Tsuruhashi station on the Osaka Loop Line is the center of Korean commerce. Under one vast roof, colorful Korean markets spread out from the station like tentacles of an octopus, north to south and east to west. Grocery stands sell fresh vegetables, fruits, meat, fish, and pickled kimchi. Small restaurants serve Korean traditional dishes, and shops sell Korean costumes. A mix of Koreans, Japanese, and foreign tourists throng the stalls.

Osaka's ancient historical ties with Korea are exemplified in the Wasso festival in Shitennoji ward. *Wasso* means "have come" in Korean (Osaka Prefecture, Osaka City, and Osaka Chamber of Commerce and Industry, 1994: 20). The festival, held on November 3, is one of Osaka's largest and is 1,500 years old. Osaka also has one of the world's finest Korean ceramics museums, the Ataka Collection.

Table 6.7. Osaka City's Distribution of Public Housing, by ward, 1991

Ward	Rented by City and Prefecture	HUDC		City and Prefecture Housing Corporation	
		Rented	Sale	Rented	Sale
North:					
Nishiyodogawa	3,484	925	—	134	814
Yodogawa	4,595	1,485	—	—	1,195
Higashiyodogawa	14,138	1,568	31	48	518
East:					
Asahi	3,677	636	—	48	1,216
Miyakojima	2,076	2,188	1,175	—	1,161
Joto	5,974	3,514	320	—	3,706
Tsurumi	8,075	—	—	—	949
Higashinari	70	—	—	—	270
Ikuno	509	72	—	—	280
Central:					
Kita	1,659	2,835	242	—	1,462
Fukushima	—	1,823	—	134	—
Nishi	—	533	—	435	1,277
Chuo	294	872	—	752	126
Naniwa	3,833	258	—	—	57
Tennoji	968	171	287	24	363
West Bay:					
Konohana	3,679	2,724	—	167	78
Minato	4,793	844	—	449	1,628
Taisho	5,010	2,544	—	—	748
Suminoe	9,056	5,780	1,038	128	1,742
South:					
Nishinari	2,781	84	—	—	159
Abeno	1,026	1,298	66	424	254
Sumiyoshi	7,137	1,086	76	576	366
Higashsisumiyoshi	2,475	499	—	480	60
Hirano	24,680	59	—	350	518
Total	109,989	31,798	3,235	4,149	18,947

Source: Osaka City, *Housing Policy of Osaka 1991,* Osaka, p. 72

Table 6.8. Major Nationalities of Registered Foreigners in Japan, 1983-1991

Year	Nationality				Total No. of Foreigners[a]
	Koreans	Chinese	Brazilians	Americans	
1983	674,581	60,984	1,637	25,041	817,129
	(83)	(7)	(0.2)	(3)	(100)
1985	683,313	67,895	1,953	27,882	850,612
	(80)	(8)	(0.2)	(3)	(100)
1990	687,940	150,339	56,429	38,364	1,075,317
	(64)	(14)	(5)	(3.5)	(100)
1991	693,053	171,071	119,333	42,498	1,218,891
	(57)	(14)	(10)	(3.5)	(100)

Sources: Ministry of Justice, *Gaikokujin toroku kokusekibetsu jinin chosahyo* (Registered Foreigners by Nationality), Tokyo, 1984, 1986, 1989, 1991, and 1992
Note: Numbers in parentheses are percentages.
[a] Includes all other nationalities.

Table 6.9. Koreans in Osaka Prefecture, 1990

City	Korean	Population
Osaka City	110,273	(59.5)
Higashhi Osaka City	21,630	(11.7)
Sakai City	7,107	(3.8)
Yao City	7,052	(3.8)
Toyonaka City	3,450	(1.8)
Ikeda City	3,218	(1.7)
Minoh City	838	(0.5)
Others	31,898	(17.2)
Osaka Prefecture	185,466	(100.0)

Source: Ministry of Justice, Registered Foreigners, 1991 and 1992
Note: Numbers in parentheses are percentages.

Photo 6.3 Wasso Festival in Osaka's inner city Tennoji Ward. Held annually on November 3, the festival is fifteen hundred years old and demonstrates Osaka's ancient ties with Korea. Photo by Richard Child Hill

Koreans, who are registered as foreigners in Japan, are treated differently from Japanese citizens across a wide spectrum of institutions: schooling, employment, marriage, medical, and pension and welfare systems (Research Action Institute for Koreans in Japan, 1990). The Japanese government does not discriminate against Koreans because they are Korean, but because they are noncitizens. Koreans maintain their cultural identity in Japan by living together and running their own schools and colleges. The Ministry of Education does not treat Korean high schools the same as Japanese schools. Like American and British branch campuses in Japan, Korean colleges are classified as "miscellaneous schools," which handicaps employment possibilities for their graduates. Graduates from Korean high schools are not qualified to take entrance examinations to attend Japanese public universities.

Koreans do not qualify for Japan's national health insurance system unless they are employed, so aging Koreans particularly suffer. There are some 60,000 elderly and disabled Koreans who do not receive Japan's welfare pension, according to the General Association of Korean Residents in Japan (Aita, 1992).

Koreans, as foreigners, are denied the right to vote,[19] and their access to public employment is circumscribed.[20] Marriage among Koreans and Japanese

Table 6.10. Osaka Prefecture's Foreigners, by Occupation in 1991

Occupation	No. of Job Holders	
Professional and managerial	7,024	(17.2)
Clerical workers	10,576	(26.0)
Production workers	11,242	(27.6)
Service workers[a]	10,767	(26.5)
Others[b]	1,103	(2.7)
Total No. of job holders	40,712	(100.0)
Total No. of Foreigners	209,587	

Source: Ministry of Justice, Registered Foreigners, 1992
Note: Numbers in parentheses are percentages.
[a] Service workers include persons in transport and telecommunication and service industries.
[b] Others include persons engaged in agriculture, fishery, forestry, and mining, and laborers.

can engender family conflicts on both sides. Japanese can be prejudiced against Koreans, and Korean parents often want their children to maintain Korean identity and heritage and not to assimilate into Japanese society.

Korean businesses and housing are concentrated among the more blighted residential areas in Osaka City. Korean markets around the Tsuruhashi station, for example, are housed in primitive buildings, the result of Korean resistance to redevelopment and the city's reluctance to force renewal on the area. This is a sore point with Osaka's urban-redevelopment authorities.

Still, social inequalities between Koreans and Japanese are diminishing. The percentage of Korean children going to college (20 percent) is catching up with Japanese children (35 percent). A recent survey by the Korean Labor League in Japan indicates that younger Koreans have experienced less discrimination than older generations. Eighty-six percent of Koreans between the ages of 14 and 25 said they had never encountered discrimination (Korean Labor League, 1991).

Korean money is visible in Osaka. Koreans established *Osaka Kogin,* a credit cooperative bank in 1980. Measured by savings, it is now the largest credit cooperative in Japan, and Osaka has two more Korean Credit Cooperatives ranking in Japan's top ten. Korean economic power lies mainly in service industries, including pachinko parlors, restaurants, and real estate.[21] As their economic power has grown, the Korean occupational pattern has come to resemble the Japanese (table 6.10).[22]

CONCLUSION

Geography is not destiny in Japan. Osaka is a reminder that urbanization need not be place stratifying, urban land markets need not be class segregating, and municipal incorporation need not be balkanizing. Much depends on the political-economic context. Intergovernmental relations, the relation of state to market in ideology and practice, and the history of class conflict and accommodation have engendered a spatial mixing of classes in the Japanese city.

NOTES

1. The research reported in this paper is based on the authors' four-month field study in Osaka in late 1992 and was funded by a Research Fellowship from the Japan Society for the Promotion of Science.

2. There are positive correlations among family income, parents' education, children's education, and children's occupational status in Japan, as in the United States, but Japanese education neither reflects nor fosters anything like the inequalities among schools and social groups found in American society.

3. Exceptions are central government sponsored "science cities" or "technopolises," including the Kansai Science City project near Kyoto.

4. Interview with Noriyuki Iwata, Shinji Matsue, and Yoichi Muranaka, Department of Planning and Coordination, Osaka Prefectural Government, November 5, 1992.

5. Interview with Yoshiaki Taguchi, Director, Urban Documentation Center, Osaka City University, Osaka, Japan, October 8, 1992.

6. The Basic Land Use Law of 1989 is an important change in direction in this respect. It declared that priority in landuse shall be given to public welfare and that land ownership is different in nature from other property rights and should be given legal treatment different from other forms of real estate (Naruse, 1990: 130).

7. Osaka city officials continue to take a pragmatic approach to land use, but they desire a stricter planning system to dampen land prices and improve the environment for housing. They admire American, British, and German planning models, which control types of building as well as land use.

8. Interview with Osamu Kimura, Director General, Economic Affairs Bureau, Osaka City, November 10, 1992.

9. Farmers retained ownership of their land, once urban development began to encroach on it, by building small factories for rent.

10. Interview with Hitoshi Konaka, Managing Director, Higashi Osaka Chamber of Commerce and Industry, October 26, 1992.

11. Osaka Prefecture has an Institute for Advanced Industry Develop-

ment. The Institute surveys small businesses every year and publishes the research results. The trend toward design shops and prototype production has
been increasing since the mid-1980s (The Osaka Prefectural Institute for
Advanced Industry Development, 1989, 1991, 1992).

12. Others include the Yodogawa Riverside project in the Asahi ward and
the Nipponbashi project in the Naniwa ward. The city has already completed
similar projects in the Abeno, Ueroku, and Tenshichi districts.

13. Interview with Yoshiaki Taguchi, Director of the Urban Documentation Center, Osaka City University, September 28, 1992.

14. Interview with Toshio Kamo, Professor of Political Science, Faculty
of Law, Osaka City University, October 13, 1992. The standardized curriculum
has come under growing criticism in Japan for stifling individual creativity.
Central and local governments are discussing ways to decentralize curriculum
decision making.

15. Public housing targets all income groups in Japan.

16. Interview with Tatsuo Tanigawa, Deputy Mayor; Shigeru Shimizu,
Mayor's Office; and Tatsuo Fujiwara, Planning Department, Kaizuka City,
November 6, 1992.

17. Japan's rules for citizenship include the following: By birth. If either
or both parents are Japanese citizens, their children automatically become
Japanese citizens. They must report the birth to a local government so that it
can be recorded in their family register (*koseki*).

By naturalization. Including foreigners married to Japanese nationals,
about 220,000 foreigners have obtained Japanese citizenship since 1945.
Resident aliens can apply for citizenship if they are at least 20 years old, have
lived in Japan for 5 years or longer, have no criminal record, and are able to
support themselves. Naturalized citizens are no longer required to adopt a
Japanese name, but it is "customary."

18. Kimbara (1986) estimates that 700,000 to 1.5 million Koreans were
forced to go to Japan. Some were brought to Osaka to labor in war-production
factories and on underground air-raid shelters.

19. Some cities in the Osaka metropolitan area are attempting to change
the law to give voting rights to foreigners.

20. Osaka Prefecture hired a third-generation Korean from Osaka Foreign Language University to teach senior high school in 1992. He was the first
Korean public school teacher hired since 1986. Osaka City and Osaka
Prefecture had long hired Koreans, despite opposition from the Ministry of
Education, but stopped in 1986. However, the new opening entailed a compro-
mise with the Ministry of Education. The new Korean teacher did not receive
the same status as his Japanese counterparts. He was hired as a permanent lec-
turer (Asahi Shimbun, 21 October, 1992).

21. Koreans own 60 percent of the 1,100 pachinko parlors in Osaka, with
annual sales of one trillion yen.

22. Since almost 90 percent of foreigners in Osaka prefecture are Koreans, data on registered foreigners by occupation can be roughly equated with Koreans. Data on the Ikuno ward show that its occupational pattern also is not much different from that of Osaka city.

REFERENCES

Aita, Kaoruko. 1992. "Korean Rights Promoted: Discrimination Being Fought through Education." *The Japan Times*, December 15, p. 3.
Asahi Shimbun. 21 October, 1992.
Bluestone, Barry and Bennett Harrison. 1992. *The Great U-Turn.* New York: Basic Books.
"Bunka No Chigai Jugyoshitai." 1992. (I would like to teach Students Different Culture). *The Asahi Shimbun*, October 21, p. 2.
Callies, David L. 1994. "Land Use Planning and Control in Japan." In *Planning for Cities and Regions in Japan.* Edited by Philip Shapira, Ian Masser, and David W. Edgington. Liverpool: Liverpool University Press, pp. 59-69.
Fahnzylber, Fernando. 1990. "The United States and Japan as Models of Industrialization." In *Manufacturing Miracles.* Edited by Gary Gereffi and Donald Wyman. Princeton: Princeton University Press, pp. 323-52.
Gordon, Andrew. 1988. *The Evolution of Labor Relations in Japan: Heavy Industry 1853-1955.* Cambridge, Mass.: Harvard University Press.
Hill, Richard Child. 1974. "Separate and Unequal: Governmental Inequality in the Metropolis," *The American Political Science Review.* 68 (4):1557-68.
Hill, Richard Child, and Kuniko Fujita. 1995. "Osaka's Tokyo Problem." *International Journal of Urban & Regional Research*, 19 (2) June:181-93.
Japan Ministry of Justice. 1984-1992. *Gaikokujin Toroku Kokusekibetsu Jinin Chosahyo* (Registered Foreigners by Nationality). Tokyo.
Japan Statistics Bureau, Management and Coordination Agency. 1990. *Population Census 1990.* Tokyo.
Kimbara, Samon. 1986. *Nihon no Naka no Kankoku-Chosenjin, Chugokujin* (Koreans and Chinese in Japan). Tokyo: Akashi Shobo.
Kodama, Tooru. 1990. "*Tokyo.Osaka ni Okeru Jutaku Kensetsu no Doko to Kadai.*" (Housing in Tokyo and Osaka). In *Tokyo.Osaka.* Edited by Masataka Ueda. Tokyo: Tokyo University Press, pp. 117-53.
Korean Labor League in Japan. 1991. "Survey on Koreans on Kandao." In *Osaka no Toshimondai* (The 12th Exchange Seminar by Tokyo Economic University Shibata Seminar and Osaka City University Miyamoto Seminar), pp. 34-37. Edited by Kenichi Miyamoto and Tokue Shibata, Tokyo.
Logan, John, and Harvey Molotch. 1987. *Urban Fortunes: The Political Economy of Place.* Berkeley: University of California Press.
Miyamoto, Keniichi. 1993. "Japan's World Cities: Osaka and Tokyo Compared." In *Japanese Cities in the World Economy.* Edited by Kuniko

Fujita and Richard Child Hill. Philadelphia: Temple University Press, pp. 53-82.

Morishima, Michio. 1982. *Why Has Japan 'Succeeded'?* Cambridge: Cambridge University Press.

Nakamura, Hachiro. 1993. "Urban Growth in Prewar Japan." In *Japanese Cities in the World Economy.* Edited by Kuniko Fujita and Richard Child Hill. Philadelphia: Temple University Press, pp. 26-49.

Narita, Kozo. 1986. "Toshiken Takakuka to Osaka Toshiken no Ichizuke." (Multicore Metropolis and Direction of the Osaka Metropolitan Area) In *Toshiken Takakuka no Tenkai* (Development of Multicore Metropolis). Edited by Yoshiaki Taguchi and Kozo Narita. Tokyo: Tokyo University Press, pp. 3-38.

———. 1990. "Saitoshika no Tokyo to Osaka (The Re-Urbanization of Tokyo and Osaka)." In *Toyko. Osaka.* Edited by Masataka Ueda. Tokyo: Tokyo University Press, pp. 3-36.

Naruse, Nobutaka. 1990. "Land Prices and Land Problems." *Local Government Review in Japan.* 8:122-31.

Nihon Marketing Kyoiku Center. 1990. *Kojin Shotoku Shihyo* (Per Capita Income Index). Tokyo.

Okugawa, Otohiko and Masataka Ueda, eds. 1986. *Perspectives on Osaka.* Osaka: Osaka Regional Development Council.

Osaka City. 1967. *Osaka Shi Sogo Keikaku* (Osaka City's Comprehensive Plan), Osaka, Japan.

———. 1974. *Osaka Shi Tobu Kogyo Shigaichi no Tochi Riyo. Control ni Kansuru Chosa Kenkyu Hokokusho* (Report on Land Use in East Osaka's Industrial District). Osaka: Osaka City Planning Bureau.

———. 1991. *Housing Policy of Osaka 1991.* Osaka: Osaka City Planning Bureau.

———. 1992. *Outline of the Osaka Economy.* Osaka: Osaka City Economic Bureau.

Osaka Prefecture. 1991*a. Osakafu Jutaku Gokanen Keikaku* (Osaka Prefecture's Sixth 5-Year Housing Plan: 1991-1996). Osaka.

———. 1991*b. Osakafu Shin Sogo Plan* (Osaka Prefecture's New Comprehensive Plan). Osaka.

———. 1992. *Sumai Zukuri Osaka 21* (Osaka's Housing Toward the 21st Century). Osaka.

Osaka Prefecture, Osaka City, and Osaka Chamber of Commerce and Industry. 1994. *Osaka: A New Gateway to Japan.* Osaka: Osaka Business Publisher's Council.

Osaka Prefectural Institute for Advanced Industry Development. 1989. *Kokusaika no shinten ni Taiohsuru Kikai Shitauke Chushyo Kigyo* (Small Machinery Enterprises responding to Internationalization). Osaka.

————.1991. *Chiiki Keizai kankyo Henka to Osaka Kogyo no Taioh ni kansuru Chosa* (Regional economic change and Osaka's Industry: The case of Metal and Machinery Industry in the Higashi Osaka area). Osaka.

————. 1992. *Asia to Tomoni Hatten Suru Osaka Kogyo* (Osaka Industry Linked to Asia). Osaka.

Ozaki, Robert. 1992. *Human Capitalism.* Tokyo: Kodansha.

Reich, Robert. 1991. *The Work of Nations.* New York: Alfred Knopf.

Research Action Institute for Koreans in Japan (RAIK). 1990. *Japan's Subtle Apartheid: The Korean Minority Now.* Tokyo: RAIK.

Rusk, David. 1993. *Cities Without Suburbs.* Washington, D.C.: Woodrow Wilson Center Press.

Seki, Mitsuhiko. 1994. *Beyond the Full-Set Industrial Structure: Japanese Industry in the New Age of East Asia.* Tokyo: LTCB International Library Foundation.

Taguchi, Yoshiaki. 1986. *"Takakuka e to Mukau Osaka Toshiken"* (Osaka Metropolitan Area with Multicore Centers) In *Toshiken Takakuka no Tenkai* (Development of Multicore Metropolis). Edited by Yoshiaki Taguchi and Kozo Narita. Tokyo: University of Tokyo Press, pp. 39-76.

Taguchi, Yoshiaki and Renei Hojo. 1992. *"Daitoshi no Restructuring to Kogyo Kasseika Mondai: Osaka Shinai Tobu no Juko Konzai Chiiki no Menteki Seibi o Megutte"* (Restructuring of a Big City and Industrial Revitalization: The Case of Housing-Industry Mixed Area in East Osaka). In *Gendai Daitoshi no Restructuring* (Restructuring of Big Cities). Edited by Masataka Ueda. Tokyo: Tokyo University Press, pp. 67-105.

Ueda, Masataka. 1986. "Strategic Policies for Revitalizing the Osaka Regional Economy," Economic Research Institute. Osaka: Osaka City University.

7 Urban Land Use and Control in the Japanese City: A Case Study of Hiroshima, Osaka, and Kyoto

DAVID L. CALLIES

On the face of it, land-use controls in the Japanese city parallel those in the American city: zoning in accordance with a comprehensive plan. As in the United States, virtually all developable land in a Japanese city is divided into a series of zones that broadly separate residential, commercial, and industrial uses. Like the United States, the zones are designated in accordance with some sort of plan. Finally, like the United States, special projects (the rough equivalent to developments of regional impact as defined by the American Law Institute's [ALI] Model Land Development Code) are subject to special rules. Also, special areas (roughly equivalent to areas of critical state concern, as defined in the ALI Model Land Development Code) are designated in the form of overlay zones or districts for urban agriculture, historic sites, and areas of aesthetic value.

There are also some major differences. The Japanese have national planning legislation, which sets out the broad requirements of land-use planning and the basic zones that most cities use to implement plans. The Japanese have adopted a more "top-down" approach to urban land-use controls than the United States (Shapira, Masser, and Edgington, 1994). Also, there is substantially more attention to economics in the Japanese plans than there is in the United States (Callies, 1994). Finally, the typical American zoning ordinance divides all land (not just part as in Japanese cities) under the jurisdiction of the local government into far more zones than does its Japanese counterpart, usually by further subdividing the basic residential, commercial, and industrial classifications into several categories according to intensity of use.

A brief summary of the U.S. system of land use controls is provided here, for the purpose of comparison, then a summary of the Japanese system is given, followed by a more detailed examination of the zoning schemes in Hiroshima, Osaka and Kyoto, three of Japan's largest cities.

THE AMERICAN CONTEXT

Land-use controls in the United States have grown enormously in kind and complexity since 1926 when the U.S. Supreme Court established the constitutionality of comprehensive zoning, which became the building block of American city planning. State, regional, and federal agencies now exercise a panoply of land-use powers, both directly and indirectly, that drastically affect the use of land (Garner and Callies, 1972). While the control of land use in the United States appears to have many roots, it was the drafting of a Standard Zoning Enabling Act and its dissemination by the U.S. Department of Commerce and adoption by dozens of states that was principally responsible for the spread of zoning, although 208 municipalities with 22 million inhabitants representing 40 percent of the urban population of the United States were zoned by 1923 (Bassett, l940: 834-35). The 1920s also saw the judicial creation of a limitation on land-use controls exercised via the police power: the theory that a land-use regulation, if it were too onerous, constituted a taking of property without compensation, contrary to the Fifth Amendment to the Federal constitution—the so-called taking issue (Bosselman, Callies, and Banta, 1973). By 1930, 981 municipalities, representing 67 percent or 46 million of its urban population, had adopted the zoning ordinance as the latest and most useful technique to control the use of land (Haar, 1977: 204).

In the United States, zoning is firmly rooted in the police power—the power to regulate so as to protect the health, safety, morals, and welfare of the people. In most jurisdictions, that power is delegated from the state—the repository of police power—to units of local government through a zoning-enabling statute. That statute is usually based on the Standard Zoning Enabling Act. Such statutes *permit* (but do not *require)* local governments to divide the land area in their jurisdiction into districts or zones and to list permitted uses, their permitted height and density ("bulk" regulation), and conditional uses in each.

The map on which the districts are drawn is called the *zoning map,* and the lists of uses, bulk regulations, and definitions are collectively called the *text.* Each district as described in the zoning ordinance text contains a list of permitted uses, together with permitted accessory (garage, carport) and temporary (fruit stands, construction sheds) uses, parking and loading requirements and limits, and so-called bulk regulations: height, side/front/rear yards, lot coverage, floor/area ratios, and the like. Some also set out what special or conditional uses are permitted in that district, together with the special conditions applicable to such uses (i.e., hours of operation, special parking, and special lighting standards for a convenience foodstore or delicatessen in a residential zone). Also, the text provides administrative regulations setting forth how the zoning ordinance restrictions on a particular piece of property may be changed. There is also usually a section in the text dealing with uses that were permitted at some past date but now fail to conform to the existing land-use regulations for the district, called, collectively, *nonconformities.*

BASIC ELEMENTS OF LAND-USE PLANNING CONTROL IN JAPAN

Japan follows the model wherein land-use regulations are based on plans with a strong, but not overwhelming, land-use component. Most local land-use regulatory schemes conform to the Urban Planning Act and the Construction Standards Act, which are discussed below. Certainly this is true with respect to the number and kinds of zoning districts found in the Hiroshima, Osaka, and Kyoto. Whereas the general thrust of planning and regulation of land use in Japan is indeed "top-down," the implementation is (at least in major urban areas) where it should be—at the local government level.

There are a variety of laws that ultimately affect the use of land in Japan, including statutes such as the Agricultural Promotion Act and the Nature Conservation Act. However, because this chapter is restricted primarily to the subject of urban-land-development controls at the city level, only a basic framework/summary of the principal statutes that are more or less enforced through the Japanese equivalent of zoning is given below.

Broad land-use policy for Japan is established primarily through the National Land Use Planning Act of 1974, or NLUPA. Administered principally by the Ministry of Construction and the National Land Authority, NLUPA was designed to help regulate land values. However, it also requires the preparation of a national land-use plan providing for the placing of land in urban, agricultural, forest, natural parks, and nature conservation areas. These are designated in regional or prefectural plans and local land-use plans. The latter are more specifically provided for in the City (or Urban) Planning Act of 1968 (Barrett and Therivel, 1991: 61-63).

City planning areas are those areas designated by the prefectural governor after consultation with the Ministry of Construction; they normally constitute already-built-up regions or soon-to-be developed areas. Altogether, they are reported to cover about a quarter of Japan's land (Barrett and Therivel, 1977: 63). These city planning areas are further divided into urbanization promotion areas (UPA) and urbanization control areas (UCA). Designed to be built up within 10 years, the UPAs are regulated by zoning. They are divided into 11 primary-use zones, the regulations for which control the use and volume of buildings constructed therein: Exclusively Low-Story Residential Districts, Categories I and II; Exclusively Medium-High Residential Districts, Categories I and II; Residential Districts, Categories I and II; QuasiResidential Districts; Neighborhood Commercial Districts; Commercial Districts; Industrial Districts; and Exclusively Industrial Districts (Building Standard Center of Japan, 1994). By the same token, development in the UCAs is, in theory, strictly controlled, although there is apparently evidence that such controls are frequently relaxed (Barrett and Therivel, 1991: 63).

The Urban Planning Act of 1968

Among the laws regulating land use in Japan, the Urban Planning Act of 1968 (referred to also as the City Planning Act) and the Building Standard Law of 1994 are most important. Both appear principally to be administered by the Ministry of Construction (Barrett and Therivel, 1991: 63; Building Center of Japan, 1994).

The Urban Planning Act permits a prefectural governor to designate cities or city centers (or village or town centers, for that matter) as urban planning zones (Arai, 1990). Once this is done, an urban plan is adopted for the area, taking into consideration environmental and social conditions, public facilities and infrastructure. The most-critical basic decision in the plan is to decide what areas within the plan's jurisdiction will be designated as an *urbanizing zone,* in which development is to be encouraged (though not without restrictions), and as a *nonurbanizing zone,* in which development is discouraged (Arai, 1990: 21). While the plans are drawn up initially by the cities or prefectural governments, it is the Ministry of Construction that finally approves how the urban plan makes these decisions.

A variety of zones, facilities and projects may or can be provided for in the urbanizing zone, as follows (Arai, 1990: 22-24).

Under the Urban Planning Act following zones may be designated:
- (a) Use area
- (b) Special use area
    - (1) Special industrial zone
    - (2) Educational zone
    - (3) Other zones established by government order (e.g., retail store zone, office zone, welfare zone, recreational zone, sightseeing zone, special business zone)
- (c) Highly developed area
- (d) Particularized district
- (e) Fire-resistant area
- (f) Beauty zone
- (g) Scenic zone
- (h) Parking place
- (i) Portside zones
- (j) Zones where historical properties are specially preserved
- (k) Neighboring zones where green zones are specially preserved
- (l) Wholesale areas

Under the Urban Planning Act, the following facilities may be designated:

(a) Traffic facilities

(b) Official open space

(c) Supply facilities or disposition facilities

(d) Waterways

(e) Educational-cultural facilities

(f) Health facilities or welfare facilities

(g) Market, butchery, or crematory facilities

(h) Public housing facilities (apartment complexes)

(i) Government and municipal office complexes

(l) Wholesaling areas

(k) Other facilities set up by government order

Under the Urban Planning Act, the following projects may be designated:

(a) Land readjustment projects under the Land Readjustment Act

(b) Projects for developing new housing areas under the New Housing Development Act

(c) Projects for improving industrial towns under the Act Concerning Arrangement of Neighboring Regions and Urban Development Zones in the Metropolitan Area, or the Act Concerning Arrangement and Development of Neighboring Zones and Urban Development Zones in the Kinkai Area

(d) Projects for redeveloping towns under the Urban Redevelopment Act

(e) New projects for maintenance of urban areas under the New Urban Maintenance Readjustment Act.

The enforcement of the urban-planning regulations depends on the zone in which the property is located (Arai, 1990: 25). A development license from the prefectural governor is generally necessary for most developments, in particular large housing developments. The development license is not issued unless the developer has already filed or first prepared a development plan. In addition, the public facilities for the proposed project must meet a certain minimum standard.

There are exceptions to the requirement for such a license for railroad and health facilities and other facilities that serve the public interest and developments serving agriculture, forestry, and fishery in nonurbanizing zones. Government projects and emergency projects are also excepted. Basically, the development license is granted only for developments classified or zoned for urban development in the urban plan for the specific city or town. If this is so, and the public facilities are adequate, a developer is in theory entitled to the development license. There is some indication that to deny a license because a different sort of development is contemplated by the governor gives the developer the right to have his land acquired by the government. Further restrictions on areas and zones are applied under the Building Standards Act, the Parking Place Act, and Act for the Preserving Ancient Cities, but these are in addition to and beyond the standards contained in a development license under the Urban Planning Act (Arai, 1990:26-27). For larger "urban-planning projects," which are usually local government sponsored, it may be necessary to obtain a license from the Minister of Construction.

The Building Standard Law of 1994

The Building Standard Law applies to all of Japan, whether or not in urban zones under the Urban Planning Act. The law is, however, more than a building code, although it has aspects of this as well. It has specific provisions "concerning overall regulations" or "overall provisions" that are designed to deal with the use of land with respect to specific projects in urban zones (Arai, 1990: 32-33). For this purpose, the Building Standard Law contains a use-zone system, one of the purposes of which is to separate conflicting uses of land (e.g., heavy industry and residences) and to encourage the concentration of buildings of similar uses in the same location. For this purpose, it uses 11 classifications:

1. Category I Exclusively Low-Story Residential Districts, which also permit schools, nursing homes, clinics, apartment houses, dormitories, and houses concurrently used as business offices, stores and similar uses.
2. Category II Exclusively Low-Story Residential Districts, which permit those uses in Category 1, but include more expanded stores and dining facilities.
3. Category I Exclusively Medium-High Residential Districts in which Category I Low-Story Residential uses are permitted, plus universities, hospitals, welfare centers, child-recreation centers, and small garages.
4. Category II Exclusively Medium-High Residential Districts (the Building Act Annexed Table 2 lists no additional permitted uses).

5. Category I Residential Districts (see 4 above).

6. Category II Residential Districts (see 4 above).

7. Quasi-Residential Districts (see 4 above).

8. Neighborhood Commercial Districts, in which a variety of industrial and commercial uses are explicitly excluded.

9. Commercial Districts, in which a variety of industrial uses are explicitly excluded.

10. Quasi-Industrial Districts, in which a long list of heavy industrial uses are excluded.

11. Industrial Districts, in which a variety of commercial (hotels) and institutional (schools and hospitals) are excluded.

The Act also permits the local government to designate yet another use zone for special uses.

The Building Standards Law also has provisions that restrict building heights in the first-class exclusive residential zone and in other zones, depending on the width of the road on which it fronts, aside from further height restrictions that depend on the materials used in its construction. There is some indication that an urban plan may contain more restrictive height restrictions (Arai, 1990: 40-43).

THE LAND-USE PLANNING SYSTEM AT WORK: THREE EXAMPLES

To illustrate how land-use controls work at the local level in Japan, the following section summarizes the relationship between local urban plans and urban zoning, which is the principal mechanism for regulating the use of urban land. The zoning itself is often divorced from the actual development process. This contrasts with zoning in the United States, where changes in zones or granting of special permissions therein is directly tied to the land-development process, even though, theoretically, development codes govern the actual development.

Hiroshima

Hiroshima is located in the south of Japan's largest island, Honshu, about 350 miles west of Tokyo. It is the economic hub of the Choguku region. It is a major governmental and industrial center, with a high concentration of companies engaged in the manufacture of automotive parts and equipment. The city faces the Inland Sea to the south and a mountain range to the north. The lowland region of principal development is the delta at the mouth of the Ota River. Much of the remaining area consists of steep hills and mountains covered with forest.

Photo 7.1 Hiroshima, which was completely rebuilt after the world's first atomic bomb was dropped on 6 August 1945, is an important city in western Honshu. The Atomic Bomb Dome (right foreground) is the only building left unreconstructed. Photo by P. P. Karan

Originally established as a municipality in 1889, Hiroshima has grown from approximately 27 square kilometers with 83,000 people to 740 square kilometers with a population of about 1.1 million in 1990. This is the more remarkable, since the detonation of an atomic bomb over the city by American forces in 1945 during World War II reduced the city's population from more than 400,000 to something over 100,000. Hiroshima was designated as a city eligible to receive aid under a 1946 Special Town Planning Law, under the auspices of the War Damage Reconstruction Institute established in 1945. In 1952, the Hiroshima Peace Memorial City Construction Plan was promulgated under the auspices of the 1949 Hiroshima Peace Memorial City Construction Law. Military installations near the epicenter of the blast were replaced by parklike open spaces of nearly 100 hectares, together with buildings and monuments dedicated to peace. A new roadway network was also planned and implemented. An additional 1,000 hectares were designated, replanned, and rebuilt under the direction of the mayor of Hiroshima and the prefectural governor,

Photo 7.2 Large blocks of apartment buildings constructed as part of the Hiroshima urban redevelopment project. Photo by P. P. Karan

who split their territorial responsibilities over the eastern and western parts of the city damaged by the blast, respectively. An example of the redevelopment is the 33.3-hectare Motomachi District Redevelopment Project, which replaced destroyed (and temporarily rebuilt) wooden dwellings with blocks of apartments numbering 4,570 units housing an estimated 12,000 people. Today, the city is governed by a 64-member town council elected from eight wards.

While city planning arguably commenced in 1589 with the construction of Hiroshima Castle, and some urban planning was applied through national legislation in 1923, modern city planning in Hiroshima did not really commence until the local implementation of the City Planning Act in 1968, subsequent to the expansion of industry and associated uses. It is the city plan and its enforcement, largely through zoning and other controls, that govern the use of land in Hiroshima today (fig. 7.1).

In common with other major cities in Japan, large parts of Hiroshima are regulated by planning districts promulgated under the auspices of the national town planning laws. A Hiroshima Region Town Planning Jurisdiction was designated in January of 1971; it covers both parts of Hiroshima and eight other nearby local governments. Withm Hiroshima, the area covered is approxi-

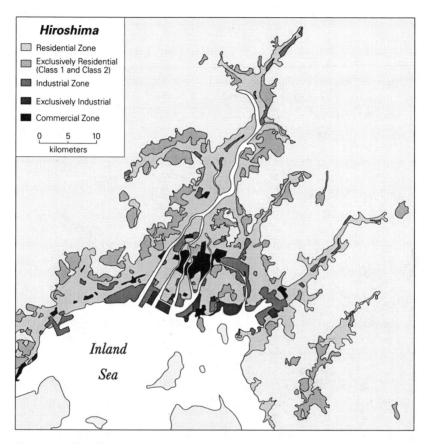

Figure 7.1 Hiroshima Land-use Zones

mately 320 square kilometers, or 31,912 hectares, from a total city land area of 740 square kilometers, or 74,037 hectares. These are the more urbanized areas of the city, particularly around its extensive waterfront.

As already described, the City Planning Act requires the division of Hiroshima's town planning area into urban promotion areas (14,045 hectares, or 19% of the area of the city) and urban control areas (17,867 hectares, or 24% of the urban area of the city). According to maps that accompany Hiroshima's town-planning literature, the remainder consists of rural and ocean areas. The town-planning law provides for the further subdivision of these two basic classifications into zoning districts with the usual restrictions on the use of land as well as external features such as floor/area ratios.

Of the 16 categories of zones provided for in the Town Planning Law, the city has "provided for" or used 7, together with "zones for certain uses." There

Table 7.1. Hiroshima Urban Zones

Zone Classification	Hectares	Percent
1. Exclusively Residential Zone, class 1	2,963	4.0
2. Exclusively Residential Zone, class 2	1,986	2.7
3. Residential zone	5,656	7.6
4. Neighborhood Commercial Zone	756.4	1.0
5. Commercial Zone	591	0.8
6. Semi-industrial Zone	1,238	1.7
7. Industrial Zone	557	0.8
8. Exclusively Industrial Zone	296	0.4

are 8 categories of such "zones for certain uses" that the city has divided into a total of 15, the first 8 of which are the most important for developmental purposes. The tabulation below lists these zones, together with the area of the city devoted to them (in hectares) and the percentage this represents of the total land area of the city.

Obtaining permission to commence development, provided the proposal is a permitted use in the zone in which a parcel falls, is a comparatively straightforward process. However, deviations from the requirements of the district are not easily permitted, whether large or small. Indeed, it may well be easier to obtain a "rezoning" by the town planning department, as noted below. In either event, contributions to public facilities are increasingly likely to be required as a prerequisite.

According to interviews with officials in the Hiroshima Planning Department in 1992, the city divides applications for development into two categories: small-scale developments of 5-25 hectares and large-scale developments of more than 20 hectares. While as many as thirty agencies and divisions of city government may be involved in reviewing projects in the larger development categories, two areas are critical in both categories: traffic (including parking) and housing. Most development proposals currently involve housing. Little or no development is permitted in urban control areas, but is limited to urban-promotion areas.

The subject of rezoning is one that apparently arises principally at planning stages unrelated to pending developments. The architectural control council is principally responsible for giving and coordinating permission to develop. Provided the property is in an urban-promotion area, the council will approve a development if it is in an area undergoing change and if it is clear that there will be a contribution by the development to needed city facilities. The same architectural control council has the authority to approve variations in standards (height, etc.) proposed by a private landowner/developer. For major development variations, a change of zone must be obtained from the city planning division. It is notable that these and other permissions may be given directly by the officials concerned. There appears to be no concept of either rezoning or the granting of substantial variations from standards as legislative acts needing the approval of the equivalent of a city council. This appears to reflect the tendency in Japan for the plans, which govern the land use through zoning, to be "top-down" through the chain of executive officers involved at the various levels of government.

Very little land development is permitted without some sort of permission. Thus, even the construction of a single-family house in an area properly zoned needs the approval of the architectural control division (although this is quickly and easily granted, often within three weeks or so), to make sure that all the district standards are met. Approval of design features is required if the house is located within the precincts of the famous Hiroshima Peace Park.

The practice of exacting public facility concessions for development permissions is well developed, although at times it is ad hoc. Thus, for example, it is quite common to require street and road dedications and school sites, and standards are in place for these requirements. The provision of open space, on the other hand, appears to proceed on a project-by-project basis. Developers may also be asked to share the cost of certain facilities as diverse as nature preserves and trails, and sanitary sewer systems. All of these are part of the urban plans applicable to Hiroshima, which target the provision of such facilities and many others by the government.

The concept of nexus between facilities and the development is not developed as it is in much of the United States. For example, in Japan officials relate that it would not be unusual to request a golf-course developer to provide a (unrelated) playground or a community center. Other developers may be required to widen a road, provide sidewalks, or traffic signalization, even if their development would not warrant such improvements. Finally, in large-scale residential construction, there does not seem to be any requirement for providing low-income housing as a condition for development approvals or permissions as sometimes occurs in other countries.

Osaka

Although Osaka City was established as a municipality only 100 years ago, it has been a commercial center since at least the fourth century (City Planning Department, 1992). Known traditionally as the *City of Water,* Osaka is bordered to the west by Osaka Bay and to the north and south by the Kanzaki and Yamato Rivers. Because of its location and proximity to these major rivers, Osaka flourished as a port city for centuries. However, the City was devastated in the fourteenth century by repeated civil wars, and did not recover until the

Photo 7.3 Residential development in the suburbs around Osaka. Photo by P. P. Karan

Ishiyama-Honganji Temple was constructed in 1496. Osaka then developed into a temple town, until the temple was destroyed in the late 1500s, culminating in a steady decline of the city until the early 1600s.

Beginning in the seventeenth century, Osaka began to flourish as an economic and financial center as well as playing a leading role in the development of modern performing arts and culture. Since this period, Osaka has continued as a consistent leader in Japanese culture, generating a wide variety of popular culture, including the theater, the development of literature, and other popular entertainments. Commerce and industry dominate Osaka's economy, characterized by a wide variety of businesses, the majority of which are wholesalers. Because of its economic vitality and central location, Osaka plays an important role as both a cultural center and a commercial leader in Japan.

Osaka has faced many crises in its long history, its population decline being the most recent one. Although Osaka had a record population of 3.25 million in 1940, in 1990 the resident population had diminished to 2.6 million, in part because of rapid growth in the nearby suburbs. Osaka has, however, maintained a heavy workday population, adding more than one million people to its total population in the daytime. In response to the downward population trend, in 1989 Osaka implemented Osaka Plan 21, a comprehensive city plan designed to establish guidelines and directions for the city planning policies for the future (City of Osaka, 1991).

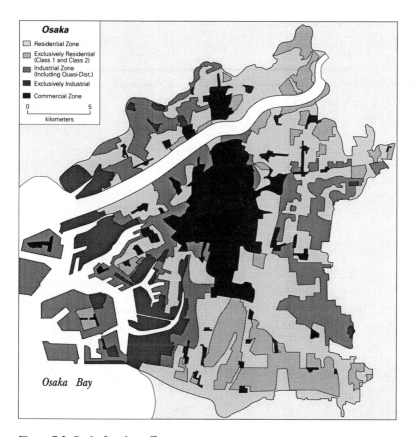

Figure 7.2 Osaka Land-use Zones

The Osaka City Comprehensive Plan for the Twenty-First Century, or Osaka Plan 21, adopts two development themes—a city that loves its people and a city that shares with the world. In order to realize its goal of making Osaka both a world-class metropolis and a pleasant, attractive city for its residents, Osaka Plan 21 sets out five urban planning objectives: a lifetime of health and safety, a fulfilling urban lifestyle, the creation and transmission of new cultural elements, a creative economic approach leading to social development, and openness to the world (City Planning Department, 1992). Osaka's future direction is geared towards urban renewal and the continued strength of Osaka's commercial and industrial center.

As in Hiroshima, which will be discussed below, Osaka is divided into urban-promotion and urban-control areas in accordance with the provisions of the City Planning Law. These are further divided into 10 zones in order to implement Osaka's city plan (fig. 7.2), all in accordance with the Building

Table 7.2. Osaka Urban Zones

Zone Classification	Hectares	Percent
1. Category I Medium-High Residential	353	1.7
2. Category II Medium-High Residential	2,070	9.8
3. Residential Category I	5,387	25.5
4. Residential Category II	1,135	5.4
5. Quasi-Residential	355	1.7
6. Neighborhood commercial	581	2.7
7. Commercial	3,550	16.8
8. Quasi-Industrial	4,658	22.0
9. Industrial	914	4.3
10. Exclusive Industrial	2,130	10.1

Standard Law (City Planning Department, 1992). However, as appears below, Osaka has further adopted a series of bulk restrictions applicable in each zone, together with a series of overlay zones dealing with such subjects as fire protection, aesthetics, and urban agriculture, together with special regulations and districts for urban redevelopment projects and its ambitious Technoport.

The 10 zoning categories mandated by the national City Planning Law and the Building Standard Law cover nearly all (21,133 hectares, all in the urban promotion area) of the city's 21,562 hectares all of which are in a formal city planning area. The districts, together with their size and percent of the city's area, are shown in table 7.2.

A series of overlay zones add additional regulations for a variety of purposes. Most of the urban planning area is divided into Fire Protection Zones (1936 hectares) and Quasi-Fire Protection Zones (15,504 hectares), in order to enhance the fire resistance of urban areas (City Planning 1925, 10). Two Building Height Control Zones actually set minimum heights (20 meters and seven meters, respectively) to encourage intensive land use and promote a dynamic appearance in the downtown area and to secure evacuation routes along certain main arterial roads (City Planning Department 1992). Seven Intensive Land Utilization Zones consisting of 31.6 hectares each set out maximum and minimum ratios of building volume to lot area, a maximum building base area-to-land ratio, minimum building area, and building wall setback. The stated purpose is to promote the intensive use of land, improve the functioning of the city by encouraging the integration of building lots, and preserve the greatest possible amount of publically accessible space.

A Port Zone of 1,672.9 hectares was created to provide for central administration by a port authority. This zone is further divided into five subzones:

Photo 7.4 Kyoto, with more than 1,600 old Buddhist temples and 270 Shinto shrines, has a large number of historic sites. Kinkakuji (Temple of the Golden Pavilion) seen here belongs to a sect of Zen Buddhism. Built in the twelfth century, it is surrounded by a fine landscape garden. Kyoto Buddhist Association has taken a lead in preserving historic sites and the city's skyline from the burst of urban development. Photo by P. P. Karan

Commercial Port, Industrial Port, Special Cargo Port, Safety Port, and Landscape Architecture and Recreation Port (City Planning Department, 1992). Aesthetic Zones covering 134.6 hectares are designated to preserve the appeal of attractive urban areas, such as the business area and government office area around Osaka Castles Seven Scenic Zones totaling 548.5 hectares are designed to preserve the city's natural beauty and pleasant environments by restricting building construction, residential land development, and tree cutting in the forests, lakes, hills, and other areas of natural beauty and to preserve structures and sites of historical or archaeological significance. Urban Agricultural Zones (651, totaling 96.45 hectares) were established to preserve farm land and other green areas, in part to help reduce pollution and in part to create a pleasant urban environment.

Finally, different plans and regulations further apply to specialized plan project areas. Thus, for example, approximately 32 hectares of urban renewal and redevelopment projects promote the comprehensive redevelopment of dense urban districts by rebuilding small buildings for fireproof multitenancy while "updating" roads, parks, and other public facilities, all in accordance with the Urban Redevelopment Act of 1969 (City Planning 1992, 32). Another 196.2 hectares are under development and redevelopment in accordance with "district planning for promoting proper redevelopment," to encourage the redevelopment of former factories and other large sites along with appropriate public facilities and their own subset of land-use controls applying to height, building ratios, and the like (City Planning 1992).

Kyoto

Established as the capital of the Heian emperors in 794, Kyoto remained the imperial capital of Japan even after real power shifted to the shoguns at Kamakura, near Edo (Tokyo), between 1185 and 1333, and subsequently to Edo itself, in the seventeenth century. During the internal struggles of the fifteenth century, Kyoto was completely burned to the ground and did not begin substantial rebuilding until Toyotomi Hideyoshi reunited Japan at the end of the sixteenth century and funded the reconstruction of the imperial palace, redesigned the city, and built a wall around it. Although arts and industry had begun to flourish in Kyoto, in 1869 Tokyo became the official imperial capital, and Kyoto's social and economic conditions temporarily declined. In 1922, the city planning areas were delineated for the first time, and in 1923 zones were designated.

After World War II ended, however, Kyoto began to grow once again, and the need for a comprehensive plan surfaced. In 1950 the Kyoto International, Cultural, and Tourist City Construction Law was enacted. This was intended to make Kyoto an international city of culture and tourism by maintaining and developing its superb historical, cultural, and artistic resources and developing cultural and tourist facilities. In 1966, the Law on Special Measures for Preservation of Historic Natural Features in Ancient Cities was enacted. Throughout this period, Kyoto saw a steady increase in population and industries, but in part because of public opinion, it did not experience large-scale sprawl such as appeared in other cities.

Topographically there was only limited room for expansion, and the beautiful natural environment and the city's many historic legacies had survived the war. It came to be generally agreed that city planning had to preserve, and be in harmony with, the city's traditional assets. In 1969 a comprehensive long-range plan entitled the "City Planning Concept" was made public (Kinoshita, 1988). Its stated goal was "city planning that improved the living environment, and respected human beings." City planning proceeded, reflecting overall ideas established in the City Planning Concept. In 1971, the city was divided into areas where development was to be promoted and areas where urbanization was to be restricted in order to prevent uncontrolled development in the suburbs and to promote the orderly development of the city. In addition, a Development and

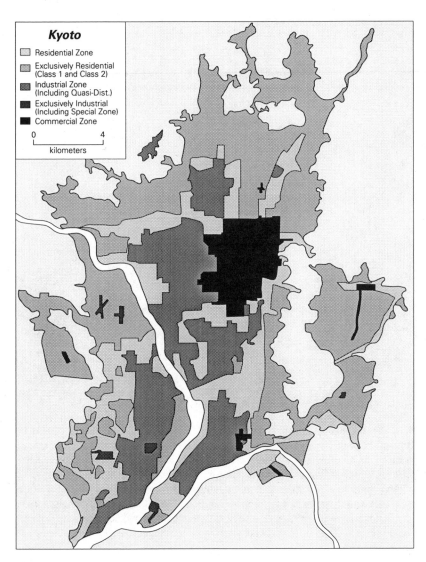

Figure 7.3 Kyoto Land-use Zones

Preservation Policy was prepared as a basis for city planning. In 1973, new land-use areas were designated that placed importance on the living environment. In 1979, the overall city planning concept was reconsidered, to place emphasis on stopping the rapid depopulation in the core and inner-ring areas while restraining the uncontrolled expansion of the population and industry in outer-ring areas. It attempted to develop areas in which residential and business functions coexisted harmoniously. With regard to transportation, stress was placed

Photo 7.5 Kyoto's historic character is being altered by a wave of ultramodern architecture. The high-density development in front of the Kyoto Railway Station is dominated by Kyoto Tower, a 430-foot-tall structure meant to look like the candles in
Buddhist temples—but with a circular restaurant and observation deck. The tower has
sparked controversy over the scale of buildings and the extent to which their features
harmonize with traditional structures. A coalition of Buddhist priests, architects, planners, and housewives has been organized to save the city's skyline from huge glass and
steel structures. Photo by P. P. Karan

on the establishment of a comprehensive transportation system based on
improvements in public means of transportation and the control of automobile
traffic.

Currently, city planning in Kyoto consists of four major categories: the
planning of urbanization promotion and control areas, guidance concerning the
use and height of buildings, the development of urban facilities, including city
roads and parks, and urban development. The Urbanization Promotion Area includes areas that have already become urbanized or are designated for urbanization within 10 years. Within this Urban Promotion Area are nine use districts:

exclusive residential category 1, exclusive residential category 2, residential, neighborhood commercial, commercial, quasi-industrial, industrial, exclusive industrial, and special industrial (fig.7.3).

Because Kyoto's urban area is quite old, urban renewal and readjustment have become important tools to revamp urban areas faced with deteriorating buildings and insufficient public utilities. Urban readjustment has become an effective means of city planning, aimed at, constructing roads and canals in relation to the land use of the area. Equally important has been Kyoto's urban development plan, aimed at a balanced and orderly new growth of the city and focusing on new construction in specific, planned areas.

Of special interest are the overlay zones for the preservation of historical, cultural, and natural resources. Presently, one fourth of the land area of Kyoto is designated as scenic areas or suburban green area overlay zones, which overlap both urban promotion and urban control areas particularly in the northern parts of the city. The idea is to protect natural landscapes. No development is permitted in these areas without the permission of the Mayor's Office for the Regulation of Development and Architectural Activities.

Moreover, under the Special Law for the Preservation of Historical Landscapes passed in 1966, about 60 square kilometers of the city are designated Special Areas for the Preservation of Historical Landscapes, or Aesthetic Areas. Additional areas are in areas or zones Restricted Against Enormous Constructions. Other select areas are designated as Preservation Areas of Historic Atmosphere, Preservation Districts for Groups of Historic Buildings, and Special Preservation Areas of Traditional Buildings. In all of these areas, it is necessary to obtain permission from the Mayor's Office for Development Activity, which is severely restricted.

CONCLUSIONS

As noted in the introduction, the Japanese system of land-use controls through zoning bears much resemblance to the American technique of local zoning. The groupings are familiar: residential, commercial, and industrial (and several zones in each category), with special development zones reflecting the need to deal with a particular large project in a separate and different fashion, as in Osaka. The planning is somewhat top-down and based on economic considerations, though recent amendments such as the Building Standard Law indicate that this is changing to reflect increasing concern about the environment, both natural and built. These concerns are often reflected in scenic, natural areas and preservation zones, as, for example, in Kyoto. The very use of a building standards law to impose land-use controls would be unusual in the United States, where zoning-enabling statutes deal only with the broad use of land and building codes deal only with the detail of structural construction, such as plumbing, electrical, and framing standards.

In a manner similar to that experienced in the United States (Callies and Grant, 1991), Japan is beginning to struggle with the relationship between infrastructure/public facilities and development permissions. As the experience in Hiroshima indicates, issues of planning gain and nexus do not yet appear to be well developed. The problems associated with such issues in the United States may never arise in Japan, given the lack of a counterpart to the Fifth Amendment to the U.S. Constitution, which has been interpreted to forbid the taking of property through regulation without compensation (Callies, 1993). For example, it would be possible for Japanese cities to require low-income housing as a condition for development permission, since they already require a variety of other "contributions" unrelated to a particular project such as development conditions, at least in Hiroshima.

Perhaps the most striking difference between American and Japanese local land-use controls is the division of the land area of the Japanese city into urbanization and nonurbanization areas, resulting in parts of the city being, in the technical sense, unzoned. In the United States, a city either adopts zoning (in most states this is a choice) or does not, but all the land area is generally zoned in those cities that choose to do so. Also, the Japanese appear to get by with far fewer zones. It is a rare American city of the size of Osaka, Hiroshima, or Kyoto that gets by with fewer than two dozen or so zones—more than twice the number of their Japanese counterparts. However, Japanese cities appear to use the overlay zone far more extensively than do their U.S. counterparts, as the experience in Osaka demonstrates. There also appears to be a tendency to use special districts (such as for ports in Osaka) to guide large developments or special development areas wholly outside the regular zoning context. The use of zoning to increase density is common to both systems, but the Japanese appear unique in requiring minimum building heights to help realize such densities.

It does not appear that Japan's relatively uniform system of plan-based urban land-use controls has changed fundamentally in the past decade or so. However, it may not need to do so. The system is general enough to accommodate a range of conditions, both social and economic. Planning has clearly responded to (or at least not impeded) a redevelopment process that, in the instance of Hiroshima, was total in both economic and physical terms. It is fair to conclude that planning would serve as well during an economic downturn as it has during a period of sustained economic growth. As some of the Hiroshima's experience indicates, the Japanese tend to target particular areas for attention when they need it, by means of special laws and districts based on, or as a follow up to special plans. The Japanese planning and land-use control framework, along with tax laws, subsidies, rising land prices, and small land-owners and property developers, have produced an interdigitated urban landscape of mixed agricultural, industrial, service, and residential uses in Japanese cities.

References

Abe, Yasutaka. 1995. "On the conservation of coastal environments by legal methods." *Kobe University Law Review* 25:1-33.

American Law Institute. 1976. *A Model Land Development Code,* complete text, adopted by the American Law Institute. May 21, 1975, with Reporter's Commentary. Philadelphia: American Law Institutes.

Arai, Hachitaro. 1990. "Land use and zoning." In, *Doing Business in Japan.* Edited by Z. Kitagawa. New York: Matthew Bender.

Barrett, B. F. D., and R. Therivel. 1991. *Environment Policy and Impact Assessment in Japan.* London and New York: Routledge.

Bassett, Edward M. 1940. *Zoning.* New York: Russell Sage Foundation.

Bosselman, Fred P., David L. Callies, and John S. Banta. 1973. *The Taking Issue: An Analysis of the Constitutional Limits of Land Use Control* Washington D.C.: U.S. Government Printing Office.

Callies, David L., ed. 1993. *After Lucas: Land Use Regulation and the Taking of Property Without Compensation.* Chicago: ABA Press.

———. 1994. *Land Use Law in the United States* (transl. by Prof. Makitaro Hotta, Ritsumeikan University) Kyoto: Horitsu Bunko Sha.

Callies, David L., and Malcolm Grant. 1991. "Paying for Growth and Planning Gain: An Anglo-American Comparison of Development Conditions, Impact Fees and Development Agreements. *The Urban Lawyer.* 23:221-248.

Garner, J. F., and David L. Callies. 1972. "Planning Law in England and Wales and in the United States." *Anglo-American Law Review* 1:292-334.

Haar, Charles. 1977. *Land Use Planning.* 3d ed. Boston, Little, Brown and Company.

Hiroshima Department of Planning, interview with Mr. Yamamoto and staff. 29 May 1992.

Kinoshita, Hiroo. 1988. New Challenges for City Planning in Kyoto: The Integration of Metropolitan Development and Conservation. *Regional Studies Dialogue* 9(3) Autumn: 87-107.

Shapira, Philip, Ian Masser, and David Edgington eds. 1994. *Planning for Cities and Regions in Japan.* Liverpool: Liverpool University Press.

Statutes, Ordinances, and Other Materials

The Building Center of Japan. 1994. *The Building Standard Law of Japan.*

City of Osaka. 1991. *Osaka City Comprehensive Plan for the 21st Century.*

City Planning Department. 1992. *City Planning in Osaka City: Planning of Osaka.*

8 Disasters Chronic and Acute: Issues in the Study of Environmental Pollution in Urban Japan

ROBERT L. KIDDER

The context of activism over issues of air pollution, as discussed in this chapter, is a long history of government-*cum*-industry "thesis" and organized citizen "antithesis."[1] Most casual observers of Japanese society and history would probably think that problems of industrial pollution date from the "full-steam-ahead" policies of industrial development that were introduced to Japan by the leaders of the Meiji restoration in the mid-nineteenth century.

Nobuko Iijima (1979) opens her methodical cataloging of Japan's pollution problems with an item from the period 1640-90 as follows: "Akazawa Dozan [a copper mining operation in what is now Ibaraki Prefecture], opened in 1591, is closed due to farmers' protests against pollution discharged from the copper mine" (3). The same page of her report contains three other listings of pollution prior to 1690 that involve obvious actions and reactions between industrial polluters and protesting citizens whose own livelihoods were being threatened. She goes on to list dozens of cases of eighteenth- and nineteenth-century (Tokugawa era) extractive development, pollution-related labor disasters (such as premature deaths among gold, silver, and mercury miners and production workers), and numerous citizen protests and governmental investigations related to issues of environmental pollution.

It is clear from Professor Iijima's work, therefore, that the patterns of action discussed later in this chapter have some amount of pedigree, both in terms of the pollution created in the pursuit of development and in the organization of citizens to deal with their own interpretations of pollution impact on themselves and their communities.

In "modern" times (the post–Meiji Restoration era from about 1868 onward), as Margeret McKean (1981) and Frank Upham (1987) have documented, pollution as a national problem came to a head in the late 1950s through the 1960s. It is difficult to sort out the specifically urban effect of these events, in part because industrial development and many of the early citizen reactions to it occurred not just in cities. Probably the most famous episode of pollution and political reaction, Minamata disease, arose in a small town that had been dominated by fishing prior to the construction of the factory that produced the poisoning waste.[2] Cadmium poisoning (Itai-Itai disease) was linked to mining operations in a variety of places, mostly rural. Examples of rural problems becoming urban problems can be seen in cases where mercury-contaminated fish are discovered in Tokyo fish markets and Tokyo infants show levels of mercury in their systems twice as high as their mothers (Iijima, 1979: 386).

Some environmental catastrophes had a similar pattern of distribution among the general population, rural or urban. They are the consequences of mass production and marketing in an advanced capitalist economy. One example is the Morinaga milk poisoning outbreak of 1955 when arsenic-contaminated powdered milk sickened more than 12,000 infants and killed 130 (Iijima, 1979: 132). A current example is the recently "uncovered" 1983-85 provision of HIV-infected blood to hemophiliac patients, which infected nearly half the hemophiliac population of Japan.

The urban environment has been the specific object of a number of environmental concerns that generally do not affect other areas. These include air and water pollution, toxic-waste dumping, and industrial accidents involving the release of toxic substances, acid rain, sunshine pollution, and noise pollution. Photochemical smog was the greatest air-pollution culprit in the largest metropolitan areas, such as Tokyo, Osaka, and Kyoto. Large industrial complexes concentrated for purposes of efficiencies of scale came to be seen as having negative effects on the population concentrations that necessarily surrounded them. The action of ultraviolet rays on emissions from factories and cars reached crisis proportions and produced strong protests in the late 1960s. In downtown Tokyo during this time, a temporary solution was to make oxygen respirators available on city sidewalks so that distressed pedestrians could get some relief from the heavy doses of pollutants that descended on the city during atmospheric inversions. The reactions in Amagasaki, part of the industrial corridor created just outside of Osaka, are spelled out later in the chapter.

Vigorous campaigns by citizens' groups and creative responses by government (Upham, 1987) produced programs to alleviate those toxic levels of pollution that were attributable to sulphur dioxide, the primary pollutant produced by industrial activity. According to data provided by the Tokyo metropolitan government in a video presentation in its City Hall building, the level of pollution was cut dramatically after 1970 and remained acceptably low until 1985. Pollution consciousness was given very concrete expression in expensive electronic signs giving new pollution particulate readings for those locations every two to four seconds posted throughout Tokyo.

In 1985, levels of nitrogen oxide began an upward trend that has continued to worsen. The source of this pollution is primarily automobile exhaust. With growing affluence, city residents have taken to automobiles in both larger numbers and larger vehicles. Population growth, meanwhile, has pressed the distribution system to rely increasingly on polluting trucks. Unlike the industrial pollution of the past, whose activities could be more easily regulated, the auto-exhaust problem is more difficult to turn around because it involves many individual actors and a market-driven and widely accepted way of spending excess income. In addition, the design of most urban areas is incompatible with the growth of large numbers of large cars. Narrow streets amid an expressway system intentionally designed by a government to induce the population out of cars and onto public transportation have produced a gridlock situation in many urban areas. While urban governments try to control this explosion through seemingly draconian regulations (such as forbidding the sale of a vehicle with an engine displacement larger than 660 cubic centimeters to anyone who cannot prove their ownership of, or access to, off-street parking), sales of big cars have continued and urban streets and highways have become increasingly congested. The battle of Amagasaki residents against the highway in their midst, reported in this paper, is a response to all of these developments.

Other "pollution" issues that are particularly urban include the fight for "sunshine" rights and reactions against noise pollution. The sunshine issue refers to the claim by property owners that construction of adjacent high-rise structures rob them of their rights to sunshine. Because of organized political and legal action over this issue, urban residents now have a legally recognized right to sunshine.[3]

Finally, anyone riding the highway between Tokyo's Narita International Airport and downtown Tokyo will see the results of noise-pollution protests—walls of sound barriers for miles as the highway threads its way through the densely populated areas of Chiba. Elsewhere, the "bullet" train is surrounded by sound barriers or required to slow down as it passes residential areas that would otherwise be pounded by the din of high-speed metal on metal. People in Tokyo are constantly reminded that noise is a form of pollution by those same electronic signs that report air particulate concentrations—every two to four second, the signs also report the decibel level in the area.

What are the sociological and psychological effects on people living in an urban setting with the ravaging consequences of environmental pollution caused by the impersonal forces of industrial development? Kai Erikson (1976: 186-259) made a general prediction of trauma resulting from chronic disasters and the loss of community in such situations. This chapter will show that the responses of air-pollution victims in Amagasaki, an industrial zone in Japan, could be used to support either the argument that Erikson's forecast has come true or the counterclaim that differences of culture, politics, and social organization in Japan have insulated these victims from the social and psychological damage that Erikson predicted. This essay offers an interpretation that casts doubt on the generalizability of Erikson's theory. Problems that are inherent in

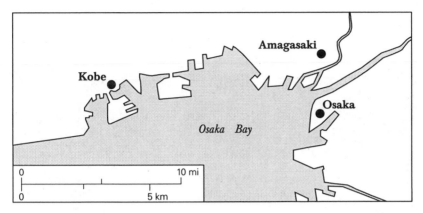

Figure 8.1 Amagasaki in Osaka-Kobe Metropolitan Area

the ethnographic research methods that both Erikson and the author have used to define and measure the sociological effects of human-engineered disasters will be discussed.

DISASTER AND LITIGATION IN AMAGASAKI

For seven years, the author has studied the experiences of a group of officially certified air-pollution victims in Amagasaki, an industrial suburb of Osaka (fig. 8.1). The mostly working-class residents of Amagasaki became "certified victims" when the Japanese government developed a compensation system in the early 1970s. The government was responding to a nationwide wave of political activism focusing on numerous widely publicized pollution disasters (Kidder and Miyazawa, 1993). The victim's diseases in Amagasaki, as in dozens of other polluted areas, ranged from emphysema and asthma to chronic forms of bronchitis. Government agencies meted out compensation to anyone who could prove one year of prior residency in the "affected" area of the city and could present a doctor's official diagnosis of one of the "qualifying" diseases. This program was institutionalized under the 1973 Law for the Compensation of Pollution-Related Health Problems (Gresser, Koichiro, and Akio, 1981). The compensation fund was created by fining the factories that were putting out the offending sulphur dioxide pollutant. Victims did not need to prove a direct connection between the pollution and their own disease. Government policy simply assumed that such connections were true for the group as a whole. In addition, a progressive municipal government—like many that were elected as an opposition force during the late 1960s and early 1970s in response to the resistance to change in the ruling national government (Krauss and Simcock, 1980)—cooperated with a victim-organized association to institute a system of 16 victim-

Photo 8.1 A view of Amagasaki looking from the train station to the sea. The elevated expressway (Highway 46) in the background passes through one of the most polluted urban areas in Japan. Photo by Robert Kidder

support centers throughout the city to serve those with special needs stemming from severe lung diseases. This compensation scheme was not unique to Amagasaki. It was instituted in dozens of polluted towns across Japan.

The gleam on this bright lamp of hope for victims, however, quickly began to tarnish. Opposition to the scheme began to form immediately among the businesses that had to pay for it. The fruits of this opposition began to appear publicly around 1980, as political pressure began to produce cutbacks in this and many other social welfare programs. As industry pressure increased, victim organizations began to respond by seeking ways to sustain the pressure that had produced the programs in the first place. By 1987, the political might of industry had produced legislation that effectively terminated the compensation scheme and declared victory over pollution.

The group that the author studied followed a strategy that had already been devised by victim groups elsewhere. Along with many other activities, they filed a mass lawsuit against polluting companies and the national government. The suit demanded full restoration of the original compensation program, additional punitive damages, and new demands for environmental cleanup, including the total shutdown of a 16-lane, multilevel highway that was built through the center of their town in 1976. The victims' organization selected 492 victim-members from its list of more than 11,000 to serve as litigant pioneers. These numbers were necessary because Japanese courts do not allow class-action lawsuits like those in the United States where only a handful of litigants could have sued on behalf of all certified victims. The litigation began in late 1988 and continues to work its way at a glacial pace through the district court in Kobe. Lawyers and victims' association leaders expect a first judgment in the case not much sooner than the year 2000. Appeals will add several more years to the cases.

The method of research involved a variety of interviews and observations with many of the participants in the litigation. These included interviews with 8 of the lawyers involved in the case, 2 doctors who treated the victims in their clinics, a high school science teacher who helped the original victims' group establish the scientific basis for their claim against the polluters, 4 of the victims' association officers who played an active role in both the association and the litigation, and 30 of the victim/litigants in their homes, some in separate interviews and some as interviews that "piggybacked" on the visits of lawyers to their clients' homes as part of their preparation for testimony in court. Since the author does not speak enough Japanese to conduct such interviews alone, he was always accompanied by interpreters who simultaneously translated what was being said. Simultaneous translations were checked with tape recordings of the interviews for accuracy. In addition to the interviews, several court sessions at each of which around 60 victim/litigators were in attendance were observed. Contact with several of the major participants in the case has been maintained in order to keep up to date on the latest developments. This work would have been impossible without the generous and informative assistance of Professor Setsuo Miyazawa of Kobe University, who has served as a coinvestigator throughout this project.

CHRONIC DISASTER AND TRAUMA: APPLYING ERIKSON'S ANALYSIS

Looking at what happened and is happening to Amagasaki's air-pollution victims, we find most, if not all, of the conditions that, says Erikson (1994), will lead to long-term, perhaps incurable, psychological trauma. Each of the paragraphs below includes a specific description of Amagasaki that would seem to make it a good candidate for the chronic disaster trauma predicted by Erikson.

First, the "disaster" of airborne toxicity leading to emphysema and asthma is *gradual* and seems to *select its victims at random*. Since other factors can also produce these diseases, victims cannot produce a "smoking-gun" proof of the source of their pain, nor can they easily sense the moment or moments when harm is being done. Evidence has to be sought in obscure scientific tests and in the pursuit of debatable logic. It was easy to observe some of the effects of these diseases: persistent coughing; shortness of breath; the need for breathing aids; the inability to climb stairs or walk even short distances beyond one's house; and, in some cases, confinement to a wheelchair or bed. Other effects were part of a litany that victims would recite in describing their problems to their lawyers. These effects included a restricted life of confinement at home; frequent visits to hospitals; frequent breathing "crises," sometimes in the middle of the night; the inability to do most kinds of paying jobs; and the prospect that the symptoms would continue to worsen. Children in affected areas have, according to victim's association leaders, a statistically much higher than normal rate of these diseases.

Second, victim conversation and, apparently, much of their anxiety, seems to be *centered on the illnesses* that define them as victims. They give detailed descriptions of their difficulties in climbing stairs, going to the store, or visiting their children's schools. They have obviously talked with each other at length about their symptoms, problems of living arrangements, and other consequences of the illnesses. They can cite statistics on the unusually high rate of asthma among their school-age children. Their relatives can describe, in patient but fatalistic tones, the hours they must spend cleaning up after parents in failing health. Victims lament the inability to get a full night's sleep. A standard part of the victim's experience, according to the people interviewed, is the sense of a confined life. It includes the inability to "go anywhere" because it is physically difficult to do so without help. One of the most central institutions in their community is the doctor's clinic, which treats about two thirds of all victims.

Third, life as a victim means a *life of dependency*. They rely on continuous support from the 16 support centers that are supported by the city government in conjunction with the victims' association for all kinds of basic activities: shopping trips to a store that may be only two blocks away; regular trips to the hospital for medicine or treatment; trips to a support group–maintained mountain house retreat, where the clear air makes breathing easier; and help in contacting government offices for needed services. Being a "victim" means, among other things, needing assistance. In other words, being dependent. Their lawsuits are mainly about extending their dependency on government and industry largess.

Fourth, the sulphur dioxide poisoning that produced these problems has been largely eliminated by new smoke-stack cleaning equipment that was installed in the 1970s, so one of the prime "enemies" in this litigation is a group of companies that cleaned up their "acts" years ago. Yet they continue to be targets of victim accusation and resentment even among victims who became ill years after these changes. In other words, like victims studied by Erikson, these people appear to be *unable to shake off their anxiety about dangers that may actually no longer exist.*

Fifth, Amagasaki has *no* obvious trappings of *"community"* in the sense that we will discuss below. When it was still a small fishing village, before being chosen as part of an industrial development zone in the early part of this century, it might well have shown aspects of community. Now, however, it is part of the urban/industrial sprawl that runs from the southern suburbs of Osaka north and west past Kobe, with no obvious distinguishing physical boundaries between the numerous political entities arrayed there. Legally, its population is around 600,000, but where Amagasaki ends and the next city begins is obvious only on maps. Indeed, the pollution originating from factories in Amagasaki was the object of a recently decided mass lawsuit in an adjacent city. Pollution, like the industrial development of this area, knew no boundaries between "communities." In light of the emphasis Erikson places on the role of community in protecting people against the ravages of disaster trauma, Amagasaki ought to be a place with elevated amounts of the kind of trauma Erikson found in West Virginia and elsewhere.

Sixth, the *polluters* (companies producing steel, glass, and power) were mostly large, remotely headquartered *industrial bureaucracies*. Some were originally divisions of the Zaibatsu (organizations that combined industry, finance, and government activity and authority, and that provided the technological muscle for Japan's activities leading up to, and during, World War II) and their postwar descendants. Headquarters, in most cases, are in Tokyo or Osaka, not Amagasaki. Many of the victims were either employees in the polluting factories or members of employee families. Some of the victims' association organizers had gained organizing experience by working as officers in the labor unions affiliated with the polluting factories. In short, Amagasaki victims had the same long-term relationship with their polluters as did the Buffalo Creek miners with the company that precipitated the disaster in their valley.

Finally, Amagasaki victims are also victimized in one additional way that Erikson did not include in his list of traumatizing events, a way that one might expect to add to the debilitating misery of the victims. Because of their special status based on pollution, they, like pollution victims elsewhere in Japan, feel they are stigmatized and treated as pariahs by many others in Japan. When Japanese people who live elsewhere in Japan, but know something about Amagasaki, are told of research there, they confirm the victims' reports that Amagasaki is a stigmatized place because of both its pollution and its general reputation as "dirty." This term probably includes many other elements in addition to air and water pollution. For example, the town is socially and economically divided between a wealthier middle-class area that is not within the pollution zone and a crowded working-class area of homes crammed in among factories and smoke stacks that visually proclaim the area as being associated with the earlier period of environmentally unrestricted growth. The stigma is probably a generalized one but its significance for victims' association members is that they experience it as being connected to the pollution that makes them victims. Their town is looked on as a bad place to be. Parents tell their children to stay away, much as suburban American parents warn their children to stay away from "bad neighborhoods" in the city. Perhaps more importantly, informants interviewed in Amagasaki find themselves regarded as polluted in some way, making them unsuitable for marriage to outsiders. Just as Hiroshima survivors found themselves excluded on the grounds that they might pass on some terrible condition to the next generation, and as residents of the infamous Minamata (site of the first and most famous scandal over heavy-metal poisoning in Japan) found that others saw them as unsuitable for marriages, pollution survivors in Amagasaki report being looked on as unclean. These stories of exclusion come from the victims, themselves. They are part of the shared self-images that come with victim status.

ERIKSON'S THESIS: DISASTER, COMMUNITY, AND TRAUMA

In the conclusion to his study of an American flood disaster, Kai Erikson (1976) speculated that trends in modern America might be producing widespread social and social-psychological conditions similar to those that he identified as resulting from the flood. These conditions, which he calls "trauma," ("the psychological process by which acute shock becomes a chronic condition, a way of keeping dead moments alive"), suggest that social and technological trends in the latter half of the twentieth century are converging to produce a rising tide of disasters that he has since come to call "a new species of trouble" (1994). His 1976 list of trauma symptoms included "a numbness of spirit, a susceptibility to anxiety and rage and depression, a sense of helplessness, an inability to concentrate, a loss of various motor skills, a heightened apprehension about the physical and social environment, a preoccupation with death, a retreat into dependency, and a general loss of ego functions." (255). Lately he has summarized these symptoms as ". . . pure dread, perfect dread, the very essence of dread" (Erickson, 1994: 140). His research leads him to the conclusion that this "dread" is what he found among victims of a variety of "chronic disasters," such as the residents who fled from the Three Mile Island nuclear emergency of 1979, the survivors of the bombing of Hiroshima, middle class homeowners who saw their neighborhood in Colorado ruined by an underground oil leak, and Americans who have joined the legions of the homeless.

Erikson argued in 1976 that " One of the long-term effects of modernization . . . has been to distance people from primary associations and to separate them from the nourishing roots of community." He was generalizing to modern society as a whole the conclusions he had reached about the importance of "community" in Buffalo Creek. He originally used his focus on the loss of community as a way to explain the unusually severe long-term trauma he observed among the flood victims in Buffalo Creek. Water and death alone, he argued, always produce some psychological trauma, but in a "normal" flood people overcome their fears and return to normal within approximately six months. So the flood alone could not account for the symptoms he observed nor for the duration of the symptoms in Buffalo Creek. *Loss of community* could explain these patterns, particularly since it involved the victims' sense that their fates had been betrayed by faceless bureaucrats in faraway offices. The coal company on which they had counted for their newfound economic security responded to the flood in ways they considered callous, even blasphemous. Because the coal company had been so intimately involved in what flood victims had thought was a unified community, its cold, calculating, legalistic reactions to the flood came as a shock and multiplied its traumatic effects. Government bureaucrats compounded the problem by insensitive "flood-relief" measures that further fractured what was left of the region's community roots.

Contributing to Erikson's prediction of rising trauma rates in late-twentieth-century America is his view that acute disasters involving human agency are likely to increase. "Advances" in technology produce an ever-expanding array of new ways to "create [man-made] havoc" (256). Disasters at Chernobyl and Bhopal, the AIDS epidemic, and wars and genocide in Kuwait, Rwanda, Sarajevo, and Chechnya, all of which came after Erikson's 1975 predictions, seem to confirm his analysis of a "new species of trouble." In every case, he argues, the disaster itself might not be enough to destroy the nurturing fabric of community, but the role of remote authoritative agencies and authorities in producing the disaster and/or failing to respond effectively to it compounds the injury, producing the "perfect dread" of trauma.

Moreover, the rise of relativistic perspectives on societal values and the trend of modern economic organization to take away meaningful work from large parts of the population create a world that is "alien to people's own instincts" (257). The resulting pattern, he says, is the lifestyle of a passive, distanced spectator who withdraws into ". . . a dulled silence, sitting out one's life in front of television sets, inventing a more active life in fantasy, nursing old resentments, and spending a good deal of time tending the aches and pains of one's own body with the help of a heavy diet of medications" (257). Erikson concluded his earlier study with a call, directed ". . . not only [at] those charged with healing the wounds of acute disaster but [at] those charged with planning a truly human future" (259), for the preservation (or restoration) of "communal forms of life."

In his subsequent exploration of other man-made disasters (1994), Erikson added the idea of chronic disasters: that technological disasters involving the release of toxic materials would have special traumatizing effects. His case studies reveal a special kind of horror at the hidden, slow spread of toxic substances, such as radioactive gas, mercury, and generic "toxic wastes" that are not easily measured and whose distribution and effects are not easily bounded in time and space. Because they may be invisible, difficult to detect, and slow moving in their cumulative production of harm, they can, he asserts, produce a special kind of dread in the people who fear they are becoming victims.

In order to fully understand Erikson's thesis, we need to appreciate that it fits into a prolonged debate within sociology over the relationship between "community" and "urbanization." For some sociologists, the essence of the city was that it was a place where community was lost. The crowding, the massification of work, consumption, mass media, and transportation all seemed to be elements working for the destruction of those "communal ties" and "humane values" that one presumably could still find in "rural" settings. In opposition, other sociologists claimed to have discovered "urban villages," cities of neighborhoods, and other patterns of community within cities. Maybe, they said, community can survive in modern settings. Others have argued that community is a mythical state romantically and inaccurately ascribed to "rural" settlements and posed in false contrast to "the city." In their view, rural poverty, like all other rural economic activity, is inexorably tied to modern economic and social conditions that sweep across all segments of society (Gaventa, 1980). Some have portrayed suburbs as failed romantic attempts to "recreate community" while hanging on to the economic advantages of urban life.

In more recent times, a revivalist movement has arisen within American sociology over the issue of community (Etzioni, 1983, 1988). Erikson's analysis, rooted as it is in the examination of connections between technology, environment, disaster, community, and trauma represents one of the earliest harbingers of this revival. In his most recent case studies, he reminds us of his earlier thesis in his comment on Hiroshima: "To the extent that communities can sensibly be thought of as organisms, as living systems, these [Hiroshima's communities] had simply disintegrated." (1994: 188). His prophetic warnings against the lurking social havoc connected to the rise of man-made, often chronic, sometimes toxic disasters does not hinge on the irrelevant rural-urban distinction. He finds the issue everywhere because of the pervasive spread of technology and the social forms that go with it. Whether among the Ojibwa Indians of northwestern Ontario or among the urbanized residents around the Shoreham Nuclear Power station on Long Island, he has found what to him has become a familiar pattern of trauma. Building from that discovery, he finds modern catastrophes beginning to blur the distinction between the acute and the chronic, so that he feels justified in projecting his conclusions from flood disasters to the "chronic" disasters of homelessness and child abuse.

PROBLEMS OF INTERPRETATION: ACUTE VERSUS CHRONIC DISASTER AND THE ISSUE OF THE NORMAL

Erikson's conclusions raise a host of interesting questions when we begin examining some of the "man-made havoc" of technological development in urban centers outside the United States, such as the situation in Amagasaki. The material presented thus far on Amagasaki all seems to support Erikson's analysis of the connection between ecological disaster, with the human agency as perpetrator, and chronic trauma. So many of the ingredients that Erikson has identified as part of this process are present in Amagasaki: the victims are victims of invisible toxic pollutants (sulphur dioxide and nitrogen oxide), both of which are directly tied to technological "progress" and the kinds of corporate risk calculations that Erikson discusses as "normal accidents" (1994: 143; see also Perrow, 1984) in his case studies. Like the flood victims of Buffalo Creek, Amagasaki victims (*a*) call themselves victims; (*b*) show evidence of permanent disability; (*c*) speak in great detail about their disabilities and the inconveniences forced on them; (*d*) worry about a future in which the services they now rely on might disappear; (*e*) direct their resentment against a force (the companies) that has long since stopped the actions that produced the disaster; (*f*) appear to be highly dependent; and (*g*) fear new developments as potential new disasters causing them further harm.

All of these features seem to place Amagasaki within the parameters of Erikson's trauma analysis, but we cannot stop at this point and conclude that Amagasaki is just one more case study supporting Erikson's thesis. When we look more closely, and with a more critical eye toward the complications of transporting analyses across lines between social systems, we find that many of the essential concepts in Erikson's thesis either fade into confusing obscurity or spring up Januslike.

We can begin by looking at Erickson's implicit distinction between the "normal" and the "traumatic." In the Buffalo Creek research, he defined the "Mountain Ethos" as the normal, the cultural context leading up to the moment of the disaster. He sets up his analysis by first establishing a conceptual device for explaining contradictory behavioral patterns: his notion of "axes of variation" within a culture. A "community," he says, may have an "ethos" that remains constant even though individuals and families display contradictory behaviors. "Normal" in Buffalo Creek meant decades of vacillation between opposite poles of several "axes of variation" he found in the mountain culture. Within this "normal" framework, the trauma of the flood would be "normal" up to a point (a point he identified as the average length of trauma responses found by others in previous disaster research—usually about six months). What he calls "abnormal" is the pattern he observed after the period when a "normal" disaster would have been put behind in favor of looking to the future and rebuilding. Trauma, he says, represents behavior patterns determined by forces that push people toward the "weak" end of the axes of variation. During normal times, mountain culture is not shattered, even if people shift toward the weak end of their axes of variation. However the flood trauma was different. It shattered the community that had sustained the psychological axes of variation and seemed to create a permanent move toward weakness. In summary, a healthy community promotes strength, while a shattered community produces weakness.

Erikson's analysis combines both on-the-spot ethnographic observation and interviews with a broad-scope cultural history of Appalachia in general and Buffalo Creek in particular. If he had ignored history and examined only the "ethnographic present" on the basis of ethnographic field work, the thesis he developed might have been significantly different. Would he see "trauma" in the behavior patterns of Buffalo Creek residents, or would the details of post-flood life be interpreted as culture, as normal for this place? Erikson meets this interpretive problem in his analysis of an oil leak in Colorado (1994: 103). He says that, among those living in the neighborhood, "the degree of dread and anxiety expressed by the plaintiff group is so sharp and so widely shared that it becomes a sociological finding as well as a clinical one, if only in the sense that it can be said to form the prevailing social temper—the culture, even—of the whole community." In other words, as one neighbor put it, " . . . you almost think that it's [the anxiety] a normal state of affairs." While there is the potential for ambivalence in the interpretation he is making here, Erikson clearly still sees the Colorado situation as one of trauma. The problem, of course, is this: how can we treat an observed social pattern as both normality and trauma when those terms are meant to be mutually exclusive? The larger analytic problem is how can we know that what we are observing is "normal" versus "traumatic"?

Problems of interpretation begin to accumulate when we look at these studies this way. Is a 150-year cultural history necessary in order to establish what is normal? Would a "straight" ethnography of Buffalo Creek, West Virginia, or East Swallow, Colorado, or Amagasaki, Japan, be inadequate if they lacked the historical context of disaster? If the ethnographer in these cases examined both cultural and disaster histories of each area, would the final interpretation necessarily be one of trauma? How can our ethnographer determine whether change from previous periods represents movement along axes of variation or social change, which constitutes a break from the past?

These analytic problems become even more damaging when we try to extrapolate from acute disasters, where sudden catastrophic events provide specific moments around which to center analysis (e.g., the infamous clock, stopped at 8:13 A.M., in Hiroshima), to chronic disasters such as toxic contamination or the general "breakdown of community" in modern society. Against what objective criterion can we measure the level of trauma, the level of community, or the interaction of forces along an axis of variation when there is no single defining historical moment of disaster? Erikson, for example, defines homelessness in America as a further case of man-made catastrophe fitting his trauma model. The author can remember an earlier period when homelessness was virtually nonexistent in most American cities. Our children, however, have never known such a period, and they and their friends are likely to think of cities as places that normally have homeless people. When did the "breakdown" that produced the current level of homelessness in the United States begin? More importantly, when do we stop thinking of it as trauma and start considering it "normal" (i.e., an element of American culture)? Similarly, when did air pollution reach a level in Amagasaki that could be defined as "disastrous"? When did it start producing disease beyond the normal (culturally defined) level of disease? Is there any way of establishing objective measures of these moments and these processes, or are we left to our own devices in simply trying to promote a consensus on the question?

We face further difficulty in applying Erikson's analysis to Amagasaki, because some of the Amagasaki victims' behavior appears to directly contradict Erikson's criteria for trauma. First, instead of "destroying community," the Amagasaki air pollution disaster appears to have created a community out of urban anomie. The randomly dispersed collection of strangers who became "victims" of air pollution coalesced into a large and active organization of people who identified with each other. Second, instead of sitting by in a passive, traumatized stupor like that which Erikson (1994) seems to have found in so many other chronic disaster sites, the Amagasaki victims have become politically mobilized and display a great deal of spirit and energy in the various political strategies, including litigation, that they maintain against the ruling parties.

Following the great Hanshin earthquake of 1995, in which most houses in the air-pollution zone of Amagasaki were damaged, the pollution victims' organization sprung into action via cellular phones to mobilize relief work in their area. Because of their prior organizing experience and the solidarity that had developed among them, these "victims" were able to become a relief organization for all earthquake victims, not just those in their own organization. In their latest show of solidarity, they have developed, and are promoting, a "green" plan for remaking Amagasaki into a site of parks, underground expressways, and water recreation. Their green dreams may be only that, a set of fond hopes, but they are a far cry from the listless, hopeless pattern of "trauma" that Erikson's studies would lead us to expect.

That Amagasaki "victims" behave this way may show us some limits on the generalizability of Erikson's thesis. Alternatively, Erikson may be right about the cases he studied, but Amagasaki may represent an alternative pattern showing ways in which victims can escape from chronic disaster trauma. The Amagasaki pattern also calls into question Erikson's practice of framing his observations in terms of the contrast between community and the loss of community. Amagasaki seems to make clear that there is no necessary connection between chronic disaster and loss of community. The Amagasaki case may even cast doubt on some of Erikson's case-study interpretations of disaster-victim behavior as stemming from trauma. If Amagasaki victims can turn their tragedy into a cause for organization and activism, perhaps the trauma Erikson observed in at least some of his case studies has other causes besides the chronic disasters he identifies. Perhaps, for example, political and legal context play a more significant role in producing the patterns of response he observed than Erikson had noticed.

On the other hand, we should keep in mind that Erikson filled most of his analysis of the flood disaster with important qualifications about the relationships between the observed trauma and the particular axes of variation that he described as unique to the culture of the mountain people in West Virginia. His concept of axes of variation explained sharp contrasts between observed behaviors of flood victims from before to after the flood and the themes that preoccupied their thinking after the flood. By saying that mountain culture had its own peculiar mixture of themes, or axes of variation, Erikson is also saying that one should expect different patterns of reaction to disaster in cultures that operate along other axes. Trauma still might occur, but it might look different because other axes of variation might predominate in other cultural settings.

For example, one important axis of variation in the mountain culture moved people between dependency and self-reliance. Mountain culture placed great importance on a man's self-reliant ability to go out into the woods and fend for himself. At the same time, "rugged individualists" could become strikingly passive and dependent on other family members in the face of crisis. In other words, mountaineers vacillated between gestures of great independence and contrasting periods of dependence. The pattern carried through into the transition of mountain people from independent farming to coal mining. This is why dependency plays so prominent a role in his definition of the symptoms of disaster trauma.

When we find dependency among air-pollution victims in Amagasaki, therefore, we face the dilemma of deciding whether to compare it with Erikson's emphasis on cultural diversity (the idea that other cultures will have other axes of variation) or his prediction of general widespread trauma as a reaction to chronic disaster. Japanese air-pollution victims do display dependency, but is dependency versus self-reliance an axis of variation in Japan? At least one scholar, Doi (1973), has identified dependency as a key personality characteristic of the Japanese. The term Doi uses is *amaeru,* and it refers to a personality trait that is reflected in particular practices that occur at the interpersonal level. However, Doi's analysis increases our difficulty in making a comparison of Amagasaki with Erikson's case studies because Doi does not present, as Erikson does, a picture of what the opposite of Japanese dependency would look like. Saying that Japanese people have a dependent personality does not offer us any model of what the alternative would be *in the Japanese context.* We can only look on with our American biases and say that Japanese people do not usually act like John Wayne or Sylvester Stallone. Ethnographic research does not provide a way of comparing levels of dependency on a Japanese scale to assess whether Japanese pollution victims are any more dependent than "normal" Japanese. Perhaps they are just being typically Japanese rather than responding to chronic disaster. Moreover, if they are more dependent than most others who are not victims, is this a sign of weakness and trauma, as Erikson says it is in West Virginia, Or are Amagasaki victims just being more "Japanese" than most others in Japan? In other words, if dependency is a Japanese characteristic, and therefore perhaps a feature in people that is valued in Japan even while it is devalued in America, does one become "better" or "worse," "stronger" or "weaker," if one becomes more dependent in Japan?

A further complication in making the leap from West Virginia to Amagasaki lies in determining how many of the behaviors we observe among

victims can be described as traumatic reaction and how much is a natural consequence of living with pollution-related diseases. Erikson's notion of disaster
trauma is that it produces behaviors that cannot be explained only in physical or
biological terms. It is a social-psychological concept consisting of a nexus between social conditions, psychological states, and behaviors. Do the Amagasaki
diseases vary in response to such psychological variables, or are they "real" in
the sense of producing similar behaviors regardless of social conditions? The
answer may lie somewhere between these extremes, but we cannot answer that
question with ethnographic data. Still, it is a question that complicates our interpretation of the Amagasaki experience as it also complicates Erikson's analysis.

PROBLEMS OF INTERPRETATION: TRAUMA, COMMUNITY, AND LITIGATION

Finally, we have to try to make sense of the actions taken by the victims in filing
their lawsuits. Litigation is often treated, in social scientific theory, as a proce-
dure that stands in contrast to the processes of community. This is one way of
characterizing much of the literature on legal pluralism (Chiba, 1989). Where
community solidarity is strong, there is little need for formal law (Black, 1976).
Where community breaks down, law may be a necessary evil for the preservation of stability. Studies in the sociology of law have contrasted Japan with the
United States over this very issue (Kawashima, 1963; Wagatsuma and Rossett,
1986; Haley, 1991). A litigious society (the United States), in which the hypoth-
esized breakdown of community solidarity has produced an explosion of formal
law (with all its attendant features—many lawyers, much formal written law,
and frequent and widespread litigation), stands in contrast to a nonlitigious society (Japan), in which strong cultural values and a heavy reliance on communal
forms of social organization produce a low demand for formal law. The
Japanese, according to this interpretation, are supposed to "grin and bear it"
(*gaman-suru*).

The litigation filed by the air-pollution victims seems to violate a variety
of expectations, including the general expectation that the Japanese will *gaman-
suru* and Erikson's analytical expectation that Amagasaki victims would be
traumatized by the chronic disaster of toxic pollution. First, the litigation seems
to contradict the communal view of Japanese society as being nonlitigious.
Japanese people, this view holds, are culturally programmed to avoid public
confrontation, to seek harmony, at least in public, and to walk away from con-
frontations. Obviously, Amagasaki's victims are going against these expectations. Their behavior is, in this sense, anomalous. Second, litigation seems to go
against Erikson's trauma scenario because litigation is not a passive, fatalistic
response to problems. The Amagasaki victims attend court in large numbers and
with great fanfare. They always notify the news media prior to a hearing and

make a grand group entry before TV cameras in their wheelchairs, on their canes, and with their breathing aids. When similar groups of victims in other towns are about to receive final court judgment on cases that are virtually identical to their own, Amagasaki victims pile onto organization-provided buses and go in large numbers to those court buildings to conduct conspicuous and well-choreographed demonstrations celebrating their wins or denouncing their losses. Saul Alinsky (1971) would applaud the variety of tactics employed by the victims' association to dramatize its issues and turn up the pressure on major corporations, politicians, and bureaucrats.

Moreover, victim-group leaders, who themselves have serious breathing problems, have developed ways of using the process of litigation as a way to expand their environmental activism to the national and international levels. One leader, with the support of the general victims' association, traveled to Thailand to appear at an international conference on pollution and was featured in nationwide newspaper reports. Others attended an international convention in Brazil.

A postmodern approach to these actions would be to observe that victimization is a *narrative* that serves to empower this particular group of persons rather than as a reflection of an inner psychological state of trauma. "Excessive" talk about symptoms and suffering may be a self-conscious act in a strategy of a group of activists rather than the mournful reflections of traumatized, psychologically incapacitated victims such as those Erikson describes.

Applying Erikson's terms of community, disaster, ethos, and trauma, we must also weigh these concepts against the fact that Amagasaki victims were not initially a "naturally occurring" group or "community" in Erikson's sense. These people had in common only their shared residence in a large city and their health problems. When a handful of doctors and patients began to suspect air pollution as the culprit in Amagasaki illnesses, those who now belong to the victims' group were strangers to each other. They had to discover each other through a long process of political organizing. The only way they could be said to constitute a community would be to say that they are all Japanese and therefore hold membership in that larger community with its shared culture, or to say that their joint political struggle has made them into a community. As pointed out already, they are acting "un-Japanese" in this instance because they are suing, so they seem to be cutting themselves off from any wider community of the Japanese people. Notice that this political interpretation turns Erikson on his head, arguing that community (in at least the minimal sense of this victims' group's solidarity) is created rather than destroyed by the disaster.

Furthermore, why should either Erikson or the author be surprised to find that, when we seek out "victims" who are self-identified that way for specific purposes, they seem to dwell on their symptoms? Erikson says such morbid preoccupation with illness in Buffalo Creek is evidence of trauma, but he was *asking* people about their suffering. He went in search of evidence of trauma. His ethnographic sampling virtually guaranteed that he would hear "sick talk." All of Erikson's subsequent research has this same problem, since, in every case study he has published on these issues, he was involved in gathering evidence on victimization for the purposes of lawsuits. The question is not whether we can be "objective" in assessing the answers to our questions or recording patterns we are looking for. It is suggested that Erikson's bleak picture may be as much a product of the identity of the "holy grail" for which he went looking (community) and the uses to which he intended to put it (support for victims in lawsuits) as it is of the events taking place in Buffalo Creek or at his later research sites. His Buffalo Creek victims did, after all, win a $13.2-million settlement as a result of the display of trauma that Erikson organized and produced.

CONCLUSION

What conclusion can we support through any ethnographic research that selects its subjects because of their political activity or significance rather than their existence as a self-contained social unit for which we can develop "thick description" (Geertz, 1973) in the traditional anthropological style and/or a thorough ethnographic cataloguing of a whole culture? Is the method of ethnography exportable to research questions other than the purely descriptive ones of the earliest ethnographers? Can we, as Erikson tries to do, for example, support claims about universal social-psychological processes in "modern societies" such as the connection between community disintegration and trauma? Can we conclude anything about the existence or breakdown of sociological abstractions such as "community" or the damaging effects of class or the insidious consequences of colonialism or the dehumanizing effects of urbanization, bureaucratization, or mass production? The author is wary of such generalization in attempting to interpret the experience of Amagasaki air pollution victims.

Perhaps we are limited to drawing conclusions about the ways in which people define their situations within particular contexts and how their definitions are related to their actions and the explanations they give for those actions. Perhaps all we can learn about Amagasaki air-pollution victims through field observation, for example, is that they see litigation as a means of exerting moral and political pressure on government and industry leaders. Perhaps we can get more detailed than this by describing different versions of this view and discovering that those versions are associated with different levels of involvement in the organization. That was the conclusion of our earlier publication on this research (Kidder and Miyazawa, 1993).

NOTES

1. Environmental scientists could probably develop a longer list of urban environmental issues noted here. This accounting is bounded by decision to include those conditions to which citizen activists and government agencies have given names and attention. "Pollution" is a somewhat slippery concept because its use does not produce just a neutral factual description. It is a characterization of an environmental condition connected to a theory about its relationship to quality-of-life issues such as health, "breathing space," and tranquility. This does not mean that pollution is not "real." It does mean that the author is applying a sociological approach to the way reality is constructed as the best means of defining pollution for purposes of sociological analysis. Because "pollution" is almost always a descriptor asserted by some and rejected by others in a contested situation, the analysis relies on the contest to produce the definition.

2. Mercury poisoning that destroys the nervous system.

3. One result has been the spread of a trademark architectural style for Japanese high-rise buildings—slanted tops that allow sunshine to reach adjacent properties.

REFERENCES

Alinsky, Saul. 1971. *Rules for Radicals*. New York: Random House.
Black, Donald. 1976. *The Behavior of Law*. New York: Academic Press.
Chiba, M. 1989. *Legal Pluralism: Toward a General Theory through Japanese Legal Culture*. Tokyo: Tokai University Press.
Doi, Takeo. 1973. *The Anatomy of Dependence*. New York: Kodansha.
Erikson, Kai T. 1976. *Everything in its Path*. New York: Simon & Schuster.
———. 1994. *A New Species of Trouble*. New York: Norton.
Etzioni, Amatai. 1983. *An Immodest Agenda: Rebuilding America Before the Twenty-First Century*. New York: New Press.
———. 1988. *The Moral Dimension: Toward a New Economics*. New York: Free Press.
Gaventa, John. 1980. *Power and Powerlessness: Quiescence and Rebellion in an Appalachian Valley* Urbana: University of Illinois Press.
Geertz, Clifford. 1973. *The Interpretation of Cultures*. New York: Basic Books.
Gresser, Julian, Fujikura Koichiro, and Morichima Akio. 1981. *Environmental Law in Japan*. Cambridge, Mass.: MIT Press.
Haley, J.O. 1991. *Authority Without Power*. New York: Oxford University Press.
Iijima, Nobuko, ed. 1979. *Pollution Japan: Historical Chronology*. Tokyo: Asahi Evening News.

Kawashima, Takeyoshi. 1963. "Dispute Resolution in Contemporary Japan." In *Law in Japan: The Legal Order of a Changing Society*. Edited by A.T. von Mehren. Cambridge, Mass.: Harvard University Press.

Kidder, Robert, and Setsuo Miyazawa. 1993. "Long-term Strategies in Environmental Litigation." *Law & Social Inquiry* 18 (4):605-627.

Krauss, Elliss, and Bradford Simcock. 1980. "Citizen's Movements: The Growth and Impact of Environmental Protest in Japan. In *Political Opposition and Local Politics in Japan*. Edited by Kurt Steiner, Ellis Kraus, and Scott C. Flanagan. Princeton: Princeton University Press.

McKean, Margaret. 1981. *Environmental Protest and Citizen: Politics in Japan*. Berkeley: University of California Press.

Perrow, Charles. 1984. *Normal Accidents*. New York: Basic Books.

Upham, Frank. 1987. *Law and Social Change in Post-War Japan*. Cambridge, Mass.: Harvard University Press.

Wagatsuma, H., and A. Rossett, 1986. "The Implications of Apology: Law and Culture in Japan and the United States." *Law & Society Review* 20 (4):461-98.

9 Urban Redevelopment in Omuta, Japan, and Flint, Michigan: A Comparison

THEODORE J. GILMAN

A company town slowly grinds to a halt. The factories that once employed thousands and made the city an engine of national growth slowly cut back output as their ability to compete declines. Production decreases lead to job cuts and layoffs, and the once-robust industrial community begins to atrophy. As the company payrolls dwindle, the supporting businesses in the surrounding municipality struggle. Slowly, they, too, go out of business. Young people, no longer able to find work, grow up and move to other, larger cities. The population ages and declines, with those left behind unable or unwilling to move. A once-thriving industrial city of 200,000 rusts quietly, dismantled by global economic forces far beyond its control. No longer do the yakitori pubs and karaoke bars hum with the vitality of Mitsui workers done with their shift.

Karaoke bars? A leading Japanese company? In what appears to be a familiar American industrial landscape? Although it may be surprising, the portrait above describes a Japanese city suffering the effects of global economic restructuring. In the United States, the story of urban decline is fairly well known. Failure to compete in the American and world markets for consumer goods and heavy manufactured items have forced the slow and painful demise of several sectors of American industry. Nationally, industrial (and thus population) growth patterns have moved away from the Northeast and Midwest, toward the South and West. The service and high-technology sectors of the American economy have experienced the greatest growth, and older, more established cities have found it difficult to attract industries in these sectors. The federal government has done little to alter this growth pattern, and state and local governments have met with only limited success (Eisinger, 1990; Brace, 1993).

Since the early 1960s, the same economic restructuring process has occurred in numerous Japanese cities as well. Given Japan's remarkable growth in the postwar period, one might not think that economic decline and urban decay would be a problem. In fact, if one looks at only national economic statistics, claims of depression and decline seem hard to believe. After all, Japan did triple its real per capita income in the 1960s, and growth in the 1970s averaged 3 to 5 percent per year. People outside of Japan are surprised to learn that Japanese industrial cities face the same problems confronting cities in other industrialized nations. But during this era of high growth, population movement from the hinterland to the cities—especially to the Tokaido region (the area in central Japan running from Tokyo to Osaka)—drained much of the younger population from the smaller industrial cities. The transformation in the Japanese economy from heavy to high-technology industries caused the decline of numerous small cities.

In the 1950s, 1960s, and 1970s, large-scale manufacturing enterprises located in the major urban centers were already attracting young people to life in the big city. At the same time, the Japanese government was helping to phase out domestic heavy industry through an active plan of rationalization. In the postwar era, coal, ship building, steel, and other basic industries were slowly pushed out of business through their inability to compete internationally and the government's unwillingness to support them. This rationalization process propelled more of the rural and small-city population toward life and jobs in the metropolis, crippling the economy of numerous small cities throughout Japan. Simultaneously, the industries around which these regional cities were built lost their international competitive edge. The resulting combination of population drain and economic "hollowing out" in Japan is identical in many ways to what has happened in the American Rust Belt.

And like Americans, Japanese residents of such communities look to the government to provide assistance and to help revitalize the local economy. Governments try to respond, but their efforts often fail to stimulate renewed growth. But governments alone are not responsible for the failure to revitalize; private sector efforts fail, too. What accounts for these failures? What types of projects are selected and implemented in Japan and in the United States? How does urban redevelopment work in these two countries? And what are the institutional structures that shape this policy process and power distribution? These questions provide the focus of this chapter.

There is an inadequate understanding of local redevelopment efforts in both Japan and the United States, although there have been a few efforts to document this process on the American side (Judd and Parkinson, 1990; Gittell, 1993). Only one such study exists for Japan (Fujita and Hill, 1993). This is unfortunate, given the emphasis in both nations (and in other industrialized countries, too) on government decentralization in the 1980s and early 1990s (Barnekov, 1989). The "New Federalism" in the United States under the Reagan and Bush administrations sought to move policy-making responsibility toward the state and local levels of government (Conlan, 1988). The Japanese movement for regional decentralization (*chihô bunken*) started later than that of the United States, but powerful members of the Japanese government con-

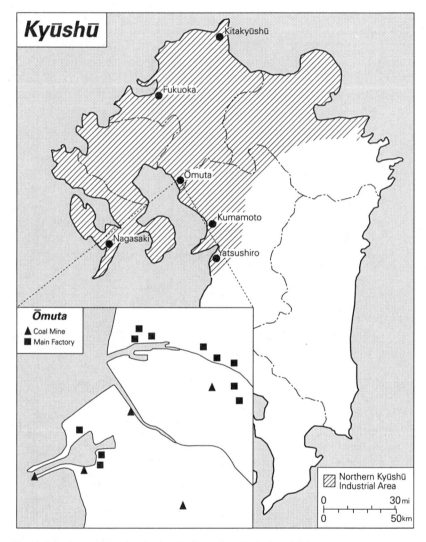

Figure 9.1 Omuta, Kyushu, in the Northern Kyushu Industrial Area

tinue to be strongly in favor of similar efforts (Ozawa, 1993). The increase in government decentralization makes studies of local development practice and policy making all the more relevant.

This chapter is divided into two sections. The first section describes the decline of Omuta and Flint that produced the conditions that exist today. In the Japanese case, these are conditions that go against our notion of the high-growth era and that prompted the need for urban revitalization. The second sec-

Photo 9.1 A dense network of railroads intersects the Northern Kyushu Industrial Area.
Photo by P. P. Karan

tion summarizes the redevelopment projects completed or underway from the early 1970s through the early 1990s. In addition to listing the projects and noting the patterns in the policy process and output, this section describes the differences in the ways the two cities went about implementing urban revitalization efforts.

An Introduction to the Case Study Cities: Omuta and Flint

Cities of all sizes face the need for economic revitalization, and this chapter does not presume to explain the politics of redevelopment for all types of city. Instead, it addresses the need to examine smaller cities. Larger cities are certainly important, and most studies of urban issues focus on the larger metropolises (Peterson, 1981; Stone and Sanders, 1987; Stone, 1989), but smaller cities must not be forgotten, since a sizable percentage of the population of both nations lives in them. In addition, smaller cities make excellent research subjects because development cycles tend to be highly visible and pronounced in these communities (Gittell, 1993: 8). In studying small cities, it is easier to get beyond

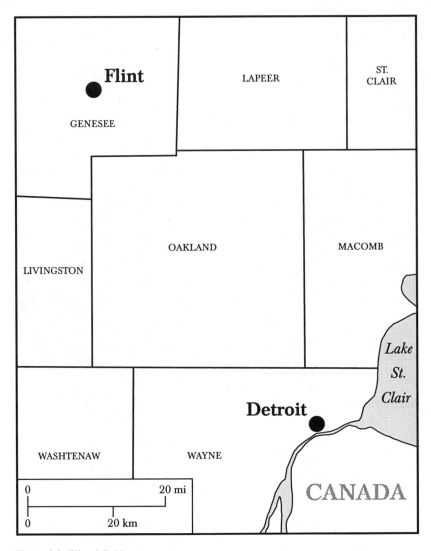

Figure 9.2 Flint, Michigan

the aggregate economic data and uncover the attitudes and behavior of individuals. Small cities are particularly useful if one wants to highlight the community psychology and the way individuals affect the process (Dahl, 1961).

Omuta

Omuta is a Japanese city (fig. 9.1) battling the effects of macroeconomic restructuring. A port city on the Ariake Sea in southern Fukuoka prefecture on the island of Kyushu, Omuta experienced a 100-year heyday as the largest coal-mining center in Japan and during that time produced much of the energy that drove Japan's rapid twentieth-century industrial growth. The Mitsui Miike (pronounced mee-kay) mine was the largest coal mine in Japan and was the center of an extensive industrial complex that included metal smelting and processing, chemical production from coal, electricity generation, and coal mining for industrial use throughout the country, but as Japan's ability to compete with other coal-producing nations declined, the demand for Miike coal declined, too.

Omuta is victim of a postwar economic double-whammy: international price competition plus a global switch from coal to petroleum energy sources. As domestically produced coal either became more expensive or held its production price per ton constant, the price per ton of imported coal fell dramatically. By 1987, top-grade bituminous coal from the Miike mine was selling for ¥23,000/ton, versus ¥7,300/ton for imported coal. This was primarily due to the fact that extraction costs overseas were so much lower than in Japan, but the rise in the strength of the yen vis-à-vis the dollar also hurt the competitiveness of domestic coal (Fukuoka Pretecture, 1992:5). For Japanese coal consumers—mainly heavy industry and electric power producers—it made little sense to purchase domestic coal. As a result, the domestic coal-mining industry entered a period of rationalization—encouraged and supported by the Ministry of International Trade and Industry (MITI)—that continues to this day. Figure 9.3 illustrates the extent of rationalization that occurred at Mitsui's Miike coal mine (Omuta City, 1992). The left scale refers to total annual coal production, in thousands of tons, while the right scale indicates the number of miners. The dramatic rise in coal output from 1955 through 1970 was the result of significant technological advances in the 1960s and labor unrest in the mid-1950s that kept the mine closed and production levels low. For Omuta residents, the key issue was, and still is, jobs. The Miike mine was the center of a huge industrial complex—the Japanese have borrowed the Russian word *kombinat*—that was built around the mine. As Miike went, so went the community. The Mitsui group kombinat is made up of 10 major companies, 9 of which are still in existence in Omuta. All but two have experienced serious job cuts in the past 30 years.

As figure 9.3 shows, the mine and other Mitsui production facilities provided almost 29,000 jobs for Omuta area residents in 1960. By 1991, that number had dropped to around 4,500. The impact of such a steep drop in the job base was catastrophic from the city's point of view. In addition to the steep drop in the number of jobs, the composition of jobs in Omuta changed as well (fig. 9.4). In the 1960s, the majority of jobs were in secondary, or manufacturing, industries. This was largely due to Mitsui's presence in the city, but, as coal rationalization took hold and the kombinat started to decline, tertiary industry jobs came to outnumber manufacturing, even as the total number of employment opportunities declined over time.

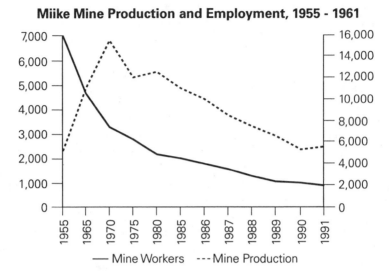

Figure 9.3 Miike Mine Production and Employment, 1955-1991

Jobs in the primary industries—farming, fishing,and forestry in Omuta—have not been a major source of employment in the postwar period, but they too have been roughly cut in half since 1960; they now account for about 4 percent of all the jobs in Omuta. This is in line with national trends. It is not clear why so many service sector jobs survive despite the decline in population. In 1960, the percentages of manufacturing and service sector jobs were almost equal, at 46 and 44 percent, respectively. By 1970, 36 percent of the jobs in Omuta were in secondary industries and 56 percent were in the service sector. This trend continued through the 1970s and into the 1980s. By 1985, manufacturing jobs dropped to 31 percent and service sector jobs swelled to 64 percent. One possible explanation is that public sector employment picked up as manufacturing employment declined. The City of Omuta is the second-largest employer in the city, after Mitsui. Another explanation is that the number of small businesses and offices has mushroomed. City statistics suggest there are more workers working in smaller offices than there were during the height of Mitsui's productive output, although it is unclear from these numbers what these workers are doing in their jobs.

Naturally, when jobs dry up in a city, people move elsewhere to find work to support their families. This has certainly happened in Omuta. The population declined from a high of almost 209,000 in 1959 to the current level—slightly over 150,000 as of the 1990 national census. The largest drop occurred between 1960 and 1970, when the city lost 34,000 residents. There was a steady, though more gradual, decline from 175,000 residents in 1970 to 150,000 in 1990 (fig. 9.5).

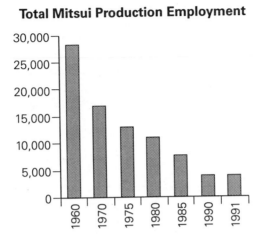

Figure 9.4 Total Mitsui Production Employment

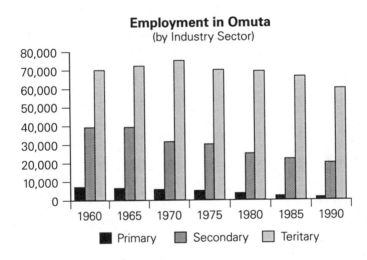

Figure 9.5 Employed People in Omuta by Industry Sector

As families have moved out of the city and the population has declined, the composition of the remaining population has changed; those who can move out of town do so, and those who cannot move remain. The population of Omuta is increasingly made up of older citizens with no children, and, as the current population continues to age, with no influx of new, younger working families to offset the trend, the number of people per family drops at about the same rate at which the population ages. This trend has not changed substantially since the major job cuts at Mitsui in the late 1960s, and the lack of

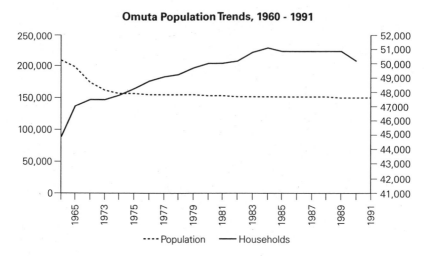

Figure 9.6 Omuta Population Trends, 1960-1991

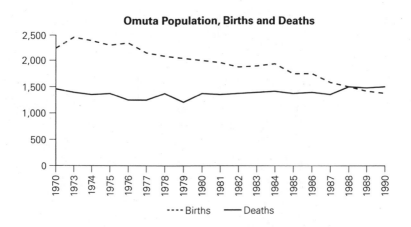

Figure 9.7 Omuta Population, Births and Deaths, 1970-1990

change in the trend indicates two things. First, the population is getting steadily older. In 1965, 10 percent of the population was age 65 years or older. By 1990, that number had increased to 18 percent. These numbers are well above the national averages: In 1965, 6.3 percent of the Japanese population was age 65 years or older, while by 1990 that number had increased to 12.1 percent (Sôrifu Shakai Hoshô Seido Shingikai Jimukyoku, 1993). Second, efforts to create jobs and attract new workers have not yet succeeded.

Another indication of the severity of Omuta's situation appears in the city's birth and death statistics. Nationally, given present trends, the number of deaths is not expected to exceed the number of births until sometime after the year 2000, but, as figure 9.6 shows, Omuta passed that threshold in 1988, and the trend shows no signs of reversing. Many nations are trying to halt population growth, but for Japan as a nation such a tendency is troublesome. Moreover, for a particular locality, the effects are readily visible and devastating. The population continues to age, with no indications of a more productive population developing in the near future. Omuta, like all of Japan, is concerned that there will not be enough younger citizens of working age to generate economic growth and support the aging population through the pension and welfare systems. This is a brief summary of the socioeconomic conditions facing local, prefectural, and national officials who are trying to help redevelop Omuta's economy. It is a hard task that officials have been working on for only a few years, relative to the length of the downward decline.

Flint

The recent history of Flint, Michigan (fig. 9.2), is fairly well known, thanks to the 1989 quasi-documentary film *Roger and Me* by Flint native Michael Moore and numerous articles in the popular press. Flint experienced a roughly 50-year heyday as a center of automobile production in the United States. Best known as the home of Buick and a labor union stronghold, Flint's history of boom and decline—and of capital versus labor—make it representative of much of America's twentieth-century industrial history. Flint's history is a good example of major trends in the politics of United States industrial development, too. The prosperity immediately following World War I sent production and employment in Flint and other industrial cities soaring.

Welfare capitalism—benevolent, privately-funded efforts at community support and enrichment—evolved nationwide after World War I. In Flint, this phenomenon was embodied in the Mott Foundation. Prior to the Great Depression, the leaders of the automobile industry in Flint built an elaborate network of privately sponsored welfare programs, insurance plans, and charitable organizations aimed at helping working people adjust to urban industrial life. They sought to preempt demands for public welfare programs or independent working-class actions (Edsforth, 1987:97). Charles Stewart Mott, one of the founding directors of General Motors (GM), established the Mott Foundation as a philanthropic organization in 1926. Just as the local industrialists sought to control politics in Flint, they strived to control social and cultural change there, too. The 1920s was a time of improving economic conditions and expanding welfare capitalism. Although their approach was somewhat paternalistic, Mott and others showed a genuine concern for the well-being of the city and its working people. It was in their interest to have a happy, healthy community on which to draw for labor.

The Great Depression catalyzed the growth of unions, which became a legitimate part of the auto industry when President Roosevelt pressured General

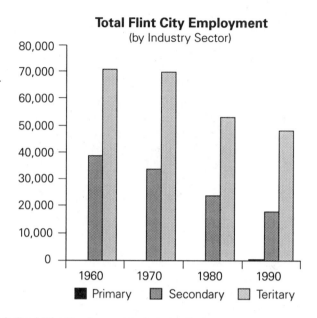

Figure 9.8 Total Flint Employment by Industry Sector

Motors into bargaining with the United Auto Workers (UAW) and the Congress of Industrial Organizations to end the Great Sit-Down Strike of 1936-37 in Flint. GM's employees and production facilities in Flint have undergone several cycles of growth and decline since the 1930s. The automobile industry is vulnerable to the rise and fall of consumer demand for vehicles, but, in addition to the cyclical rise and fall of the American auto industry, Flint gradually lost production to other communities that offered cheaper labor, lower utilities costs, better factory facilities and infrastructure, or other investment incentives. Production moved out of Flint, bound for communities in the South and West. Flint's recent past is similar to that of other cities in what is now known as the *American Rust Belt.*

The oil crisis of 1973 marked a new era for Flint, just as it did for Omuta. Gas prices rose rapidly, and the demand for smaller, fuel-efficient cars made it difficult for GM to compete with imported vehicles. Over the next decade, GM cut jobs and production from its older Flint facilities, or transferred them to other sites in an on-going corporate restructuring effort (United States Bureau of the Census, 1930, 1950, 1970, 1980, 1990).

The changes in the industry and the sudden uncompetitiveness of GM had a profound effect on the Flint populace. Auto industry jobs declined, and people were forced to find jobs outside of manufacturing. Figure 9.8 indicates the total number of full-time jobs in Flint, broken down by broad industrial

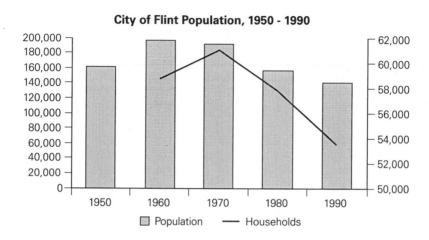

Figure 9.9 Flint Population, 1950-1990

sector. Although service-sector jobs stayed roughly constant or even increased slightly, the number of manufacturing jobs in Flint has dropped drastically since 1970. This is due to plant closings within the city limits.

People cannot support themselves and their families without jobs, and the population of Flint has changed accordingly. Figure 9.9 demonstrates that, following a rapid rise to a peak of almost 197,000 inhabitants, the city population dropped to slightly over 140,000 in 1990. The number of households in Flint has fallen from a high of almost 61,000 in 1970 to just over 53,000 in 1990. With no jobs available and living conditions deteriorating, people are looking elsewhere for jobs and housing. The city of Flint faces a daunting challenge if it hopes to recover the prosperity of its recent past.

It is interesting that there is no mass exodus of young people away from Flint the way there was in Omuta. As figure 9.10 suggests, the median age in Flint has consistently hovered between 25 and 30 years in the postwar era, although it was lowest in 1980 and has since rebounded to 1950 levels. Flint is not becoming a city of old people. However, the number of persons per household is steadily declining. This may indicate that people feel they cannot support larger families on their current sources of income. It is certainly not a sign of prosperity.

Several interesting trends emerge from this demographic comparison. First, both Omuta and Flint started dealing with these challenges around 1970. Larger political and economic issues changed the playing field for both cities, causing once-prosperous company towns to slide into decline. Second, the declines in both Omuta and Flint have been the result of declining domestic heavy industry. Although Omuta was driven by coal and Flint by the comparatively high technology of automobile manufacturing, both cities suffered from

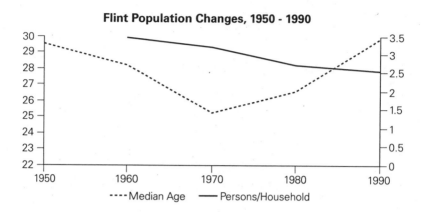

Figure 9.10 Flint Population Changes, 1950-1990

an influx of cheaper products from abroad. Japanese industrial consumers could buy coal more cheaply abroad than at home, while American consumers could buy more-fuel-efficient and reliable cars from foreign manufacturers. Japan's vaunted industrial policy did no more to save Omuta than America's comparatively laissez-faire industrial policy did to save Flint. In both cases, private-sector (corporate) decisions dictated the fate of the local community. Finally, all the money and energy invested by both public and private sector players produced little in the way of positive results, but in both cases city officials, determined to help stimulate a renaissance in the city continue to hammer away at the problems.

REVITALIZATION EFFORTS

Omuta

Omuta's responses to economic decline were late in coming, relative to the timing of the city's economic decline. While the city's economy was clearly going downhill in the early and mid-1970s, real efforts at redevelopment and revitalization did not start until the mid-1980s. The focus of policy responses in the 1970s and early 1980s was on compensation for displaced workers rather than new sources of jobs and economic growth. The policy focus from the mid-1980s into the 1990s was a mixture of quality-of-life improvement issues for city residents and attempted innovations in economic redevelopment to create jobs and attract people to the city. The shift in local focus was clearly due in part to changes in the national policy landscape, and the quality-of-life efforts were more successful than the job creation and economic growth measures: Omuta is a nicer place to live—it is cleaner and has more park space and new

Photo 9.2 Smokestacks and factories dot the industrial landscape of Northern Kyushu. Built on coal and steel, energy-intensive industries once dominated the region, which has now been cleaned up and has attracted high-technology industries. With a tenth of the country's population, this part of the Megalopolis accounts for about 12 percent of the national gross domestic product with an economy as large as those of Indonesia, Thailand, and Malaysia combined. Photo by P. P. Karan

civic facilities—than it was before the mid-1980s, but few new jobs have been created and the economy continues to sputter along.

The overall effect of institutions in Omuta reflects the unitary nature of Japan's governmental system in many ways, although there are some distinct areas of functional fragmentation, too. Starting at the local level, the major institutional factors in the urban redevelopment arena are as follows. The directly elected mayor is strong, and therefore the local political system generally facilitates elite-led policy making. The city assembly is weak, never seriously challenging the mayor or city hall bureaucrats on any of the plans generated by the administration. However, although veto points are few, they can be (and have been) used effectively by those opposed to a particular project. In addition, the primacy of bureaucrats over politicians is evident in Omuta's redevelopment efforts, *with the exception* of the fact that the current mayor was the primary catalyst for the city's redevelopment efforts. Japanese local bureaucrats serve two masters. The mayor is their areal superior, while national ministries and agencies are their functional superiors. Local officials must be responsive to both. The final salient local institutional feature is the lack of fiscal autonomy, which constrains city budget decision making. Since the city generates only about one third of its budget revenues directly, it is heavily reliant on disbursements from prefectural and national accounts.

Above the local level, Fukuoka prefecture acts as a conduit for redevelopment funds and expertise from Tokyo. Japan is divided into 47 prefectures.

Prefectures are headed by a directly elected governor and a prefectural assembly. The former is more powerful. Although there is some discretionary power at the prefectural level, most participants characterize the prefecture as a pipe through which national resources flow to the localities. Prefectures are free to make policy that is "not in conflict with the law." However, according to Reed, "the central ministries have broad authority to interpret the law in the absence of court decisions, and they guard their authority jealously. Each time a local government has attempted to enact an innovative policy, the concerned ministry has argued that the ordinance conflicts with the law and is therefore illegal." (Reed, 1986: 25).

The central government assigns numerous functions to the prefecture and provides finances for the implementation of these programs. While these assigned functions seem overwhelming when viewed from an American perspective, Japanese local governments have somewhat more authority than do local governments in a typical unitary state (Reed; 1986).

The budgetary constraints placed on localities by the Tokyo government prompt Omuta and other cities to look to national programs for fiscal assistance. Local taxes account for roughly one third of local revenues. Of the remaining two thirds of the local budget, the two most important taxes are the transfer tax (*jôyozei*) and the allocation tax (*kôfuzei*). Both are collected by the national government and returned to the locality by the Ministry of Home Affairs (MOHA). The transfer tax is a straight tax, meaning the amount collected from the locality is the amount disbursed to that locality from the central government, while the allocation tax is a form of general revenue sharing. The MOHA calculates the demand for a list of services provided by the locality, subtracts the actual revenues of the local government, and disburses the difference up to a total representing a fixed percentage of three national taxes. These three sources comprise general revenue for the locality and come with no strings attached. All other disbursements are made for specific purposes.

MOHA is arguably the most powerful ministry from the local government's perspective. All local borrowing is subject to MOHA approval. An interesting change to note is the steady increase in MOHA's budget through the 1970s and 1980s, depicted in figure 9.11. The budget grew much faster than both the MITI and Ministry of Construction (MoC) budgets and did so despite serious administrative reform efforts at the national level. The MOHA budget more than quintupled between 1975 and 1990, while the MoC budget barely doubled. The MITI budget quadrupled in the same time span, but in absolute terms the MOHA budget was 20 times the size of the MITI budget (*Zaisei Tôkei*, 1992). However, these figures are somewhat deceptive because most of the MOHA budget simply passes through the ministry to the local level. MOHA is a key institution for localities borrowing money, but it exerts little or

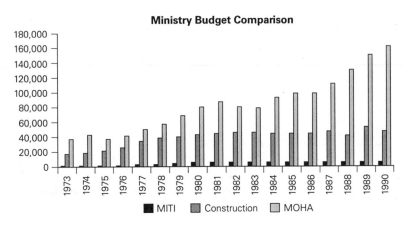

Figure 9.11 Ministry Budget Comparison

no control over the budget or general administration beyond enforcement of conservative budgeting criteria and formulae. The MoC and MITI are more important in these areas.

The programs implemented at the national level thus make up the universe within which localities must operate. From the local perspective, these programs are the most important factor determining policy choices and outcomes.

Omuta's change in policy focus in the mid-1980s did not result from any direct, immediate changes in the local political structure. In fact, Omuta's local government structure did not changed significantly in the postwar era. Since the Occupation reforms, Omuta—like every other city in Japan—has had a directly elected mayor and a city assembly. The number of representatives in that assembly is determined by formula, on the basis of population.

The threat of change in the national policy landscape prompted new policy priorities and developments. Starting in the early 1960s, Omuta benefited from a steady stream of subsidies to coal-producing areas. In the mid-1980s, these rationalization subsidy programs began to draw to a close. The change in priorities at the national level catalyzed a change in priorities at the local level. The shift from coal policies to postcoal policies is described in the following section.

Is change in the policy environment a case of institutional change? It is argued that it is. The coal policies described below were backed by a series of laws passed by the national Diet. This legal framework was the institutional basis for 30 years of local government activity and routinized behavior. With the impending expiration of these laws, national bureaucrats and local officials were forced to find a new raison d'être. Omuta's local economic policy making was habitually predicated on national laws, priorities, and directions. When these changed, Omuta was forced to change, too.

Policy Responses   This section describes the strategic change in Omuta's policy efforts from coal preservation and rationalization to coal replacement. Generally speaking, how did Omuta and Flint construct redevelopment policy? In a nutshell, both cities tried to revitalize using as much outside capital—both public and private—as possible. There are numerous ways to break down their redevelopment policy efforts. Policy pronouncements in both Omuta and Flint focus on seven different types. Omuta lists infrastructure development, industrial promotion, "living environment," resident welfare, education and culture, international cultural exchange, and taking advantage of regionally focused policies in its revitalization documents. Flint's Urban Investment Plan of 1993 focused on infrastructure, economic development, education and training, health care and social services, housing, law enforcement, and parks and recreation. Broadly speaking, policies in both Omuta and Flint aim to improve either quality of life or economic growth. How can we explain the difference in focus? To a large extent, each city planned programs that it believed could be financed with outside resources. So each applied for whatever was available.

How does one rebuild a small city like Omuta? Functionally speaking, there appear to be two types of policy used to revive slumping cities. The first type is designed to improve the quality of life in the city. One Omuta official pointed out that company towns—especially industrial centers like Omuta—are often severely lacking in infrastructure and public lifestyle amenities such as parks, pleasant roads and waterways, extensive sewer systems, and nice city centers (Muto interview). Government policies and plans to improve these facilities are aimed at making the former company town (*kigyô jôka machi*) a better, more pleasant place to live. The words *machi tsukuri* (community-building) and *sumiyasui* (easy to live in) appear repeatedly in such infrastructure-improvement plans. This type of policy is construction oriented, with modest goals and tangible results that make them rather easy to accomplish.

Making Omuta a more pleasant place to live has two purposes. First, it is an attempt to raise the level of public amenities so they are on a par with those in other communities. Omuta has less green public space than other communities its size, although it has worked hard to remedy this problem (Omuta City, 1979-1989). Second, the city seeks an image makeover that residents hope will make it a more attractive place for outside firms to locate. It is a widely held article of faith that firms will be more likely to locate to places where their employees will want to live, although I am not aware of any study that confirms this notion. Omuta also has dreams of becoming a bedroom community for workers in Fukuoka City, an hour north by express train.

The second type of redevelopment policy is designed to attract people and job-creating firms to the city. A type of local-level industry-promotion policy, these efforts target industries and even individual firms and try to entice them with "soft" projects such as participation in government projects, tax breaks, investment credits and other industry-promotion incentives and "hard" projects such as industrial parks and transport-network improvements. These projects are more ambitious and take time to show success or failure. While they, too, require construction, they also demand salesmanship and other elusive skills that contribute to a city's changing image.

Of course, these two types of projects overlap, support, and complement each other, and cities do not undertake one type without the other. Omuta has numerous projects in both policy areas, although, so far, the quality of life projects appear more "successful" than the industrial promotion efforts. Quality of life appears to be improving—there is a new city library and an improved park system, with plans for a new hospital on the drawing board—while few jobs are being created in Omuta. In addition, the city is working to improve its reputation as a destination for tourists; toward this end, plans are well underway to develop an amusement park, city zoo, and other leisure facilities. Tourism falls into both categories of the redevelopment project. Residents use such facilities during their own leisure time, and tourism facilities create jobs either directly or indirectly (through increased sales by local merchants, for example).

Coal Policy Environment, 1970 to mid-1980s For the better part of the 1970s, Omuta's revitalization policy consisted primarily of efforts to extract compensation payments for workers who were laid off or retired early. This support money came from the continuation of the Coal Area Assistance and Promotion Policy, a long-running national government program aimed at the long-term rationalization of Omuta's main industry by stabilizing areas and communities hurt by the decline of the domestic coal industry. It is the earliest governmental attempt to control and soften the decline of Omuta and similar cities. Managed primarily by MITI, with the support of other government ministries and agencies, the policy encompasses numerous laws and policies aiding many groups and individuals related to the coal industry. There are six laws related to the coal industry decline on which coal area policy is based. The oldest law, aimed at cleaning up pollution in coal regions, was passed in 1952. The most recent, which uses tax revenue from petroleum sales to help regions cope with labor, pollution, and new industry issues, was passed in 1967. One law will expire in 2001, while the rest are slated to expire in 2002.

Under these laws, a series of Coal Programs (*Sekitan Taisaku*) was promulgated by the national government for use in localities throughout Japan. The First Coal Program took effect in 1963, and ran for two years. Programs Two and Three also had two-year durations, but subsequent policies specified longer terms as regions became more stable and less-frequent adjustment was required. The current program—the Final Coal Program, which took effect in 1991—is functionally the ninth coal policy, but it is not called that, because it is intended to be the final iteration in the series. According to one Fukuoka Prefecture official, simply calling it the "Ninth Coal Policy" would imply an intention to make a tenth, eleventh, on so on. This is the government's way of communicating the termination of this industry rationalization policy series (Sato interview).

What was the local government's role in the coal-program era? Local actions in the 1970s and early 1980s closely resemble the top-down, insulated system one might expect in a unitary political system. Since the early 1950s, the Omuta city government has regularly joined with related coal industry and labor groups to pressure Tokyo to keep the subsidies flowing. Through the 1970s, the community was quite unified in its movement toward this goal. Coal was Omuta's lifeblood, and the thought of that industry no longer supporting the community was unimaginable. Until 1986, the mayor of Omuta was always a Mitsui company employee. Articulating the priorities of the city, company, and union, he would travel to Fukuoka, the prefectural government seat, and to Tokyo to push for more funds for his increasingly depressed city. Supported in his efforts by both labor and big business, it is not surprising that for so long the city's economic policy consisted primarily of successfully extracting subsidies from the national government. Business, labor, and government wanted the money, and the Tokyo government was willing to continue its largesse.

This program was a continuation of national government efforts to rationalize (downsize) the Japanese coal industry. Initial rationalization efforts—begun in 1950—were aimed at improving efficiency and corporate strength in the coal industry. Rationalization was designed to revive the industry, and its collapse was an unplanned event. Despite the government's best efforts, coal-mine output efficiency did not improve. By 1955 the rationalization plans had already begun to focus on managing decline rather than on planning improvements (Hein 1990, 230, 248). The national government was more interested in compensating the "losers" in Japan's postwar industrial transformation than in preserving the Japanese coal industry. The government adopted this approach because of pressure from coal consumers, such as steel producers and the electric power industry. Neither wanted to subsidize the inefficient coal industry by agreeing to pay higher-than-market prices. These coal consumers argued that such subsidies would slow national growth and the coal industry was not worth such a sacrifice. Government officials listened, and they made policies designed to manage the decline of coal (Samuels, 1987: 108-24, 131).

Nevertheless, the top priority for the local government through the mid-1980s was the preservation of the coal mine and related industries. This was still the engine driving the local economy, and the major political and economic actors worked to maintain this situation. Since public opinion was unified on this point, it was easy for the local government to set the same priorities year after year. The national government responded with subsidies for this prominent sunset industry, and it maintained a set of institutions that worked toward this end. Ultimately, funds for the gradual rationalization of the industry flowed from the national to the local level for several decades, in large part because of standard programmatic inertia: such programs, once established, are difficult to disassemble. As Campbell puts it, "[i]n all organizations, participants will usually follow the rules and do today what they did yesterday, inhibiting policy change" (1992: 353).

There was no perceived need for policy innovation during this time, since the major interests were satisfied with the status quo, and coal policy implementation went smoothly because of the centralization and bureaucratization of the program. National ministry officials worked with prefectural and local officials to distribute benefits, cushioning the industry's decline for decades.

Coal Policy, Mid-1980s to the Early 1990s   As production at the Mitsui Miike mine was cut and jobs were lost, the national government provided money and advice to cushion the decline. Nationally, assistance to coal-mining areas was provided by a wide range of government ministries, although MITI and MOHA led the way in bureaucratic authority and budget disbursements, respectively. The era of job cuts, early retirements, and payments to affected former workers and families was coming to a close. The Coal Policy's main focus became forward looking and developmental. Financing regional promotion plans, new coal-technology research centers, symposiums on clean coal technology and regional development, and overseas study missions emerged as the heart of the last two coal policies.

A change in institutional *balance* occurred in the 1980s. Although there was no structural change, and the same important institutional players were going through the same institutional channels, a fragmentation of priorities occurred at the local level. Two camps developed in Omuta politics, one that wanted to preserve the status quo that centered on coal and coal-related industries and a second that saw the dependence on coal coming to an end. The latter sought to move forward and create a new economic era for the city, thus leaving the coal era behind.

Why did this division occur at this time? There are several possible explanations. From a political perspective, Mitsui employment dropped to a level that made the unions and the company less politically powerful in Tokyo. At the national level, this made it safe for Tokyo to cut back—with an eye toward eventually eliminating—the long-standing coal area subsidies. But the coal lobby had been weak for years, so this is not a likely explanation. From a bureaucratic perspective, the rationalization in other coal areas was even further advanced than in Omuta, so MITI saw a declining need to cushion this sunset industry as a whole. Smaller mines had been closed for years, and coal extraction efficiency (tons per man per month) rose steadily through the 1970s and 1980s (Kyushu Trade and Industry Bureau, 1992: 13-14). Subsidies could not be stopped cold, but the change in economic factors prompted a change in subsidy strategy.

An intergovernmental perspective offers a third possible explanation. At the local level, the division between status quo supporters and progressives came to a head in the 1986 mayoral election, and the splits were visible in previously unified sectors of the community. The outcome of this local contest sent a signal to Tokyo that it was finally safe to stop the subsidy programs, although there is no solid evidence that Tokyo was paying any attention. The signal was in the form of the new mayor, who began a campaign to change Omuta's image and to initiate a postcoal era. The changes in Omuta alone did not cause the change at the national level. Other coal areas experienced similar changes, but Omuta's history as the site of the largest mine was important. Other mining areas had not held onto coal as long as Omuta had.

Mitsui was changing, too. Older industrial concerns were phased out in favor of new ones: metal smelting and aluminum refining moved up-scale to more high-value activities such as aluminum fiber production (*Nikkan Kôgyô Shimbun*, April 21, 1989); technologically advanced rare earth refining was started (*Nikkei Sangyô Shimbun*, November 9, 1988); coal chemical plants were retooled to produce fine ceramics and other products demanded by high technology industries (*Nikkan Kôgyô Shimbun*, April 4, 1989); and, as the coal mine slowly decreased production, it increased its research and training (of miners from other parts of Asia) in the fields of coal extraction and safety techniques. The Mitsui Coal labor union experienced evolutionary pains, too. Some workers sought to keep the coal industry alive, while others argued for retraining and new jobs within the company. Ultimately, the union split into two factions, the "old union" (*kyû kumiai*) and "new union" (*shin kumiai*) (Nishimura interview). These two camps continue to exist, but both are growing increasingly weak as time goes by and membership decreases.

These local political and economic changes catalyzed a shift in the national policy environment. As mentioned briefly above, MITI decided it was time to bring the special coal policy series to a close. It made this decision on the basis of evidence that the coal industry was finally a fraction of its former size (Goto interview), but, rather than end the program abruptly, MITI changed the focus of its grants to coal areas. The ministry has a strong postwar tradition of promulgating and implementing industrial policy, and some at MITI saw a phoenix rising from the ashes of the coal industry. MITI became a sponsor of coal technology research and development in the hope that new products and technology might be developed for export to coal-producing nations. MITI began funding research into clean coal technology and more efficient, safer coal-extraction processes. For Omuta, this change produced the World Coal Techno-Center project, a research and development facility intended to use the old Miike mine facilities. More generally, MITI developed a Coal Area

Promotion Policy that included such efforts as infrastructure improvement, luring firms to former coal areas (*kigyô yûchi*), and aiding small and medium-sized businesses in these areas. These efforts were undertaken under the auspices of MITI's Regional Promotion and Facilities Public Corporation (*Chiiki Shinkô Seibi Kôdan*) (Overview of the Coal Area Promotion Policy). As the largest producer of coal in Japan, Mitsui jumped at the opportunity to receive further government grants, and, as the site of the largest mine in Japan, Omuta cooperated in the directional shift. Perhaps there was a postcoal future that included coal, too.

In 1986, the forward-looking forces scored a decisive victory when, for the first time, Omuta elected a mayor who was not from the Mitsui establishment. The election of Shiotsuka Kôichi says a lot about the changes that happened in Omuta politics. An Omuta native who graduated from prestigious Tokyo University, he worked in the national Ministry of Construction until he was elected mayor at age 40. During his tenure at the Construction Ministry, he spent two years on loan to the United Nations' Development Agency, working on development issues in Manila. By far Omuta's youngest mayor ever, he represents a technocratic vision of a new Omuta that seeks to change the city from a coal town to a more economically diversified community. The city slogan, *sekitan mo aru toshi* (The City That Has Coal, Too), symbolizes this goal; it received wide play in the local newspapers. The 1986 election was ultimately a referendum about the future course of the city, and the conflict has seldom surfaced since the election. Although the post–oil crisis unified coalition has fragmented somewhat, Omuta politics still functions much as it did in the 1970s and early 1980s, with a strong executive, high elite cohesion, and few veto points. There are a few distinct differences, mostly in policy content rather than the process.

Mayor Shiotsuka provides the strong executive leadership of past mayors; he may even be a stronger leader, since he is charting a new course for the city that will not show quick results. In the first six years of his administration, the population continued to decline, though at a slower rate, and there were few new jobs created in Omuta. The biggest change in Omuta can be seen in efforts at new policy development. Until Shiotsuka, there was none; now, this is a central focus of local politics. Shiotsuka was clearly the catalyst for this change, and the centralized, vertically tracked institutional structure facilitated his ability to set city priorities. However, there is little true innovation in Omuta, since the revitalization and diversification policies underway now are the kinds of projects that other cities have been attempting for years, though they are new to Omuta. Shiotsuka catalyzed a change in policy direction, but the national institutional framework—including the various policies implemented elsewhere—dictated what was actually done. Omuta's new master plan of 1991 described the general direction in which the city wanted to go. Industrial park zones and infrastructural improvement, supported by quality of life and leisure facility projects were the core of the plan. Table 9.1 gives a list of the major projects in Omuta.

The idea for these projects came mainly from examinations of what other cities were doing to foster economic development (Muto interview). Visits to other cities and consultations with prefectural and national officials prompted Omuta officials to try similar policies and projects. While none of these projects is particularly innovative, they all represent a dramatic departure from the policy inertia of the years prior to the Shiotsuka administration.

Changes in national-level programs—not statutory changes, but changes in administrative policy focus and emphasis—available to localities promoting economic development encouraged Omuta to move away from welfare-oriented subsidies and toward policies focused on growth. But although the intent of the programs changed, the structure through which they passed, and the way they were managed went unaltered. The mayor is still a central figure in the process, primarily in setting the local policy agenda. His endorsement virtually assures a project will move forward. Although all projects must be cleared by the city assembly, the assembly is functionally just a rubber stamp; it holds hearings and grills city hall officials on project proposals, but they have never had much input on any redevelopment programs (Nishimura interview). The assembly role is purely oversight, a formality in the policy process.

As the list of revitalization projects shows, bureaucrats—from city hall up to the national level—dominate the pursuit of redevelopment project ideas. From the planning through implementation stages, they call the shots and really make things happen. In light of the fiscally top-down nature of Japanese government, one of the local officials' most-important functions is serving as the actual link with the prefectural and national levels. From the standpoint of Japanese political studies, this is somewhat counterintuitive. Many of the projects listed could be classified as pork-barrel appropriations. Road improvements, downtown development projects, and other upgrades to the physical infrastructure are usually assumed to be the domain of politicians—in the local, prefectural, and national assemblies—seeking electoral security (Dore, 1978: 236-41; Calder, 1988). But in this policy area, in Omuta at least, there is little evidence to support this notion. Although the mayor is involved in many of these efforts, he is not closely connected to any local representatives. His past experience in the bureaucracy seems to account for this bureaucratic focus.

Bureaucratic primacy exists in this policy area for other reasons, too. Although money is available from various national sources, getting it can be difficult. Cities compete for funds, so having an idea of what the ministry in control of the purse strings wants in a proposal is important. The system places a higher value on systemic savvy and technical knowledge than on political contacts and clout. The application forms required for such grants are long and contorted, and

Table 9.1. Redevelopment Projects in Omuta, 1970-92

Project Name	Sponsor/ Applicant	Funding Sources	Main Funding Source	Innovation Source	Early 1970s to Early 1980s	Early 1980s to Present	Policy Type	Dominant Player Type
Farm Subsidies (cadmium problem)	3	1	1	N/A	X	X	redistributive	political
Coal Policy (continuing)	3	1	1	N/A	X	X	redistributive	political
Ariake GeoBio World Theme Park	3, 4	1,2,3,4	1	lateral		X	growth	bureaucratic
Downtown Area Activity Plan (Community Mart Model Project)	3, 4	1,2,3,4	4	vertical/lateral		X	facilities imp.	bureau/busi
Kattachi Area Development Project	3	3,4	4	vertical		X	facilities imp.	bureaucratic
Omuta Zoo Revitalization	3	3	3	self		X	growth	bureaucratic
Suwa Park Facilities Project	3	3,4	3	vertical		X	facilities imp.	bureaucratic
New City Hospital	3	planning stage	N/A	?		X	facilities imp.	bureaucratic
Area Road Improvement	3	1,2,3	1,2	vertical		X	facilities imp.	bureaucratic
Industrial/Regional Promotion and Corporate Invitation	3	3	3	lateral		X	growth	bureau/busi
Omuta Central Industrial Park	3	3,4	3	lateral		X	growth	bureaucratic
Omuta Technopark Inland Industrial Park Development Project	3	1	1	vertical		X	growth	bureaucratic
Product Distribution Center	3	3,4	3	self		X	growth	bureaucratic
World Coal Technology Center	3, 4	1	1	vertical		X	growth	bureau/busi
Miike Port Facilities Improvement Plan	3, 4	2	2	self		X	growth	business
The Central Ariake Region Activity Promotion Council	3, 4	1,2,3,4	N/A	lateral		X	growth	political
Ariake Coastal Summit	3	1,2	N/A	lateral		X	growth	political

Note: 1 = national government; 2 = prefecture; 3 = Omuta; 4 = private capital; NA = not available demand a technocratic expertise that politicians do not necessarily have. Books are written by experienced local and national career officials explaining the various ways of accessing national coffers (Local Financial Affairs Association, 1992; Planning Section of the Ministry for Local Autonomy, 1993; Yokota and Ebata, 1993). Although officials from different sections work together closely at the local level, this is not the case at the prefectural and national levels.

The ministries are quite fragmented on a horizontal scale; MITI, the MoC, and MOHA all have programs for urban redevelopment that functionally overlap one another, but there is little cooperation among these agencies to avoid duplication. In fact, the Six Coal Laws required a number of agencies and ministries to each create their own plan to assist each coal area. The Prime Minister's Office, along with the Ministries of Finance, Agriculture, Transportation, Health/Welfare, Labor, Construction, Local Affairs, and International Trade and Industry were required to generate and implement such programs (Summary of the Six Laws Relating to Coal). Each had to reach down to the local level and provide subsidies to struggling coal regions, Omuta among them.

In this policy area, bureaucrats are more important than politicians, and bureaucratic intergovernmental relations are deep. One manifestation of these deep vertical ties is seen in the practice of *jinji kôryû*, the personnel exchange system all national agencies use. National officials are dispatched to the prefectural or local level for a year or two, where they serve as section chief and gain practical project management experience. During that time, they still receive their preassignment salary, paid by their ministry of origin. On returning to their home ministry, they usually move up a level in the bureaucracy. MITI, the Ministry of Construction, the Ministry of Health and Welfare, and the Ministry of Local Affairs all have sent employees to Omuta. Prefectural officials are sent to the local level under the same system. Personnel exchange seems to only work from the top down. Local officials do not go to higher levels to gain experience, but localities benefit from the presence of officials from higher levels. Personal contacts in various offices, expertise at grant applications from the receiving end, and knowledge of available programs all help localities take advantage of national ministry resources.

Flint

Redevelopment efforts in Flint started in the early 1970s and have been largely unsuccessful at bringing prosperity to the city. These efforts started earlier than they did in Omuta, relative to the start of local economic deterioration. Flint's redevelopment history can be divided into three distinct periods, each prompted by changes in federal government policy toward cities. The early 1970s marked the end of the urban renewal era, which started well before the 1973 oil crisis. Urban renewal was a federally driven attempt to revive cities throughout the United States by razing whole sections of urban blight and starting over from scratch with federal funds priming the pump. It was the first federal legislation to deal with the central city, and it was no more successful in Flint than anywhere else. Urban renewal did little to change the face of cities. The procedural red tape involved in the program drove private investors away. Local officials used the program for high-priced projects rather than for neighborhood community redevelopment. In general, urban renewal was treated like a real estate enterprise rather than as a social program (Gelfand, 1975).

The second era—the focus of this research—changed the emphasis from urban renewal to locally determined downtown economic growth, which was to be sparked by winning and using federal funds in the form of Urban Development Action Grants (UDAGs) and Community Development Block Grants (CDBGs) from the U.S. Department of Housing and Urban Development (HUD). Started during the Carter administration in 1978, UDAGs could be awarded only to urban projects financed primarily by private investments. These funds went toward big downtown projects aimed at achieving a critical mass of commercial activity to catalyze growth. Flint was very successful in winning these grants. By the end of 1984, Michigan had won a total of 112 UDAGs, with 30 going to Detroit. Flint was second with 10, and Pontiac was third with 8 grants (*Flint Journal*, December 9, 1984).

From the mid-1970s through the mid-1980s, revitalization efforts consisted mostly of programs led by Flint's private sector economic elite. Large, private, capital-intensive projects appeared in the downtown area, where they were supposed to lure businesses and consumers away from the burgeoning suburbs. Although private capital—provided by the Mott Foundation and by investment syndicates—paid the largest percentage for most of the projects, none moved decisively forward toward completion until federal grants were won. Most of these projects did not achieve their intended goals, and a few became notorious white elephants because the goals set for the projects were unrealistic. These goals were set by private-sector consultants and project specialists who sold the project ideas to the city. Their economic interest in the projects—they benefited, whether the projects succeeded or failed—encouraged the replication of ideas from other localities and discouraged innovations that might have been more realistic and more successful.

Following this string of failures, the pattern of redevelopment efforts shifted again. This shift was caused in part by the end of the CDBG and UDAG programs in 1988. This forced city officials, in conjunction with smaller capital interests in the community, to change the focus of revitalization from large urban icons to small business job-creation efforts. These have been marginally successful, but their success is overshadowed by GM's decisions and their impact on Flint. Even if several smaller firms can create a couple of hundred jobs in a year, these gains are often obscured by large employment decisions—

either hirings or layoffs—involving thousands of workers in the automobile industry.

Redevelopment in Flint is a mixture of what we would expect to find in a fragmented federal system and a centralized unitary system. Politicians are more important in Flint's revitalization efforts than they are in Omuta. This is an institutionalized fact of American politics, where the primacy of politicians is the norm. In this policy area at least, American congressional representatives appear more active in policy making than their counterparts in the Japanese Diet.[1] At the local level, the mayor is a central policy figure, too. Career civil servants are certainly players—especially at the Flint city hall—but they do not wield the clout and authority of their Japanese counterparts. Funds for redevelopment are secured by politicians in the United States, and by bureaucrats in Japan. Both systems are quite open to citizen participation in the process, though the higher degree of local business elite involvement in revitalization planning and implementation in Flint demonstrates the lower barriers to entry into the redevelopment policy arena on the American side. In Omuta, bureaucrats take the lead on the larger projects. In Flint, private sector business people lead.

In the United States, there is considerable fiscal autonomy at the local level, which should encourage innovation. Grants from the national to the local level have more strings and control associated with them in Japan than in the United States There is also more room for creative grantsmanship in the American system.[2] In addition, there are no limits set by the federal government on local bond issues. American cities have the freedom to mortgage themselves into oblivion, and the concept of city bankruptcy is not unheard of in the United States. The notorious case of Watertown, Wisconsin, in the 1860s is a classic case of a city floating bonds and then getting burned. Watertown issued railroad bonds for two fledgling railroad companies, using the city's credit to capitalize the railroads. In an era of rapid rail expansion, the city hoped to enjoy a growth boom that would help it capture the potential economic benefits. The railroads failed, and by 1870 Watertown's debt plus interest equaled one-half of the city's assessed property value (Monkkonen, 1988: 148-51). Although failures to honor debt have been relatively few, even large cities such as New York and Washington, D.C., have flirted with debt crises in recent memory.

Japanese cities float bonds, but they never approach bankruptcy, thanks to the oversight and control exercised by the MOHA in Tokyo. American local fiscal autonomy allows for more flexible use of locally derived revenues. Tax increment bonds, revenue-sharing bonds, rehabilitation bonds, and other financial instruments give United States cities a larger toolbox with which to construct redevelopment efforts.

But Flint has been caught between the fiscal freedom to do what it wants, and federal government programs that urge it to do what Washington wants.

The state of Michigan has had a limited impact on Flint and has not really helped or hindered local efforts financially. Flint might have received more state support if Detroit had not demanded so much assistance, but the Lansing government did little to push Flint in one direction or another. Ultimately, Flint has sought many grants and loans from the federal government, allowing grant availability to dictate what—and whether—projects are implemented. In this way it has behaved more like a city in a unitary state. Flint has spent less energy on innovation and more on using the governmental system to its own advantage.

Policy implementation in Flint looks more centralized than one would expect of a fragmented political system in another way, too. The same people and organizations were responsible for realizing policy ideas, especially in the first decade of revitalization efforts. The remarkable continuity in the names and faces involved with revitalization in Flint suggests a centralized decision-making process with few veto points and high barriers to entry, and in many ways this is an accurate description of the city's redevelopment process. The fact that such centralized activity has happened highlights an interesting point about the flexibility of the American governmental structure: although localities have the freedom to go it alone to a great extent, they are not forced to exercise this autonomy. Rather, independent governmental action is but one stategy option.

The policy structure at the federal level played an important role in determining the direction of revitalization efforts in Flint. Flint was forced to change its policy stategy and responses in the late 1980s by structural changes in its environment. Specifically, the availablity of grants diminished, forcing Flint to find other funding sources for revitalization efforts. HUD's UDAG and CDBG programs started in the mid-1970s but ran their course and were not renewed by the Republican administrations after 1988. While these grants were by no means the only source of redevelopment funds used in Flint, they were often the lynch pin that held a project idea together and kept it moving forward.

Certain aspects of the UDAG program pushed Flint toward a reliance on developers and consultants. In particular, although the city was charged with submitting the application and funneling funds to the project, private developers and consultants were required to provide the extensive documentation required in the application.

Three requirements in particular gave experienced developers an edge and provided incentives for cities to hire developers and consultants with UDAG project experience: evidence that developers/managers had the capabilities to do the project, market studies to substantiate the feasibility of the project, and a demonstration of the methodology used to calculate the number of jobs to be created. Flint hired nationally known developers and consultants for all its major projects, including Recreation Consultants, Inc., which developed the Marriott Corporation's Great America theme parks in Chicago and

San Francisco; Randall Duell Associates, which helped develop 22 theme parks, including Busch Gardens (Virginia) and Hershey Park (Pennsylvania); and James Rouse, head of the Enterprise Development Corporation, who headed the development of Boston's Quincy Market, Baltimore's Inner Harbor area, and other large retail projects. These specialists brought their recipes for success to Flint and tried to replicate them.

The point here is that Japan has local bureaucrats who handle details such as those listed above. In the United States, although cities file the grant applications, much of the work is done by private-sector consultants. Consultants operate in Japan, too, although they are less common there than in the United States (Cole, 1989: 44). Research suggests that their participation in urban redevelopment may vary by policy type. Consultants were quite active in the quest for an amusement park in Omuta, but they were less involved in shopping district revitalization and not involved at all in the industrial park efforts.

The end of the federal grant program forced a change in tactics at the local level: Flint now had to fund redevelopment efforts in an environment where capital was less freely available. A multimillion dollar surge in capital-intensive development in the late 1970s and early 1980s resulted in the $14 million Riverbank Park, opened in 1979, the $40 million Hyatt Regency Hotel complex, opened in 1981, the $73 million AutoWorld, opened in 1984, and the $29 million Water Street Pavilion, opened in 1985 (*Flint Journal*, August 21, 1985). The result was that no large, new revitalization initiatives were started after the early 1980s. Instead, a plan composed of smaller projects aimed at small-to-medium businesses emerged from the local (city and county) government. Capital became tight, the large outlays of the past had not produced results, and both the public and private sectors did not want to get burned financially again.

Policy Responses   Redevelopment efforts in Flint have focused less on compensatory demands and special programs for unemployed workers than have those in Omuta. Although workers certainly took advantage of existing federal unemployment and welfare benefits following layoffs and plant closings, there was no effort on the part of city representatives to extract any new or additional payments from the federal government for those affected.

For most of the 1970s, Flint focused on rebuilding the traditional downtown area with large capital-improvement projects. The beginning of this downtown makeover was a new University of Michigan–Flint campus. The idea was first revealed in 1972 at a meeting of the Flint Area Conference, Inc. (FACI), and ground-breaking occurred in 1974 (*Flint Journal*, March 7, 1972; July 23, 1974). Table 9.2 lists the major redevelopment projects in Flint. In addition to these explicitly developmental projects in the downtown area, another industrial park was built at the city's Bishop Airport. Sponsored by the city, the park was financed with a city bond issue and money from the federal Economic Development Agency (EDA).

The net effect of these projects on the economy of Flint was small compared to the capital expended: $568.5 million was the total cost for all projects combined. Buick City—which alone cost $295 million—created more jobs in the auto industry, but the other projects cost more than $273 million and created few jobs, lured few new businesses, did little to stem the tide of flight to the suburbs, and did not effectively address the issues that caused Flint's decline in the first place. Federal funds, allocated almost entirely from HUD grant programs, accounted for only $65 million but were the catalyst for a number of projects. Five million dollars came from an Army Corps of Engineers flood control project on the Flint River. The remainder was HUD grant money for urban revitalization projects. Unfortunately, such comprehensive data were not available about Omuta.

The largest single project—Buick City—was quite different in many ways from the other redevelopment projects in Flint in that it sought to revitalize the auto industry. Most other projects tried to diversify the local economic base, expanding into light manufacturing, tourism, and service/retail sectors. The Buick City experience was also a political home run for the mayor (Rutherford), the kind of coup that had happened infrequently in Flint's recent history.

Redevelopment Efforts from the Mid-1970s through the Mid-1980s
Much of the discussion of Omuta's redevelopment centered on the Omuta city government, but the city government has played a less central role in the story of Flint. This alone highlights a significant difference in the political structure and function between the two cities. To compare some of the key governmental issues we must ask, what was the role of government in Flint's revitalization efforts that started in the early 1970s? In the last 20 years, Flint's city government has acted primarily as a conduit for federal funds and has helped monitor the use of those funds for the federal government. The Omuta government did a lot of this type of activity, but, whereas the Omuta government was active in the planning and implementation, too, the Flint government—while in attendance on a consultative basis and as a monitor—largely left priority setting and project implementation to the private sector.

Why did Flint pursue a strategy of capital-intensive downtown redevelopment? The end product was a narrowly focused, construction-based strategy. The federal government policy environment, the fiscal structure, and the existence of private consulting firms largely account for the shape of Flint's redevelopment strategy. At all levels, government structure was important in a passive sense: it provided the legal means for the organization of interests in a nonprofit corporate format, and it permitted these interests to operate in a quasi-official capacity with a high degree of fiscal autonomy. The Mott Foundation and the Downtown Development Authority were central private sector players in the process, and neither could exist without statutes that permitted their creation. The policy environment at the federal level further shaped the playing

Table 9.2. Redevelopment Projects in Flint, 1970-1992

Project Name	Sponsor/ Applicant	Funding Sources	Main Funding Source	Innovation Source	1960s to Early 1970s	Early 1970s to mid-1980s	Mid-1980s to 1993	UDAG/CDBG Assisted	Policy Type	Dominant Player Type
UM–Flint Campus	2,3	2	2	lateral	X	X			growth	bureaucratic
Riverbank Park	3	1,3,4	1.3[a]	vertical/lateral	X	X		facilities imp.	facilities imp.	bureaucratic
St. John Industrial Park	3	1,2,3,4	1.3[a]	lateral	X	X		X	growth	bureau/busi
River Village	3,4	1,3,4	4	lateral	X	X		X	growth	bureaucratic
Riverfront Center	3,4	1,3,4	4	lateral		X		X	growth	political/busi
State office building	2	2	2	?	X	X			growth	bureaucratic
Windmill Place†	3,4	1,3,4	4	lateral		X		X	growth	bureaucratic
Autoworld	3,4	1,2,3,4	4	lateral	X	X		X	growth	political/busi
Buick City	3,4	1,2,3,4	4	lateral		X		X	growth	political/busi
Water Street Pavilion	3,4	1,2,3,4	4	lateral		X		X	growth	political/busi
Carriage Factory	3	1,4	4	lateral			X	X	growth	business
Schafer Square	3	1,2,4	2	lateral			X	X	growth	business
Oak Tech Park	3	3	3	lateral		X	X		growth	business
Oak Business Center	3, 4	3,4	4	lateral		X	X	X	growth	business

Note: 1 = national government; 2 = state; 3 = Flint; 4 = private capital
[a] Largest and second largest funding sources within $1 million of each other.

field, and this is the most proactive aspect of the institutional structure. Congress directed HUD to establish programs that Flint exploited on almost every major project. Had these programs not existed, Flint's redevelopment efforts would have been quite different, but there was little bureaucratic oversight—beyond the proper allocation of funds—in Flint. Local bureaucrats made sure that HUD grant money was spent as the national government intended, but they did not evaluate any programs for the redevelopment projects. Planning was rooted in the private sector, and the executive branch did not evaluate Flint's projects after completion and then adjust future spending accordingly. In terms of developing a proactive strategy for economic revitalization, government did not take the lead in organizing community interests. In this regard, Flint and Omuta are quite different.

An additional reason for Flint's capital-intensive redevelopment strategy was that such an approach was feasible. Large sums of money were available in both the public and private sectors for urban revitalization. The cooperative federalism of the 1970s strengthened federal-city relations and made local access to federal funds relatively easy (Conlan, 1988). The economic recession of the late 1970s and early 1980s made Flint an excellent candidate for revitalization efforts. Flint was one of the hardest-hit cities in the country. Unemployment soared to nearly 30 percent, and Flint's plight was covered extensively in the media. The mayor and other local elites saw Flint as a strong candidate for redevelopment and pushed government and private sources to help the city out of its slump. Their solicitation efforts were successful, since they attracted a great deal of redevelopment capital.

Private developers—hired as consultants and project managers—also account for Flint's capital-intensive redevelopment strategy. Developers sold ideas to the city and helped Flint copy ideas from other localities. Developers, architects, and other idea entrepreneurs were active in Flint's riverfront redevelopment, shopping-area revitalization, and tourism-promotion escapades. Skilled grant winners, they brought successful formulae from other cities and pushed Flint to emulate the efforts of other cities. Flint followed their lead, and ended up on a one-way path to mediocrity and failure.

Both cities demonstrate a degree of centralized policy making, but in different ways. City hall was the heart of the planning and priority process in Omuta, while in Flint economic elites quickly developed a private institution to focus (or centralize) the process, simultaneously legitimizing their interests and taking an early start in generating a policy response. The organization of interests seems to account for much in the Flint case, and the leading economic elites were well organized in the early 1970s when redevelopment plans were being formed. The president of the Mott Foundation and the Foundation's program officers, the mayor, and executives from local banks and from local General Motors facilities set the tone for 20 years of development in Flint.

FACI was a crucial institution that drove Flint's revitalization. In April 1970, 34 Flint area executives and civic leaders met at the Consumers Power Co. lodge at Tippy Dam (on the Big Manistee River) and made plans to establish FACI. Registered with the federal government as a private, nonprofit corporation in 1971, FACI's main purpose was to plan projects and programs in the Flint area. Its tax-exempt status limited the activities in which FACI could participate, so in May 1973 FACI established Flint Renaissance, Inc, under a different tax-exempt status. Flint Renaissance, Inc. was the "action" wing of FACI and had broader functional powers, such as the ability to obtain and preserve land and to accept gifts and donations from the private sector. Such funds and property could be used as seed money for project development (*Flint Journal*, May 2, 1973). The officers of both corporations were identical, and Harding Mott—whose family established the Mott Foundation—was the first chairman of the board. Saul Seigel, a prominent local businessman, was president.

Through the 1970s and 1980s, FACI was a leading force in Flint's revitalization efforts. Its major accomplishment was a comprehensive 10-year plan, called *Centric '80,* for Flint's downtown redevelopment. Five of the major projects done to renew the downtown area evolved from this plan: the University of Michigan—Flint campus; Riverbank Park, a flood control and beautification project on the Flint River; two industrial parks—St. John Industrial Park and Bishop Airpark; River Village, a planned residential community with a market component called Windmill Place; and Riverfront Center, comprising the Hyatt Hotel and a state office building. The City of Flint and the Mott Foundation cooperated with FACI to bring these projects to completion (Minutes of the Flint Area Conference, Inc., Board of Directors Meeting, August 12, 1987).

FACI helped set the agenda for Flint's redevelopment efforts in the 1970s and 1980s. The group's board of directors met every few months, and printed newsletters updated participants on the details of projects it had put in motion. In 1984, FACI expanded from a small group of local business elites to include a slightly broader "membership" of dues-paying participants (Wilson, 1985). Organizations and individuals could join FACI for $100 (or more). Conference members provided a willing pool of available local business talent that supported the organization personally and financially, contributing time, expertise, and organizational support to FACI projects. FACI was the coordinating arena for individuals from various local associations, including dominant players like the Downtown Development Authority and the Mott Foundation, and smaller (and shorter-lived) organizations such as the Center City Association, Forward Development Corporation, Flint Neighborhood Improvement and Preservation Project, Urban Coalition, and the International Downtown Executives Association (Sheaffer, 1981). Top city administrators and the mayor also attended meetings and were kept informed via the FACI information loop.

This description of FACI and the privatization of priority setting provides a structural explanation for the way in which priorities were set at the local level but not for the content of those early plans. As in Omuta, policy diffusion explains much of the local decision content, but, in Omuta, this diffusion occurred vertically and laterally: the city fit its ideas into the national government policy menu offerings, and the city gleaned ideas from other localities in Japan. Both types of diffusion exist in Flint. Industrial parks, amusement parks, and shopping malls were being built in other cities long before Flint caught on to them. Thus, on the issue of policy innovation Flint also resembles Omuta to some extent. Projects in both cities were innovative, in the sense that they were new to the city, but they were not innovative, in that they were already successful solutions elsewhere and had been truly new ideas in other localities first. There was little innovation in Flint's redevelopment policy, in part because local institutional machinations channeled the redevelopment process into a particular groove: FACI's organization and creation of a tightly knit local in-group tied to the Mott Foundation made it difficult for those with diverging ideas to become part of the process.

However, there is a second, more-compelling force that worked to discourage local innovation and push revitalization decision making in one definite direction: the availability of federal funding and the array of subsidies proffered by the federal government. It is probable that the intent of the federal programs was not to hinder local creativity in coming up with solutions. There certainly are examples of cities generating successful revitalization solutions that are not driven or dictated by national program priorities (Gittell, 1993), but, functionally speaking, that is exactly what happened. The funding available at the federal level solidified the priorities of local elites in Flint, and these priorities became the city's course of action. Once started down that path, the city won many grants and was thus able to implement the list of projects above. Flint became "path dependent" (North, 1990) to the extent that other innovative options appeared too costly, and continued work in this direction seemed the best approach.

Federal government grants are complicated to win and to administer. The paperwork involved is voluminous, and navigating the application, administration, and oversight report requirements demands special knowledge (Jurkiewicz interview). However, once a city figures out the formula, it can be quite successful in winning such grants. Flint administrators—in conjunction with several private development firms that specialized in winning and using such grants—discovered a "path of least resistance" by which they could receive large sums of money for projects they felt were risky. In essence, the city became addicted to federal development grants and spent the 1970s on a long capital-improvement high during which the city received more than $65 million from Washington (Department of Community Development Flint City Hall). This helps explain why Flint pursued subsidies from the federal government so diligently and why new innovative ideas in urban revitalization were not explored.

The UDAG funds were the key to implementing the major revitalization projects, even though the amount was only around 10 percent of the total final cost. Before the grants were approved, little real work occurred. After the grant approval came through, the Mott Foundation affirmed its large financial commitments, acquired land was cleared, and the projects really began to gel. The city, the state, and private developers also contributed substantial amounts, but the projects would not have moved forward without the prior votes of confidence from both HUD and the Mott Foundation.

Redevelopment Efforts from the Mid-1980s through the Early 1990s
By the mid-1980s, the succession of projects listed above had finally run their course. Plans and grants were completed, and the face of downtown Flint was dramatically different from the early 1970s. Unfortunately, there were no more people living in, working in, or using the downtown than there had been a decade earlier. Although city officials claim that 5,300 jobs were created by the $568 million in implemented projects (Department of Community Development, Flint City Hall), the population indicators suggest that Flint continued to decline. The perceived need for revitalization—or the need to keep doing something that at least seemed to be addressing the city's decline—prompted a new strategy based on smaller projects and programs. Business incubator programs and "buy local" campaigns signaled a resignation to the fact that Flint would have to struggle on in its present condition.

Having sunk substantial capital into a failed revitalization effort, local private-sector elites had little financial strength left for a renewed development offensive. This time the local government—in conjunction with more moderate private sector efforts—played a larger planning and implementation role. Government efforts sought to improve the economic security of those remaining residents and businesses in Flint. Small business loans were made possible through the Flint Economic Development Corporation (EDC), capitalized in 1979 with a revolving fund made up of city, federal EDA, and leftover CDBG money. This use of leftover federal funds is one of the truly innovative uses of the institutional structure found in Flint. The city realized that the enabling federal legislation and administrative guidelines called for the allocation of grants to cities, but it did not specify that the city had to use the money for grants to others; funds could be disbursed as loans, too. Flint officials found that these funds could be used to set up local revolving loan instruments and could thus be used over and over again once allocated (Kump interview). The Flint EDC made almost 100 loans between 1980 and 1993, two thirds of which were for business start-ups. The main point here is that these were *small* business initiatives: the average loan size was $45,000, and the maximum loan value was $200,000 (Kump interview).

The impact of these small business loan efforts is small in comparison to the large layoffs and cyclical employment trends of the automobile industry. But this program is part of the reshaping of Flint. Local strategists admit that Flint's goal should not be to rise to power in automobile manufacturing once more (King interview). The Mott Foundation's *1983 Annual Report* states, "Downtowns cannot be restored to their previous role as the single focal point for a city's shopping and office work. But neither are they doomed to extinction. In many cities, downtowns are developing new economic rationales and emerging as centers for specialty retailing, for retailing and dining out, and for knowledge-based professional services. . . . Thus, they are assuming different, but no less important roles in their communities" (39).

This change in Flint's redevelopment strategy, from a focus on large capital-intensive projects to an emphasis on small-business support, was caused by attitudinal changes at the local level. The city government found itself controlling foreclosed property that it did not want to own—the Auto-World facility and the Water Street Pavilion complex. The companies originally set up to manage the properties defaulted on their loans, and the city was thus forced to take possession. Moreover, following the series of large and risky projects of the 1970s and early 1980s, private capital was harder to come by. The Mott Foundation suffered from its own"Vietnam Syndrome," and it was reluctant to participate in large-scale projects in Flint, having been burned numerous times. Relations between the foundation and the city remained close, but neither side initiated big projects the way they had during the previous decade (King interview. Since HUD grants were to be used to leverage private capital investments and private capital was tight, city development administrators may have seen further efforts at federal grants as having a marginal return.

Changes in the fiscal environment do not provide much of an explanation for Flint's change in strategy. Although the federal block grant program went through a transformation under the Reagan administration, these changes do not appear to have had much of an impact on Flint's revitalization strategy. The block-grant application process was simplified and streamlined in the 1980s, but Flint submitted fewer grant applications during this decade. In addition to his campaign promise to get the government off the backs of the American people, President Reagan also sought to get the federal government off the backs of state and local officials. The new president met these goals in the housing and urban development policy area. Block-grant applications became smaller, and less detailed information was required prior to the start of a program. Although Congress opposed the reduction in oversight advocated by HUD, the agency used a variety of administrative tactics to carry out its goals (Rich 1993, 43-49). Under such a system of relaxed regulations, one might have expected Flint to apply for more federal grants. However, the city filed fewer applications.

One possible explanation lies in the political nature of the HUD grant application process. All of Flint's applications were supported by the city's most prominent congressional representatives, Representative Dale Kildee and Senator Donald Riegle, both Democrats. Flint's most-successful grant solicitation efforts came during the Carter Administration, when the Democratic administration looked favorably on a city with strong ties to organized labor in a state that had a Democratic governor at the time. Michigan was a strongly Democratic state during the Reagan years, too, a fact that may have made Flint's administrators pessimistic about applying for further grants.

The emphasis on small businesses did not prohibit support for larger business concerns as well. The Flint EDC also issued tax-exempt revenue bonds of up to $10 million, but these could be used for manufacturing only. Until 1986, bonds for commercial use were issued, too, but the Internal Revenue Service changed the rules for such commercial use of bonds, since too few jobs were being created and too many physicians and lawyers were using these funds to open offices (Kump interview). The rate on such bonds is 75 to 80 percent of the prime rate, and the bond is guaranteed by the city or the EDC. Local banks buy most of the bonds, for which the prices are negotiable; they are not set by legislation. Since 1980, roughly 20 of this type of bond issues have been conducted (Department of Community Development, Flint City Hall).

In the immediate aftermath of the big-project era, smaller ad hoc projects were conceived and implemented in Flint. The push for local business support and stabilization received a small boost in 1984, when FACI organized the first Flint Wares Fair, which generated business for area firms. The fair brought purchasing agents of area companies, school systems, and governmental agencies together at one site so representatives of area companies with goods and services could make contact. The idea behind the fair was to keep as many purchases by area businesses and agencies as possible in the local economy. In 1985, the fair generated $40 million in contracts to area companies, and it was credited by the state governor's office with creating roughly 2,000 new jobs in the years 1984 through 1986 (*Flint Journal*, August 6, 1986).

In an effort to learn from its mistakes, the city formulated a different approach to revitalization. FACI ceased operation in 1988 and was replaced by a new institution aimed at small-business promotion. The Genesee Economic Area Revitalization, Inc. (GEAR), a private, nonprofit corporation, was formed in 1989. Its stated (and apparently self-selected) purpose was "to oversee and coordinate economic development efforts in Genesee County" (*Flint Journal*, June 9, 1991). GEAR's origins are unclear, despite the fact that it emerged in the late 1980s. In his dissertation, Steven P. Dandaneau offers an extensive discussion of GEAR's economic redevelopment strategy for the Flint area. Dandaneau unsuccessfully sought information on GEAR's origins. He quotes Mark Davis, a Lafayette, Indiana, native who became GEAR's first executive director in 1990 as saying, "To be honest, I've never looked, it wasn't important, and it's not important. It's only important to academics. In the real world, what is important is what are they doing, OK?" (Dandaneau, 1992: 436).

Dandaneau cites a member of GEAR's strategic planning committee responding in a similar way, saying it is "hard to remember, and probably not real productive to try to sort out who started what" (436). Like FACI, GEAR was the product of local elites interested in promoting economic revitalization in Flint.

Dandaneau calls GEAR's efforts an "'enlightened' plan because no longer would Flint's elites depend upon the Mott Foundation, General Motors, nor any other benefactor for its progress and prosperity" (431). GEAR's earliest strategic document was the "Genesis Project," a 1989 Price Waterhouse, Inc., report commissioned by GEAR and paid for with the help of a federal EDA grant. It was a vague statement of priorities that called for the expansion and diversification of Flint's economy and a clearer vision of what diversification meant. Using this document as a springboard, GEAR developed a Strategic Economic Development Plan for Flint/Genesee County in 1990. Dandaneau claims the organization then shopped this plan around to more than 40 community groups, gatherings, and elected officials to solicit feedback and to generate local support for the report (436-37). The final version of the strategic plan was approved by GEAR's Board of Directors on July 9, 1991 (*Flint Journal*, July 10, 1991). Discussing the GEAR plan, Dandaneau states that the "... vision statement was originally drafted by an informal group headed by Flint businessman Dallas C. Dort (whose grandfather, J. Dallas Dort, was an important business partner of Billy Durant's). The membership of this group included the heads of the GM's Flint Automotive Division, AC Rochester Division, and the University of Michigan—Flint, the Mayor of Flint, Doug Roos of the Corporation for Enterprise development (whose organization was chiefly responsible for drafting GEAR's strategic plan), as well as others who would eventually hold positions on GEAR's strategic planning committee." (443).

The plan set out four overarching goals: (1) to develop a competitive, world-class workforce; (2) to diversify the economy by creating new non-GM manufacturing and skilled service jobs by supporting entrepreneurship and helping existing companies; (3) to make Flint/Genesee Counties a world center for applying information technology to manufacturing; and (4) to support and complement GM, UAW, and community efforts to retain jobs by understanding and responding to changing global trends (Dandaneau, 1992: 448-49). Toward this end, Dandaneau asserts, "GEAR seeks to reorganize the community's political administrative response away from what the Mott Foundation or any public sector institution might 'want it to be'" (464).

Although this strategy may look like a conscious choice on GEAR's part, in reality the city had few other options. The Mott Foundation was unwilling to lead a renewed redevelopment movement and was content to fund smaller projects while still licking its wounds from the previous decade of failure. Lists of funded projects included in the Foundation's annual reports indicate the shift from large projects requiring substantial capital investment to smaller projects aimed at improving quality of life, social welfare, and small-business opportunities. Large-scale government capital was not available for Flint to use either.

Flint did provide small businesses loans, 60 percent of which were given to small local start-up firms, but the city started following this strategy well before GEAR picked up on it. Flint started offering these loans when the EDA began its small-business loan program in 1979. My research suggests that federal program availability, not local elite enlightenment, prompted the shift in strategy and that it happened earlier than Dandaneau and GEAR would argue.

But the city was not ready to ignore the industry responsible for its booming growth earlier in the century. Flint was also eager to help Buick and other General Motors concerns and suppliers to increase production and create jobs locally. To this end, the city still granted tax abatements and declared special industrial zones for GM facilities. Between 1977 and 1988, Flint granted 20 tax abatements for GM concerns. From 1988 through October of 1993, Flint approved an additional 17 tax abatements for the automaker, not including abatements for GM suppliers and related businesses (Kump interview). Although these were always disputed and mulled over by the city council—the loss of property tax revenue was usually cited by those opposed to an abatement—the council never rejected an application for such a break or designation. Flint continued to be a struggling auto industry city.

CONCLUSIONS AND OVERVIEW OF FINDINGS

Local officials consistently take advantage of programs offered by national agencies. They use the existing system to the best possible advantage (meaning they extract as much as they can from the national government) and adapt local goals and plans to fit national policy frameworks. From the 1960s through the early 1980s, Omuta consistently capitalized on Tokyo's willingness to subsidize the rationalization of the coal industry, but this institutional environment did not encourage or facilitate conversion to other industries or any growth-oriented activities. And from the mid-1980s to the present, Omuta used national program incentives to implement projects focused on growth. From the early 1970s through the late 1980s, Flint used the federal block-grant programs to catalyze and legitimate large-scale projects intended to spark growth. Just as coal subsidies dried up for Omuta, the block-grant programs ended for Flint and the city was forced to change to a different strategy, this time based on small-scale capital and small business promotion.

Redevelopment efforts in Omuta and Flint failed because of a lack of innovation in the revitalization process. Both cities tried to use proven policies to address their economic woes, and few of their efforts produced positive results. Similar strategies emerged from distinctly different institutional structures, and these strategies focused on attracting new firms to the community, promoting tourism, and improving the quality of life in the community, to retain remaining residents and to entice people (and companies) to move there. Although the general strategies themselves were not inherently bad, the projects implemented to fulfill these strategies were copied closely from other cities. Expensive amusement parks that never achieved their goals, elaborate downtown shopping facilities that failed to draw shoppers to the city center, and industrial parks with standard incentive packages all added up to a lackluster revitalization scheme in both cities. Neither city devised a truly innovative plan to spark growth, although innovation might have provided a way out of their downward spiral.

What explains this failure to think problems through intelligently? The overall conclusion is that, despite some crossnational similarities in the situations facing each city, the local redevelopment strategies and processes in each country are remarkably different. The most notable similarity is that the institutional structure in both nations pushes cities to replicate successful projects from other communities rather than encouraging them to innovate new solutions appropriate to their own specific problems. "Supply-side" government programs that reward local compliance with national government programs, a heavy reliance on private sector consultants interested in replicating their own past successes, and a local tendency to copy other cities' successes all caused Omuta and Flint to choose redevelopment efforts that faced strong odds against them from the beginning.

Although neither city achieved truly successful revitalization, Omuta was far more successful at avoiding the pitfalls of a truly bad redevelopment policy. Put more bluntly, Omuta had more government involvement in its revitalization efforts, and these efforts, though not rousing successes, did not become embarrassing failures either. Omuta avoided making a bad situation worse. Flint had comparatively less government involvement in its revitalization efforts, leaving most of the funding and idea access to private interests. These private sector actors drove two large, expensive, keystone projects straight into blatant and decisive failure. The one truly successful redevelopment effort in Flint was accomplished only through a bit of luck and some local political intervention.

Despite the widely acknowledged differences between Japan and the United States, the impact of intergovernmental relations on urban redevelopment appears similar in both nations. In Japan, the recent rhetoric of local autonomy was caused by the reality of strong central government influence and local dependence on national programs. In the United States, where federalism ostensibly confers greater autonomy on localities, reliance on national programs and subsidies is strong, too.

The role of the national government in urban revitalization differs in Japan and the United States In a nutshell, the differences are as follows: In the Japanese case, political events do not affect the redevelopment process; bureaucrats dominate the game, and they operate in and around a set of stable national policy programs that do not change over time. The government finances much of the revitalization effort directly through grants, and indirectly through grants and loans from an array of public corporations, which control funds accounting for about 40 percent of the national budget. Such enterprises perform many different functions, although this study is concerned only with how they affect urban redevelopment efforts. According to Johnson, Japan's public corporations "make loans to implement official industrial policies and to aid low productivity or declining sectors of the economy. They also spend funds to strengthen the industrial infrastructure or to develop resources. They help stabilize prices; they produce revenue; and they do research" (1978, 16). For Omuta, the Japan Development Bank and the Regional Promotion and Facilities Corporation (*Chiiki Shinkô Seibi Kôdan*) are two of the more important public corporations.

On the American side, politics matters more than bureaucracy. This accounts for the variation in federal programs over time. As new administrations assume control in Washington, they change the policy environment within which cities must operate. Unlike their Japanese counterparts, whose policy options seldom change, American cities are constantly faced with updated and newly refocused grant programs from which they must extract benefits. Political connections and clout seem to count for more than technocratic savvy in the American grant system. Although federal programs are an important part of Flint's redevelopment effort, their main function is to leverage private investment. Private funding sources are even more important, and these include private nonprofit foundations and venture capital investors. Philanthropic organizations are a crucial part of urban revitalization in America, and they present an interesting dilemma for cities benefiting from their generosity. On the one hand they provide the means to implement large projects that might not otherwise come to fruition. On the other hand, they are not accountable to anyone, and they carry ideological baggage that can constrain cities and push them down one particular developmental path.

NOTES

1. This is a controversial observation based only on two cases presented here. It is not necessarily true in other cities and policy areas. Some Japanese policy areas are far more politicized than others. Construction and agriculture are highly politicized, for example, while industrial policy is more bureaucratic (Muramatsu, 1986; Sakakibara, 1992).

2. Reed (1986) supports this statement. However, Samuels tempers this comparison. He points to the duplication of programs in the Japanese system—

caused by *tutewari gyosei*, the vertically fragmented system of administration—as evidence of room for creativity (Samuels, 1983:247). Duplication does exist in both systems, as it does in Western European nations, but Reed asserts that the epidemic of duplication in the United States is the worse than the instances of duplication in Japan. Japan is comparatively centralized and orderly. For example, the case of rampant social service spending without oversight depicted by Derthick (1975) would be unimaginable in the Japanese system.

INTERVIEWS

Goto Kanichi. Director, Research Division, Kyushu Bureau of International Trade and Industry, MITI. February 16, 1993.

Jurkiewicz, Nancy. Special Operations Coordinator, Flint Department of Community Development. March 8, 1994.

King, Richard. Economic Development Administrator, Flint City Hall. March 8, 1994.

Kump, Frederick. Economic Development/TIFA Manager, Flint City Hall. March 8, 1994.

Muto Yasukatsu. Planning and Promotion Section Chief, Omuta City Hall. December 22, 1992.

Nishimura Satoru. Omuta City Assembly official. May 24, 1993.

Sato Seiji. Coal Mining Area Development Section Chief, Regional Development Division, Fukuoka Prefecture. May 27, 1993.

REFERENCES

Barnekov, Timothy K. 1989. *Privatism and Urban Policy in Britain and the United States*. Oxford: Oxford University Press.

Brace, Paul. 1993. *State Government and Economic Performance*. Baltimore: Johns Hopkins University Press.

Calder, Kent E. 1988. *Crisis and Compensation: Public Policy and Political Stability in Japan*. Princeton: Princeton University Press.

Campbell, John C. 1992. *How Policies Change: The Japanese Government and the Aging Society*. Princeton: Princeton University Press.

Cole, Robert E. 1989. Strategies *for Learning: Small-Group Activities in American, Japanese, and Swedish Industry*. Berkeley: University of California Press.

Conlan, Timothy J. 1988. *New Federalism: Intergovernmental Reform and Political Change from Nixon to Reagan*. Washington, DC: The Brookings Institution.

Dahl, Robert. 1961. *Who Governs?* New Haven: Yale University Press.

Dandaneau, Steven P. 1992. *Ideology and Dependent Deindustriali-zation: A Study of Local Responses to Flint, Michigan's, Social and Cultural Decline from a Critical Theory Perspective.* Ph.D. dissertation, Brandeis University.

Department of Community Development, Flint City Hall.

Derthick, Martha. 1975. *Uncontrollable Spending for Social Service Grants.* Washington, D.C.: The Brookings Institution.

Dore, Ronald P. 1978. *Shinohata: A Portrait of a Japanese Village.* New York: Pantheon.

Edsforth, Ronald. 1987. *Class Conflict and Cultural Consensus: The Making of a Mass Consumer Society in Flint, Michigan.* New Brunswick: Rutgers University Press.

Eisinger, Peter. 1990. "Do the American states do industrial policy?" *British Journal of Political Science* 20:509-35.

Fujita, Kuniko, and Richard C. Hill, eds. 1993. *Japanese Cities in the World Economy.* Philadelphia: Temple University Press.

Fukuoka Prefecture. 1992. *Conditions in Coal-Producing Regions of Fukuoka Prefecture (Fukuoka-ken Santan Chiiki no Genjô),* Fukuoka.

Gelfand, Mark. 1975. *A Nation of Cities: The Federal Government and Urban America, 1933-1965.* New York: Oxford University Press.

Gittell, Ross J. 1993. *Renewing Cities.* Princeton: Princeton University Press.

Hein, Laura. 1990. *Fueling Growth: The Energy Revolution and Eco-nomic Policy in Postwar Japan.* Cambridge, Mass.: Council on East Asian Studies, Harvard University.

Johnson, Chalmers. 1978. *Japan's Public Policy Companies.* Washington, DC: American Enterprise Institute.

Judd, Dennis, and Michael Parkinson, eds. 1990. *Leadership and Urban Regeneration: Cities in North America and Europe.* Beverly Hills, Calif.: Sage Urban Affairs Annual Reviews.

Kyushu Trade and Industry Bureau. 1992. *Present Conditions of Kyushu Coal Production Areas (Kyushu Santan Chiiki no Genkyô).* Fukuoka: Kyushu Tsûsho Sangyô Kyoku.

Local Financial Affairs Association (*Chihô Zaimu Kyôkai*). 1992. *How to Understand Local Independent Projects (Kore de Wakaru Chihô Tandoku Jigyô).* Tokyo: Local Financial Affairs Association.

Minutes of the Flint Area Conference, Inc. Board of Directors Meeting, August 12, 1987.

Monkkonen, Eric H. 1988. *America Becomes Urban: The Development of United States Cities and Towns, 1780-1980.* Berkeley: University of California Press.

Mott Foundation, *1983 Annual Report,* Detroit, 1984.

Muramatsu, Michio. 1986. "Center-Local Political Relations in Japan: A Lateral Competition Model," *Journal of Japanese Studies* 12:303-27.

Nikkan Kôgyô Shimbun, April 21, 1989.

Nikkan Sanyô Shimbun, November 9, 1988.

North, Douglass S. 1990. *Institutions, Institutional Change, and Economic Performance*. New York: Cambridge University Press.

Omuta City. 1979-1989. *Citizens' Lives (Shimin no Kurashi)*, annual fact publication.

"Overview of the Coal Area Promotion Policy," January, 1993. Infor-mation provided by the Kyushu Bureau of International Trade and Industry, MITI.

Ozawa, Ichirô. 1993. *Nihon Kaizô Keikaku* (A Plan for Remodeling Japan). Tokyo: Kôdansha.

Peterson, Paul E. 1981. *City Limits*. Chicago: University of Chicago Press.

Planning Section of the Ministry for Local Autonomy. 1993. *Tandoku Jigyô Handobukku (Independent Project Handbook)*. Tokyo: Dai-Ichi Hôki.

Reed, Steven R. 1986. *Japanese Prefectures and Policymaking*. Pittsburgh: University of Pittsburgh Press.

Rich, Michael J. 1993. *Federal Policymaking and the Poor*. Princeton: Princeton University Press.

Sakakibara, Eisuke. 1992. "The Japanese Politico-Economic System and the Public Sector." In *Parallel Politics*. Edited by Samuel Kernell. Washington, D.C.: Brookings Institution.

Samuels, Richard J. 1983. *The Politics of Regional Policy in Japan: Localities Incorporated?* Princeton: Princeton University Press.

————. 1987. *The Business of the Japanese State: Energy Markets in Comparative and Historical Perspective*. Ithaca: Cornell University Press.

Scheaffer, James S. 1981. Report to the Board and Members of the Flint Area Conference, Inc. October 1.

Sôrifu Shakai Hoshô Seido Shingikai Jimukyoku, ed. 1993. *Social Security Statistical Yearbook (Shakai Hoshô Tôkei Nenpô)*. Tokyo: Hôken.

Steiner, Kurt. 1965. *Local Government in Japan*. Stanford: Stanford University Press.

Stone, Clarence N., and Heywood T. Sanders. 1987. *The Politics of Urban Development*. Lawrence: University Press of Kansas.

Stone, Clarence N. 1989. *Regime Politics: Governing Atlanta, 1946-1988*. Lawrence: University Press of Kansas.

Summary of the Six Laws Relating to Coal (*Sekitan Kankei Roppô no Gaiyô*). Internal document received from Fukuoka Prefecture's Regional Development Division, Coal Mining Area Development Section.

United States Bureau of the Census, *County Business Patterns*. Wilson, John R.
    1985. Notes from address delivered June 4, 1985. Wilson was the
    Chairman of the Flint Area Conference, Inc., and General Manager of
    General Motors' AC Spark Plug Division, located in Flint.
Yokota, Mitsuo and Ebata, Kenji. 1993. *Kôkyô Shisetsu Zaigen Benran (Public
    Facility Finance Handbook)*. Tokyo: Gyôsei, Inc.
Zaisei Tôkei, Ministry of Finance Shûkei-kyoku Chôsa-ka, 1992.

Written in 1970, Origas's essay is among the earliest of those dealing with Sôseki as a writer of "city fiction." He contrasts Sôseki's vision of London with an earlier depiction of Berlin by that other doyen of Meiji era Japanese literature, Mori Ogai. Being another well-known Meiji intellectual who had lived (much earlier than Sôseki) in the West, Ogai, too, is frequently seen as a model of modern Japan's encounter with the West. Origas addresses more specifically these authors' very different literary approaches in their respective depiction of these two cities of Europe. Ogai's laudatory description of Berlin in the story *Maihime* (The Dancing Girl, 1890) begins, "But suddenly here I was, standing in the middle of this most modern of European capitals":

> My eyes were dazzled by its brilliance, my mind was dazed by the riot of color. To translate Unter den Linden as 'under the Bodhi tree,' would suggest a quiet secluded spot. But just come and see the groups of men and women sauntering along the pavements that line each side of that great thoroughfare as it runs, straight as a die, through the city . . . Carriages ran silently on asphalt roads. Just visible in the clear sky between the towering buildings were fountains cascading with the sound of heavy rain. Looking into the distance, one could see the statue of the goddess on the victory column. She seemed to be floating halfway to heaven from the midst of the green trees on the other side of the Brandenburg Gate. All these myriad sights were gathered so close at hand that it was quite bewildering for the newcomer. (153)

Traveling to Europe 15 years earlier than Sôseki, closer to the apex of the Western-influenced "civilization and enlightenment" (*bunmei kaika*) period in Japan, it perhaps should not surprise us that Ogai shows such enthusiasm for the avenues and neoclassicist architecture of Munich. Well read in Western literature and philosophy, Ogai appreciated well the philosophical underpinnings of this idealized landscape. He uses this knowledge in constructing his own literary representation of the scene. As described by Origas, Ogai mixes the assorted elements of the city as an artist would the colors of his palette; these he orders into a classical model of a city, drawn in linear perspective, as a composite of its major avenues and monumental architecture. Indeed, Ogai's relation of the uncanny order and synchronism in which these at first multifarious elements are gathered "so close at hand" seems an Occidentalist exaggeration of the rational ideal.

Although Berlin and London were always very different cities, in his depiction of the latter Sôseki seems to despair of finding any workings of logic in the modern city. In contrast to Ogai's idealized panorama of the city, the narrator of London Tower appears to find it difficult to see beyond the madness of the crowds and traffic swirling about him: "On the street I was afraid of being carried away by the surging crowd. In my lodgings I was afraid a railway train might crash into the wall. Night and day I could have no peace of mind. A two years' stay among so many people might well, I feared, turn my nerves into a state like that of heated glue" (23). Origas views Sôseki's enumeration of these dispersive elements, the surging crowds and the confusing network of trains and city cars, as the discovery of a modern aesthetic of the city. These elements certainly are a great contrast to the more classical organization of Ogai's Munich where "men and women saunter . . . along the pavements," and "carriages run . . . silently on asphalt roads."

Particularly important in Origas's interpretation is Sôseki's use of the more dispersive spider-web system of the train line, as opposed to the avenue or monumental architecture, as the organizing principle of his view of the city. Origas suggests that it is this less concentric description that makes Sôseki's description of the early twentieth-century city so persuasive, and (though not stated by Origas in these exact terms) so "modern." Yet, as much as by the innovative style of London Tower, readers are likely to be struck by Sôseki's at times dark view of the city. Of significance to a following discussion of the manner in which the depiction of the city has changed over the years, the contrast seen between Sôseki' and Ogai's above descriptions may be due more to a difference in chronology than to artistic philosophy. In the intervening 30-year period between Ogai and Sôseki's accounts, depiction of the modern city in many Western accounts as well had passed from early enthusiasm to more critical renderings of the dark side of city life.

From this earliest piece, one can see a reflection of Sôseki's philosophy of modernism and modernization. Although Origas treats Sôseki's London experience as formative in his developing philosophy of the modern city, Sôseki appears to have had a more general view of modernization, seeing it as a process taking place in all countries, if only belatedly in Japan. To date, many critics have been interested in Sôseki's works as examples of a Japanese literary modernism, often speaking of the "isolation of the individual" or the "modern self" (kindai jiga) in Sôseki's fiction; these being seen as signs of his standing as a modernist literary figure. Less frequently considered are the many examples in Sôseki's fiction of the more physical aspects and origins of that alienation. In its urban settings, whether in London or Tokyo, Sôseki's fiction includes the urban crowd, often seen as alienating in itself, as well as the street cars, electrical lines, asphalt, dust, and general salmagundi of the modern city. These elements are not presented by chance, but according to a philosophy of both modernism and modernization. In the speech "Civilization of Modern-Day Japan," Sôseki gives a simple yet astute synopsis of such a philosophy: "We have these two intertwining processes: one involving inventions and mechanisms that spring from the desire to conserve our labor as much as possible, and the other involving amusements that spring from the wish to consume our energies as freely as possible. As these two intertwine like a textile's warp and woof, combining in infinitely varied ways, the result is this strange, chaotic phenomenon we know as our modern civilization" (268). Although Sôseki's depiction of the city was given less attention in previous periods of scholarship, the author here and in other writings is clearly interested not only in the psychological but also in the physical dimensions of modernity. While this paper acknowledges the significance of Sôseki's fiction as products of "international" modernism, of more immediate interest here are indications in his novels of repercussions brought by modernization on the landscape of Tokyo.

Treating Sôseki's well-known novel *Sanshiro* (1908) as city fiction, this chapter will examine the author's depiction of Tokyo in that time when much of the literal landscape of the city was rapidly changing. In attending to local detail, it is not the intent of this paper to remake Sôseki as a "local-color" writer, but to demonstrate how, as part of his interest in the issues of modernity, Sôseki was interested in the specific question of Tokyo's increasing modernization.

SANSHIRÔ AS GEOGRAPHIC IRONY

One of Sôseki's better-known longer fictions, *Sanshirô* has commonly been read in universalist terms as a classic tale of the country lad lost in the big city. Elements of the novel highlight the great distance between the capital and the protagonist's, Sanshirô's, birthplace of Kyûshû, and, although we will look later at representations of more localized settings in the novel, the first chapter of *Sanshirô*, especially, prompts broader interpretations. For the reader less familiar with Sôseki, the following section will attempt to give some indication of how *Sanshirô* can and has been read in broad national, international, or universalist terms. Later, it will be argued that, among these often quite ponderous broader themes, which we might think of collectively as associated with the question of modernism, Sôseki weaves an ironic counter-narrative dealing more with the effects of modernization, which counter-narrative (and hence the title of this section) often involves local geography.

In the first chapter of *Sanshirô*, the main character makes the long train trip from his home town of Kumamoto to Tokyo, where he is to begin studies at Imperial University. To mark the ontological boundaries crossed by Sanshirô in this trip, the narrator notes how the complexions of the local women, "at first very dark, almost black, turned lighter and lighter as the train drew closer to Hiroshima, then Osaka and Kyoto" (3). The spatial and temporal distance between Kumamoto and Tokyo is extenuated by such observations of otherness, and this first chapter as a whole may elicit a reading as an allegory of the relationship of the provinces to the capital. Another important broad theme is the main character's cognizance that he is setting out on the great adventure of life.

The opening chapter thus switches between what we might define loosely as
themes involving a "national" perspective, or the consideration of province and
capital, and themes of a more "universal" nature. As a coming-of-age narrative,
the chapter introduces several mock-epic elements. For instance, during the
train ride, Sanshirô dreams of the new world that awaits him in Tokyo: "He was
going to Tokyo. He would enter the University. He would meet famous scholars,
associate with students of taste and breeding, do research in the library, write
books. Society would acclaim him, his mother would be overjoyed" (10). In this
universal coming-of-age narrative, throughout the novel Sanshirô acts the archetypal innocent, a naive idealist who, like Candide, encounters a reality so at
odds with what he had been led to expect. Such universalist themes in *Sanshirô*
have certainly helped secure its popularity to the present; another reason perhaps that some are reluctant to consider the more local aspects of his works.

Sanshirô and other of Sôseki's novels encompass a wide range of themes.
While James Fujii writes that as part of the modern Japanese canon Sôseki's
novels often "avoid marking the text with . . . the aspect of modernity that man-
ifests itself as international aggression," *Sanshirô* includes consideration even
of such larger political issues. The theme of Sanshirô as the naive provincial
coming to the city is complimented actually by a narrative of Japan as the neo-
phyte player on the international stage. Toward the end of the ride to Tokyo,
Sanshirô meets up with a man "the likes of whom," the narrator relates, "he had
never expected to meet . . . after the Russo-Japanese War." As they approach Mt.
Fuji, the man comments on this national symbol: "It's the finest thing Japan has
to offer, the only thing we've got to boast about. The trouble is, of course, it's
just a natural object. It's been sitting there for all time. We certainly didn't make
it" (15). In still other details of his conversation, this man presents the view that
Japan's material accomplishments do not measure up to those of the West. To
these comments, Sanshirô answers, "But still, . . . Japan will start developing
from now on at least." To this the man replies, "Japan is going to perish" (15). In
seeming contradiction of Fujii's picture of Sôseki, elements of this chapter contain other such critical evaluations of Japan's modernity.

Sôseki certainly provides material for the debate of the emergence and
character of modernity East and West and other larger themes. Engaged in such
issues, readers often overlook however the implications in Sôseki's novels of
the repercussions of modernity at the local level. In *Low City, High City*, a history of modern Tokyo to the earthquake of 1923, Edward Seidensticker writes
that "the story of modern literature is, like the story of prime ministers,
philosophers, and the like, a national one, something that happened in Tokyo
but is not of it" (1983:251). However, read with an eye for local circumstances,
even fiction by such a grand figure of modern Japanese literature as Sôseki can
be seen as part of the story of Tokyo.

To return to our discussion of the first chapter of *Sanshirô*: Learning that
Sanshirô is travelling to Tokyo to enter the university, the man he encounters on

the train makes the following rather peculiar comment: "Tokyo is bigger than Kumamoto. And Japan is bigger than Tokyo. And bigger than Japan . . . even bigger than Japan, surely, is the inside of your head. Don't ever surrender yourself—not to Japan, not to anything. You may think that what you're doing is for the sake of nation, but let something take possession of you like that, and all you do is bring it down" (15). This passage has been interpreted in different ways by critics, for this phrase in a humorous way manages to include such diverse and broad themes as nation, regionalism, or the humanist ideal of the inalienable spirit of the individual. This strange man, both the reader and Sanshirô later discover, is actually a professor, Hirota, from the Imperial University, which Sanshirô is to attend. In the critical essay accompanying his translation of *Sanshirô*, Jay Rubin (1977) sees Hirota as a model of what he calls the "modern urban individualist," interpreting the above remarks as the words of "a man intent on preserving his own broad inner world" (227). Although such a universalist ideal is apparent in the phrase that the inside of Sanshirô's head is bigger than Japan, elements such as the caution against surrendering oneself to nation seem more directly political. It would probably go against the intent of the passage to suggest that it includes also consideration of locale, for the inclination of the passage moves from the local and specific to the general and universal, from Kumamoto to Tokyo to Japan to the unbound universe of the imagination. Largely on the basis of this first chapter, in which Sanshiro moves from Kumamoto to the new world of the modern city, critics have seen the work as a whole as a discussion of modernity in broadest terms. Rubin writes that Sanshirô does not begin to understand the meaning of Hirota's words until "he has gotten a taste of the big city"; however, as we shall see, the Tokyo of *Sanshirô* only rarely lives up to the ideal of the city as playground of modern individualism.

In the last lines of this first chapter, Sanshirô concludes that, although he had never met such a man in Kumamoto, "there were bound to be men like this everywhere in Tokyo" (16). Sanshirô's first impression of Tokyo, seen at the beginning of the second chapter, is indeed of a world completely different from Kumamoto: "Tokyo was full of things that startled Sanshirô. First, the ringing of the street-car bells startled him, and the crowds that got on and off between rings. Next to startle him was Marunouchi, the busy commercial center of the city" (17). Through the enumeration of the multifarious sounds and scenes of the city—the streetcar bells, the commercial center, the crowds—Sôseki creates an image of the modern capital as demographic center of the nation and locus of material progress. However, introducing the equally important theme of the cost of modernization, more specific details of locale describe a city undergoing particularly severe change: "Everywhere he walked there were piles of lumber, heaps of rock, new homes set back from the street, old warehouses rotting in front of them. Everything looked as though it were being destroyed, and at the same time everything looked as though it were under reconstruction" (X).

Though at times neglected by critics, themes of philosophical modernity in Sôseki's works are counterbalanced by the above types of descriptions of often destructive physical modernization.

Present-day readers of Sôseki may not be aware of the great changes taking place in Tokyo at this date. It is odd, however, that critics too seldom take into account the literal transformation of Tokyo when considering the question of modernism and Sôseki's works. In *Dai-Tokyo no Shisô* (The Topography of Greater Tokyo), Noboru Haga defines the period 1906 to 1910 as the final phase of a series of projects through which the lineaments of modern Tokyo were set (9). Giving a more contemporary and participant view of modernization, an official guide in English to the city of Tokyo compiled by "The Municipal Authorities" in 1914, reports that in these years the "main streets of the city have been widened, entailing the removal and rebuilding of all the houses on one side of the street, at a labour and expense so vast and complicated that very few cities would have attempted it" (58). It is hard to imagine that any author of a work set in the city in this period could not be affected by such changes, and, written in 1908 during which the most drastic of these changes were taking place, we see clear images of the "piles of lumber, heaps of rock, new homes set back from the street, old warehouses rotting in front of them" such renovations entailed.

In the work *Visions of the Modern City*, critics William Sharpe and Leonard Wallock (1987) present three transitions undergone by the modern city, the stages of "concentrated settlement," "center city with suburban ring," and "decentered urban field." In fiction, too, they assert, "it is possible to distinguish three major periods of metaphoric reevaluation and changing terminology that correspond roughly to the three phases of urban growth" (11). Thus, we are given Dickens, Mayhew, and Engels as authors who "attempted to portray an unprecedented urban environment" (i.e., the "concentrated settlement phase"); Joyce and T.S. Eliot are cited as examples of the modernist, metropolitan sensibility that celebrated representations of city life ("center city with suburban ring"); and, finally, Pynchon, or, on the more popular front, Tama Janowitz, and Jay McInerney, as writers who "doubt . . . whether the contemporary city has any logic at all" (24) ("decentered urban field"). Though useful, this definition seems overly determined. As we will see in the following section, Sôseki, though writing in a more traditional idiom, was perhaps as skeptical of the logic of the modern city as is Pynchon. Unlike London or Paris, which had undergone successive periods of reconstruction in their development as modern cities, Edo, as Seidensticker demonstrates in *High City Low City,* went through a much more rapid transformation in its recreation as the capital of modern Japan. In considering literature written and published in Tokyo, it seems that writing was only rarely afforded the envious opportunity to metaphorically "reevaluate" the actual established city but more often seems to chase the apparition of what the city might be, or might have been. Details of Sôseki's works include signs of the tensions of that rapid growth which would perhaps qualify Tokyo as the original "decentered urban field" of modern cities.

Sôseki, in the second chapter of *Sanshirô,* gives a vision of a city more complex than suggested by the convenient definitions of "concentrated settlement" or "center city with suburban ring." The scale of Marunouchi and the commercial center of the city, the narrator relates, startle Sanshirô, but what startled him most of all "was Tokyo itself, for no matter how far he went, it never ended." This description seems to respond directly to the rapid growth then occurring in Tokyo. This growth was so rapid that, along with the renovations that accompanied it, it nearly subsumed the older city. The city authorities attribute the rapid spread of the city to the new electric street car system: "With the introduction of the electric car system a marvelous transformation has taken place. Being no longer compelled to live within easy reach of daily work the labourer now can take a house in any part of the city and arrive at his work in a few minutes by tram. This has caused a rush of the poorer inhabitants toward the suburbs, and even many of the better classes are moving thither, causing a rapid expansion of the city limits" (31). This "marvelous transformation" of course continues today, although more often it is the salary man who must commute, not a few minutes, but an hour, or even a few hours, to his work in the city. Even by the time of the publication of *Sanshiro,* as the handbook relates, the numerous villages about Tokyo were fast being swallowed up by the expanding city. Though often overlooked in broader readings of *Sanshirô,* the effects of this rapid expansion can be seen in the local landscape of the novel. It is in this very literal sense that the local landscape—scarred by modernization—of *Sanshirô* is used as an ironic counter-narrative to its more often noted themes of modernism (fig. 10.1)

As metaphor of modernization, trains play an important role in this and other Sôseki works. As we have discussed, the opening chapter of this novel could be regarded as a relation of the train line as modus operandi connecting the capital to the provinces. Writing not long after the "civilization and enlightenment" period during which Japan enthusiastically adopted elements of the political institutions and culture of the West, Sôseki's works record the concurrent and continuing changes in the landscape of Tokyo. In this, they depict tensions involved in the attempt to transform Edo into Tokyo, the "chief structural metaphor," as Berque calls it, of modern Japan (1993:46).

The city authorities quoted above relate pointedly that "being the metropolis of the Empire people from all quarters are constantly making visits to take in the sights. All the great railway lines have terminals in the capital and all passengers pass through Tokyo" (63-64). Among the more promising characteristics of tram traffic in Tokyo, the authorities continue, are "not only the increase of population and tourist business . . . but the manner in which the average citizen is acquiring the riding habit, which is developing very remarkably" (64)

Figure 10.1 Tokyo 1916

This seems to be given as further proof of Tokyo's modernity. A chart is presented, in fact, for the average rides per inhabitant in Tokyo versus figures for major western cities: the citizens of Tokyo, they report, average 109 trips per year; the citizens of London, 199; those of New York, 316 rides; those of Paris, 213 rides; and the citizens of Berlin ride the trams 237 times a year. In the train's role in the process of modernization, however, the national and other major train lines worked hand in hand with the growing network of city-bound public transportation. It is in these more local circumstances, in Sôseki's novels, that we see the impact of modernization.

Written in a period when the extensive system of public transportation now recognized at the Yamanote line was all but set in place, the authorities exuberance is to be expected. In *Sanshirô*, however, characters are much less enthusiastic about such new developments, a sign of their ambivalence regarding modernity in general. Nonoshiro, a professor at Imperial University who plays the more conservative counterpart of the individualist Hirota, comments of the system of street cars, "Don't you hate those things: They're so noisy! . . . I don't know how to transfer by myself. . . . The conductor has to help me. They've built so damned many lines the past few years, the more 'convenient' it gets, the more confused I get. It's like my research" (25). Although attention has been given to broader readings of Sôseki's novels as discussions of Japan's place in the modern, international world, we can see here, again, Sôseki's consideration of the impact of modernization at the local level.

The trains, as well as the upheaval entailed in the projects above described, certainly contributed to the flight of city inhabitants referred to poetically by Seidensticker as "the diaspora to the suburbs and beyond of the children of the Low City" (1983:210). Paradoxically, this occurred in the same period that large numbers of provincials, of whom Sanshirô would be one example, were drawn to Tokyo by the promise of the modern city. In the following, it will be discussed further how Sôseki contrasts the ideal image of the city as modern utopia, or as powerful central capital, with less ideal local conditions.

While Sharpe and Wallock speak of the three major periods of the city and their "metaphoric reevaluation" in literature, in *Sanshirô* the city is not strictly an account of actual conditions. Although, on the basis of details discussed thus far, we should consider Sôseki as a writer who did not shrink to depict unsettling aspects of the modern city, critic Isoda Kôichi has argued that most Japanese writers responded to modernization in fact by recreating Tokyo in their fiction as a village, in which traditional practices and associations between characters still persisted much as we imagine they had done in the Edo period. Influenced perhaps by Isoda, Paul Anderer, in his essay "Tokyo and the Borders of Modern Japanese Fiction," is especially critical of what he sees as a failure of modern Japanese fiction to address the challenges of the new modern city landscape: "This city, whose population doubled between 1895 and 1923, and whose topography, architecture, and transportation systems underwent change . . . has functioned in literature as a largely alien and intrusive presence, and lies as far beyond the borders of Japanese fiction as a foreign country" (1987:227). While Isoda's and Anderer's points can be supported by numerous works that seem only able to approach the topic of Tokyo by recreating it as a provincial *furusato*, there are others (often by lesser-known writers) that do attempt to depict various sides of the modern city. Although Sôseki has not in the past been regarded as a writer specifically of city fiction, Maeda Ai has called him the "only writer of his generation who diligently pursued the meaning of the changing Yamanote topos and the manner of lives engraved therein" (1982:419). Although at times he may embellish the picturesque in his novels, Sôseki attempts to deal at least with the growth and changes of the city and the depiction of those newer areas Seidensticker derisively calls "that great abstraction 'suburbia'" (1983:251).

In an approach representatively universalist, Donald Keene describes *Sanshirô* as "an archetypal tale of the boy from the hinterland who is at first impressed by everything he sees in Tokyo, even the crowded trams . . ." (1984:326). Critics often details how, at first enthusiastic, Sanshiro gradually becomes alienated by the city, this taken as a representation of the isolation of the modern individual. We get such an impression of that isolation in the narrator's synopsis of Sanshirô's view of Tokyo: "His own world and the real world were aligned on a single plane, but nowhere did they touch. The real world would move on in its uproar and leave him behind. The thought filled him with a great unease. Sanshirô stood and watched the activity of the streetcars and the trains, of people in white and people in black, and this was how he felt" (18). The word *unease* (*fuan*) in this passage has been used in fact by Japanese critics as a catch word for Sôseki's representation of the dislocation of the modern self. However, as seen, in his novel *Sanshirô,* Sôseki is also quite specific as to the more direct stimulus of that unease, i.e., the uproar and activity of the city, its construction projects, its streetcars and trains, and its crowds of people.

Following sections of the novel as well might be read, in ironical fashion, as a provincial's disappointment with the lavish promises of the city. One aspect of this novel, however, that has discouraged those interested in Sôseki as a writer of city fiction is that it is only in the second chapter (discussed above) that we get a view of central Tokyo. The principle setting of the novel is the outlying ward of Hongô, where Sanshirô lives in a boardinghouse and attends Imperial University. To older inhabitants of the time especially, this northern ward might have been considered only marginally part of Tokyo (fig. 10.2).

More difficult to characterize than the low city areas, Sôseki creates a new space for his fiction by using these areas often as ironic commentaries on both the issues of modernism and other rapidly modernizing areas of the city. In including such areas, collectively *Sanshirô* presents the reader with two images of Tokyo, one of the crowded, chaotic construction zone of the more central areas, which we have seen, and another of the outer areas, which vary in their depiction as either idyllic preserves of nature or, somewhat contradictorily, as wastelands teeming with new émigrés.

Influenced as we are by the conception of the Yamanote region in general as the more settled and prosperous area of Tokyo, Hongô may not at first strike us as an incongruous setting for a tale of "modern" Tokyo. In the restoration period, however, this area was nearly emptied, regaining in population only from mid-Meiji. It is a curious contrast to compare the presentation of Hongo in maps created in the first decade of the twentieth century with those from 20 or even 30 years earlier, for, perhaps because of the large blank area occupied by the university, the ward seems little changed from the time in which it was part of the large Maeda family estate. Edward Seidensticker (1983) describes

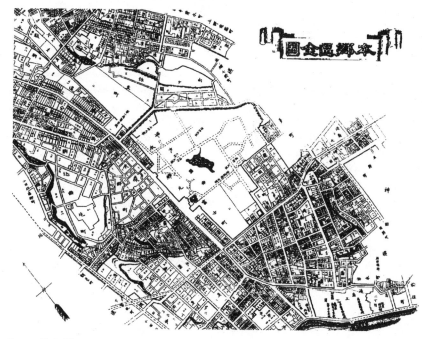

Figure 10.2 Hongo

the shifting boundaries of Tokyo from Meiji to the present by suggesting that a line drawn north and south from the westernmost point of the Meiji city would divide the present city into approximately equally populated parts. Hongô was neither of the old centers nor directly in line with this great population shift to the west. Despite the presence of Imperial University—which, incidentally, had only been moved to the site in the 1880s—Hongô at that time could be considered rural in areas. Regarded as a backwater of sorts, Hongô was separated by the Imperial palace from both the old downtown areas of Kyôbashi and Nihonbashi and the flourishing modern district of the Ginza.

In focusing on the locale of Hongô, the more patently "modern" areas of the city do not disappear from the book but are cast into relief, rather, by the esoteric modernism of the academic world at Imperial University, with its contradictory surroundings. Less than through the crowds of the city, Sanshirô's isolation increases as he enters university life in this (in selected areas) almost bucolic setting. The location and atmosphere of Hongô and the Imperial University are used as a geographic joke of sorts in the novel, a parody of both the ideals of modernism and of modernization.

This latter section of *Sanshirô* at first concentrates on the philosophical modernism (a rather imprecise term I use as a contrast to modernization) attained at the university. Sanshirô, however, is disillusioned by the lectures he receives on such tedious topics as "twenty definitions of literature that had been formulated by men of letters down through the ages," or "how the word "answer" came from the Anglo-Saxon *andswaru*, or "the name of the village where Sir Walter Scott had gone to grammar school." He complains of his dissatisfaction to a classmate, Yojiro, who tells him that the only cure is to "get on the streetcar and ride around Tokyo ten or fifteen times" (34). In this and other instances, there is a deliberate contrast between Hongô as the host ward of the university, a center and symbol of philosophical modernity, and the low city, areas where actual modernization is going on at a frantic pace. In this scene, Sanshirô uses the city car to escape the tedium of the one site to return to the excitement of the other. The novel as a whole can be seen as a contrast between local conditions in Hongo and a broader discussion of philosophical modernism.

In this scene, Sanshirô and Yojiro ride from Hongô Yonchôme to Shinbashi, turning back at Shinbashi and going as far as Nihonbashi. The two get off finally at Nihonbashi, have dinner and saké, and go to see "an authentic variety theater," which, the narrator relates, Sanshirô did not in fact appreciate that much. This is one of the few instances in the novel where we see Sanshirô physically leave Hongô and environs to explore the city proper. There seems little hope that he will attempt to join the "real" world of the modern city, for after the trip Yojiro remarks, "The only thing that will satisfy you from now on is the library," signaling his return to the world of letters and philosophical modernity.

Fortunately, Sanshirô does not prove a serious scholar or the remainder of the novel might have taken place among rows of dusty books. In another of the notable diversions from academic life, Sanshirô, Professor Hirota, and Mineko, a very modern coed to whom Sanshirô is attracted, travel to the Chrysanthemum Festival at Dangozaka, just north of the university. Although Sôseki's depiction is less cheery, Paul Waley writes that this festival, in which customers would enter booths to see dolls made of chrysanthemum act in romances or battles, was one of the most colorful events of Meiji Tokyo (1991:91). In 1887, 20 years prior to the publication of *Sanshirô*, the carnivalesque atmosphere of this festival was described in Futabatei Shimei's novel *Ukigumo* (Drifting Clouds): "What a crowd! Shaven-headed priests had come and long-haired men, men with half-shaven heads, and men with topknots. And they, too, had come, those beloved of the gods, the darlings of destiny . . . our so-called 'public-servants.' Businessmen came and the meek and humble. . . . Dangozaka was in a state of the wildest confusion. Flower-sellers stood by the usual signboards waving the flags of their respective establishments in the attempt to lure in customers" (63). Although the language and details of the scene seem of Edo, Futabatei relates how people of all walks of life, representing both the old and new Japan, could be found at the festival. This seems more the sort of location one might find in a work by Kafu or Tanizaki celebrating the vitality of earlier times. It is more this image of the festival that Edward Seidensticker perhaps has in mind when he writes, "Sanshirô lives in Hongô, and does not have a very exciting time of it. He sees a performance of *Hamlet*, which strikes him as full of odd remarks, but the pleasurable event described at greatest length is a viewing of the chrysanthemum dolls at Dangozaka, just north of the university" (1983:243). In *Low City, High City*, Seidensticker preferences the more traditional "low-city" areas and he seems here to regard the market at Dangozaka as a sort of Hongô equivalent of Asakusa. This preference seems in accordance with his general regard for writers such as Nagai Kafu and Tanizaki (writers whom Isoda sees as influential in the preservation of the image of Tokyo as provincial village).

Sôseki's depiction of the fair and Dangozaka in *Sanshirô*, however, concentrates more on the squalid and plebeian than on the picturesque. From the vantage point of the festival exhibition sheds at the top of Dangozaka, the narrator relates, "People seemed to be plunging down into the valley below. Those who were plunging down and those who were crawling up came together in a chaotic jumble that clogged the street and gave it a grotesque sort of movement, a fitful squirming that quickly tired the eyes. "This is horrible!" exclaimed Professor Hirota, standing atop the slope. He was obviously ready to go home" (89). While Seidensticker seems to see an image of fading Edoesque exuberance in the fair, Sôseki's characters are appalled by what they regard as the uncouth atmosphere there. Most of the crowd, the narrator relates, "was composed of local shopkeepers. There were very few people (there) who seemed to be educated" (89). To focus on these stark observations of class perhaps skews the overall tone and import of the scene. It is interesting, however, how different interpretations of this episode and locale can be. In contrast to Seidensticker's sentimental depiction of the Dangozaka episode as "the pleasurable event described at greatest length" in the novel, Jay Rubin, in a more universalist approach, comments that, to the individualist Hirota, who is "hyper-sensitive to the artificial—particularly that most cramped and constraining man-made creation, society," "the milling throng (at Dangozaka) is a vision of Hell" (1977:225).

Whatever observations we might make on this view of class in the novel, more to the point of this paper is the way Sôseki depicts here a scene at odds with the image of Hongô as strictly rural and which clashes also with the pursuits and mind-set of the more upper-class students and professors of the university. I believe there is a correlation between this depiction of a Hongô teeming with people and the earlier images of the more central areas of the city where "everything looked as though it were being destroyed, and at the same time everything looked as though it were under reconstruction" (17). Both depictions can be seen as examples of deleterious effects of modernization. Although such a connection may be less apparent to present-day readers, this and most major novels by Sôseki were originally published in the Asahi newspaper, whose urban readers would have been more aware of ironies of locale.

There seems to be a deliberate juxtaposition in the novel of the twin effects of modernization: its transformation of the Tokyo proper and the rapid and haphazard expansion of the city limits.

Sôseki's depiction of a more lower-class crowd at the Chrysanthemum Festival and Dangozaka reflects documented changes in the demographics of the area. In *Dai-Tokyo no Shisô*, Noboru Haga (1992) relates that in the rapid rise of population in Tokyo, Koishigawa-ku, the ward later incorporated with Hongo as Bunkyô-ku, saw the highest rate of growth of all Tokyo's then 15 wards, quadrupling in population in the 15-year period between 1883 and 1913 (this contrast can be seen by looking at the areas of concentrated settlement north of the university in the contemporary map).

The contradictory images of a district at once rustic and yet burgeoning with the poorer masses is supported by a description given by a popular travel writer of the period, Itô Gingetsu. In the work *Latest Record of Tokyo's Prosperity*, originally published in 1906, Itô's depiction of Hongô as a whole is quite disparaging: "As Hongô is a post town, it is not actually in Tokyo; However, half of Hongô itself is not in Hongô, being no more than a path for manure carts. In front of the First Higher School, at a corner on the cross-roads of Oiwake and Katamachi, there is a soba house; serving very bad soba. Everything up to this soba house is within Hongô's jurisdiction, however you measure it. The remaining tail of Hongô, however, is, even for a post town, a very sorry place. Foolish people have continued to build rough worn-out shacks so that the town has been stretched out as long as a cow's piss" (388). Although Sôseki does not resort to scatological comparisons, we can see a similar attention in *Sanshirô* to the unrefined side of Hongô as well as to its rapid growth.

Published just two years before *Sanshiro*, Gingetsu's work describes many of the same scenes as found in this novel, and often with a similar alarm concerning the rapid expansion of the city. In the minds of both authors, this expansion is not the clear sign of progress for which it is taken by the municipal authorities. Itô's chapter on Hongô begins with a *kyôka* (comic verse) fragment *"Hongô, too, as far as Kaneyasu, is within Edo."* Kaneyasu is a dry goods shop in the Hongô ward. It was here that Edo ended and the provinces north of the city were said to begin. In his account, Itô adds, however, that the market in Hongô had been in decline for quite some time: "Although it had some merit in the Tenmei era (1781-1789) when Kaneyasu was within Edo, these days anything beyond the Myôjin Temple in Kanda is outside Tokyo limits" (388). Although technically part of Kanda, the Myôjin temple can be located on the southwesternmost corner of the attached map of Hongô, leaving all of the ward, by Itô's reckoning, outside Tokyo.

The Kaneyasu is also mentioned in *Sanshirô*, and still stands today, though, as Seidensticker notes, it is now considered practically downtown. In an early episode of the story, Sanshirô and Professor Nonomiya pass the

Kaneyasu as they exit the southern gate of the university and enter one of the most crowded intersections in the Hongô area: "Streetcars turning the corner thundered between them, bells ringing. The dense traffic made it almost impossible to cross, but Nonomiya pointed to the shop on the other side and announced, 'I'm going to buy something over at the Kaneyasu'" (26). While this touch of transportation madness at Sanchôme, the last stop actually on the line into Hongô, seems to qualify this southernmost area of the ward at least as part of the modern city, Itô maintains that it was not. Though given perhaps partly in jest, his note of the decline of Hongô throughout Meiji might help account for the drastically differing depiction of Dangozaka and the Chrysanthemum Festival made by Futabatei and, 20 years later, by Sôseki.

As noted, passages of the novel contrast the philosophical modernism of the university against its setting in this more prosaic locale. A final example of this contrast between philosophical modernism and locale in the story involves Professor Hirota, the character seen by Rubin as the modern individualist of the story. Yojiro, who enjoys deflating the presumptions of academics, relates how Hirota "talks about how dirty Tokyo is," though he has never been abroad: "He studies the West in photographs. He's got lots of them—the Arc de Triomphe in Paris, the Houses of Parliament in London—and he measures Japan against them. Of *course* Japan looks bad in comparison. Meanwhile, he can live in a shack and not give a damn. It's very strange" (130). This seems another example of the frequently noted theme of Japan's modernism versus that of the West. But as part of that dialogue, Sôseki is sensitive to Tokyo's current stage of development and the unreason of those who believe that it should aspire to the same standards as these European city monuments. Here as elsewhere it is possible to read the local circumstances of Tokyo into this broad East/West equation. Hirota does live in a shack. As Itô relates, aside from the buildings of the university, the majority of structures in Hongô were little more than shacks. In *Sanshirô*, Sôseki is successful in pointing out the contradictions both of modernism and of the rapidly expanding Tokyo of this period.

Although this paper has concentrated largely on the depiction of more squalid aspects of Hongô as an ironic commentary on both philosophical modernism and the modernization of Tokyo, before closing, we should also note that Sôseki constructs a quite different image of areas of the ward. Though a poor student, Sanshirô is described as an amateur naturalist of sorts. He spends much of his time wandering Hongô and environs, taking in the sights. On one occasion, he turns at the top of Dangozaka, the scene of the melee at the Chrysanthemum Festival, and comes out to a broad avenue in Sendagi-chô. The narrator relates: "These days, ideal autumn weather made the skies of Tokyo look as deep as those of the countryside. Just to think that one was living beneath skies like this was enough to clear the mind. Walking out to open fields made everything perfect. The sense unwound and the spirit became as broad as the heavens ... This was not the irresponsible balminess of spring. Gazing at the hedges to either side, Sanshiro inhaled Tokyo's autumn fragrance for the first time in his life" (98). In the essay "*Ogai, Sôseki no mita Tokyo*" (Tokyo as seen by Sôseki and Ogai, 1989), critic Yoshimoto Takaaki suggests that contrasting features of crowds and confusion and elements of unspoiled nature can be found in Sôseki's works as a whole. In the significant sites of his fiction, Yoshimoto writes, Sôseki always returns to his typical image of Tokyo as nature (140).

Sôseki describes the area lying on the Ueno Park side of the university as a near wilderness. This can be seen in the details of the view from a hill in Yanaka, not far from the above scene. After escaping the tumult at the Chrysanthemum Festival, Sanshirô and Mineko observe these surroundings: "They saw a thatched roof in the distance. The entire wall below the roof was red. Moving closer they found the color was that of red peppers hung to dry.... The stream ran by just below them. It was shallow, now that the water level had fallen with the coming of autumn, shallow enough for a wagtail to fly over and perch on a jutting rock. Sanshirô gazed long into the clear water. It slowly began to grow muddy. A farmer upstream, he saw, was washing radishes" (91). Of the tranquillity of this side of Hongô, one of Sanshirô's professors relates, "the academic life demands a place like this," and one might imagine a Thoreauesque setting conducive to study. It may be that Sôseki is attempting to create a pastoral image in noting these details. Nature in this work, however, is not used simple as an escape. Other details of this scene, the growing muddiness of the water, the farmer upstream washing radishes, can be read as a more critical commentary on the backwardness of the locale, to its rusticity. Similarly, in a later chapter of the novel, professor Hirota is described thus: "He can't keep his mind on any one thing. He's like that little stream near Dangozaka: shallow and narrow, the water constantly changing. There's no discipline to what he does" (120).

Depiction of nature in Hongô, similar to depictions of chaotic development, can be used by Sôseki as another example of the ironies of philosophical modernism and modernization. As opposed to the beauty of nature, the isolation of the Imperial University in such a setting is often emphasized. The intellectual aloofness of the students and professors, who posture as philosophical modernists, is thereby satirized through the physical isolation and barrenness of their surroundings. On first arriving in Hongô, after an uneventful first day at the university spent talking with Professor Nonomiya about his experiments on "the pressure exerted by light," Sanshirô stops beside the body of water then known simply as "University pond": "It was extraordinarily quiet. Not even the noise of the streetcars penetrated this far. One streetcar line was to have run past the Red Gate, but the University had protested and it had gone through Koishikawa instead. Kneeling by the pond, Sanshirô recalled this incident that he had read about in the Kyûshû papers. Any university that refused to have streetcars near it must be far removed from society" (21). Today, this pond is officially known as "Sanshirô's pond." It is ironic that Sôseki should be so honored, since, as clearly seen in this passage, the pond serves as an image of the isolation of academic life, particularly at this university, which refused even to allow streetcars in its vicinity.

In conclusion, in his essay "Sôseki and Western Modernism," critic Fredric Jameson (1991) poses several questions regarding Japan's place in the modernist literary tradition. He asks, for instance, whether in Japan the modern period was accented by the same stages of realism and antirealism as occurred in the West: "Any speculation about Sôseki ought to include a discussion of whether in Japanese social life in this period there existed the same kinds of bourgeois stereotypes about everyday life that were constructed in the West during the realist period and which had in the modern already entered into crisis and become the object of satirical or utopian contestation" (131). In his query regarding Sôseki and Japanese modernism, Jameson seems to regard modernism was an exclusively Western phenomenon. There is little question in *Sanshirô* that Tokyo is modern, even in the more exclusive literary or philosophical sense. More important to Sôseki is the manner and implications of Japan's modernization. In the speech "Civilization of Modern Japan," we recall that Sôseki defines civilization as the "intertwining processes (of) inventions and mechanisms that spring from the desire to conserve our labor as much as possible, and the other involving amusements that spring from the wish to consume our energies as freely as possible" (268). These processes, he explains, had formerly moved at a slower rate in Japan than they had in the West. He concludes that Japan developed at an unnaturally rapid rate as these two spheres came closer together throughout the Meiji era. Sôseki's answer to Jameson's question thus might be quite simple: that, yes, in Japan there was served the same dishes of realism, antirealism, and other artistic and philosophical trends as in the West but they were often served in the same course, and rather too quickly. As Sôseki comments in his speech: "In the normal order of events, wave A of a civilization yields to wave B only when people have drunk their fill of A and have become satiated, at which time new desires arise from within and a new wave develops . . . It is like sitting at a dinner table and having one dish after another set before us and then taken away so quickly that, far from getting a good taste of each one, we can't even enjoy a clear look at what is being served" (268). Sôseki speaks here of civilization in the broad sense, but this view can be seen in his depiction of the city. Wallock and Sharpe write of distinct phases of city literature; in Sôseki's works, however, the physical manifestation of the city is often contradictory, transitory, or even illusory, manifesting in the local landscape the ironies of modernism and modernization.

Haga writes that the history of modern Tokyo is centered in the residential areas opened up in the Yamanote region. Although in other works Sôseki writes of other areas of the city, it is with the Yamanote region that he is frequently associated. In his depiction of this and other parts of the city, Sôseki appears to have foreseen some of the major lines of development of Tokyo to the present. This is part of what makes him today one of the most accessible and widely read authors of the Meiji era. His depiction of the city, however, is neither simple nor predictable. Wallock and Sharpe propose distinct phases of city literature; in Sôseki's works, however, the physical manifestation of the city is often contradictory, transitory, or even illusory, manifesting in the local landscape the ironies of modernism and modernization. A most paradoxical aspect of *Sanshirô* is the contradictory depiction of the isolation of Hongô as an area only recently assimilated into the city and that is at the same time very crowded. Although critics often speak of the international or universal nature of Sôseki's fiction, many modern readers overlook some of the more subtle ironies Sôseki uses to question Japan and Tokyo's chosen path of progress in the modern age. The setting of *Sanshirô* in Hongô is not used as an escape from such problems but as a means of throwing into relief the upheaval of the older city and the effects of the rapid growth of the city.

REFERENCES

Anderer, Paul. 1987. "Tokyo and the Borders of Modern Japanese Fiction." In *Versions of the Modern City: Essays in History, Art, and Literature.* Edited by W. Sharpe and L. Wallock. Baltimore and London: The Johns Hopkins University Press, p. 27.

Berque, Augustin. 1993. *Du geste à la cité: Formes urbaines et lien social au Japon.* Paris: Éditions Gallimard.

Futabatei, Shimei. 1956. "The Drifting Cloud." In *Modern Japanese Literature.* Edited by D. Keene. New York: Grove Press.

Haga, Noboru. 1992. *Dai-Tokyo no shisô.* Tokyo: Oyamakaku Shuppan Kabushikigaisha.

Isoda, Kôichi. 1990. *Shisô to shite no Tokyo.* Tokyo: Kôdansha.

Itô, Gingetsu. 1992. *Saishin Tokyo Hanjôki.* Edited by J. Aikawa. 12 vols. Vol. 2, *Bungaku Chishi 'Tokyo' Sôsho.* Tokyo: Taikûsha.

Jameson, Fredric R. 1991. "Sôseki and Western Modernism." *Boundary 2* 18 (3):122-41.

Keene, Donald. 1984. *Dawn to the West.* New York: Henry Holt and Company.

Maeda, Ai. 1992. *Tôshi no naka no bungaku.* (Literature of the Urban Realm) Tokyo: Chikuma.

Natsume, Sôseki. 1912. "The Civilization of Modern-Day Japan." Translated by Jay Rubin. In *Kokoro.* Washington, D.C.: Regnery Gateway. 1989.

Natsume, Sôseki. 1977. *Sanshirô.* Translated by Jay Rubin. Seattle: University of Washington Press.

Natsume, Sôseki. 1978. *Sorekara* (And Then) Translated by Norma More Field. Baton Rouge: Louisiana University Press.

Natsume, Sôseki. 1992. *The Tower of London*. Translated by Peter Milward and Kii Nakano. Brighton: In Print Publishing.

Ogai, Mori. 1975. *Maihime (The Dancing Girl)*. Translated by Richard Bowring. *Monumenta Nipponica* 30: 151-66.

Origas, Jean Jacques. 1970. 'Kumo no te' no machi: Sôseki shôki no sakuhin no ichi danmen. In *Kindai Nihon Bungaku Sosho*. Tokyo: Showa Joshi Daigaku Kindai Bunka Kenkyujo.

Rubin, Jay. 1977. "Sanshirô and Sôseki: A Critical Essay." In Sôseki Natsume, *Sanshirô*. Seattle: University of Washington Press.

Seidensticker, Edward. 1983. *Low City, High City: Tokyo from Edo to the Earthquake*. Cambridge, Mass.: Harvard University Press.

Sharpe, William and Leonard Wallock. 1987. "From 'Great Town' to 'Non-place Urban Realm': Reading the Modern City." In *Versions of the Modern City: Essays in History, Art, and Literature*. Edited by W. Sharpe and L. Wallock. Baltimore and London: The Johns Hopkins University Press.

Waley, Paul. 1991. *Tokyo: City of Stories*. New York, Tokyo: Weatherhill.

Yamamoto, Hirofumi, ed. 1993. *Technological Innovation and the Development of Transportation in Japan*. Edited by H. Yamamoto. Tokyo: United Nations University Press.

Yoshimoto, Takaaki. 1989. *Zo Toshite no Tokyo: toshi ronshu*. Tokyo: Yudachisha

Contributors

William Burton is a research associate in the Department of East Asian Studies at the University of Washington, Seattle. His major research interest is in modern Japanese literature.

David L. Callies is Benjamin A. Kudo Professor of Law in the William S. Richardson School of Law at the University of Hawaii. His principal research is in land-use law and urban planning in Japan, the United States, and Britain. He has authored numerous papers, including "Land Use Planning and Control in Japan" in *Planning for Cities and Regions in Japan* (1994).

Roman A. Cybriwsky is Professor of Geography and Urban Studies at Temple University, Philadelphia. Between 1984 and 1994 he was on the faculty of Temple University Japan at Tokyo. He is the author of *Tokyo: The Changing Profile of an Urban Giant* (1991), the most authoritative study on the urban geography of Tokyo.

Kuniko Fujita teaches industrial sociology and urban sociology at Michigan State University. Her major research is on urban industrial restructuring in Japan. She has authored a number of studies on Japanese cities, including a paper on restructuring of the Tokyo metropolis in *International Journal of Urban and Regional Research* (1991).

Theodore J. Gilman is on the faculty of the Department of Political Science at Union College, Schenectady, New York. His major research is on urban redevelopment strategies in Japan and the United States. His research on the process and characteristics of urban redevelopment in the Japanese and American cities have made a major contribution to the comparative study of local redevelopment efforts.

Richard Child Hill is Professor of Sociology and Urban Affairs at Michigan State University. He is the coauthor with Kuniko Fujita of *The Japanese Cities in the World Economy* (1993) and the author of several research monographs on urban restructuring in Japan and the United States.

P. P. Karan is Professor of Geography and Chair of the Japan Studies Program at the University of Kentucky. His current research is on the cultural geography of Japan. In 1985-86 and 1992-93 he was Research Professor at the Institute for the Study of Languages and Cultures of Asia and Africa at the Tokyo University of Foreign Studies, Tokyo. He is coauthor with Cotton Mather and Shigeru Iijima of *The Japanese Landscapes* (Johns Hopkins University Press and The Geographical Society 1998).

Robert Kidder is Professor of Sociology at Temple University, Philadelphia. His major research is on urban environmental aspects of Japan. He was on the faculty of Temple University Japan at Tokyo and has published several studies on Japan.

Cotton Mather is former chair of the Department of Geography at the University of Minnesota, and is currently the President of The New Mexico Geographical Society, Messila, New Mexico. He is the world's leading scholar of cultural landscapes and has authored numerous studies on cultural geography of parts of the United States, Europe, Latin America, and Asia, including *The Japanese Landscapes* with P. P. Karan and Shigeru Iijima.

Kohei Okamoto is on the faculty of the Department of Geography at Nogoya University. His principal research interest is on suburban development in Japan. He is the author of several monographs on the suburbs of Tokyo and Osaka.

Kristin Stapleton is Assistant Professor of History at the University of Kentucky. Her major research interest is East Asian history. She is the author of several papers on urban history of East Asia.

Index